Beyond Humanitarianism

What You Need to Know
About Africa
and Why It Matters

D1417145

Beyond Humanitarianism

What You Need to Know
About Africa
and Why It Matters

Edited by Princeton N. Lyman
and Patricia Dorff

Council on Foreign Relations / FOREIGN AFFAIRS

Library of Congress Cataloging-in-Publication Data

Beyond humanitarianism : what you need to know about Africa and why it matters / edited by Princeton N. Lyman and Patricia Dorff.
    p. cm.
    Includes bibliographical references and index.
    ISBN 978-0-87609-371-9 (pbk.)
    1. United States—Foreign relations—Africa. 2. Africa—Foreign relations—United States. 3. United States—Foreign economic relations—Africa. 4. Africa—Foreign economic relations—United States. 5. Africa—Foreign economic relations—China. 6. China—Foreign economic relations—Africa. 7. Africa—Politics and government—21st century. 8. Africa— Foreign economic relations. I. Lyman, Princeton N. II. Dorff, Patricia.

DT38.7.B49 2007
327.7306—dc22

2007024191

Contents

Foreword

In 2006, the Council on Foreign Relations published the report of an Independent Task Force, *More Than Humanitarianism: A Strategic U.S. Approach Toward Africa.* This report, which, according to the State Department, "raised the profile of Africa among policymakers," detailed the growing importance of Africa to the United States and to U.S. foreign policy.

This book draws upon a variety of Council content: *Foreign Affairs* articles, Independent Task Force reports, Council Special Reports, the Council's website—CFR.org—as well as other pieces by Council senior fellows. These articles address underlying trends on the continent, such as the growth of democracy, the rising activity of China, and the political and economic prospects of the most important African countries. Conflicts and the terrorist threats in Africa are addressed as well. Princeton N. Lyman, the Council's adjunct senior fellow for Africa policy studies, has written an introduction that provides an overview of the major issues as well as section essays that briefly highlight the context for better understanding each chapter. The book concludes with recommendations for U.S. policy toward Africa—recommendations drawn from the original Task Force report that remain highly relevant.

Of course, the issues discussed in this book evolve daily. On CFR.org, the Council on Foreign Relations maintains an updated review of African issues, links to important publications, and interviews with senior staff. I encourage readers to access this site on a regular basis to stay abreast of African developments and other major foreign policy issues.

Richard N. Haass
President
Council on Foreign Relations
June 2007

Introduction

AFRICA HAS RISEN steadily in importance to the United States in recent years. Traditionally, Africa has been thought of primarily as an object of humanitarian concern. That perception has been highlighted by popular figures, such as Bono, Bob Geldof, George Clooney, and others, focusing public attention on Africa's poverty, conflicts, and major diseases. Worldwide concerts such as Live 8 in July 2005 focused on these themes and urged leaders of the industrialized world to devote more aid, debt relief, and opening of trade to assist Africa. The leaders of the G8 responded that year, pledging to double aid to Africa to $50 billion annually by 2010 and eliminating the debt of some of Africa's poorest countries.

Africa has further captured worldwide attention because of the conflict in Darfur, Sudan. Because the United States has judged the Sudanese government's campaign in the region to be genocide, the conflict has taken on enormous moral importance. Unfortunately, despite many UN Security Council resolutions, special envoys, and various peace agreements, not to mention the experience in Rwanda, the violence continues and has even worsened.

But Africa has other reasons, beyond these critical humanitarian issues, to command America's attention. Africa is currently the scene of major competition for access to its natural resources. China, India, Malaysia, South Korea, Brazil, and other countries with rapidly growing economies are turning to Africa for oil, minerals, timber, and other resources. China in particular has led in this competition with significant amounts of aid along with financial backing for hundreds of Chinese companies to invest in Africa. China's aid for infrastructure projects, long ignored by the United States and other Western aid programs, and its readiness to set aside issues of governance, human rights, and economic transparency—issues of growing importance to the West—has made it a formidable competitor for both influence and lucrative contracts on the continent.

This new competition comes at a time when Africa's oil is becoming more important to the United States. Currently, 15 percent of U.S. oil imports come from Africa, as much as from the Middle East. Moreover, Africa is poised to double its output over the coming decade and potentially could provide as much as 25 percent of U.S. imports. African capacity to export natural gas is also growing rapidly, with American and British companies making billions of dollars in investments in liquefied natural gas (LNG) plants along the Gulf of Guinea. Yet nearly all of Africa's oil reserves are in countries experiencing violence or instability, and in some cases serious violations of human rights. As the United States is discovering in the Middle East and Latin America, it is impossible to count on a continuing supply of oil from Africa without attention to the quality of governance, the degree that indigenous populations are benefiting from oil, and long-term stability.

Africa's importance is also growing in trade negotiations. With 40 of the World Trade Organization's 185 members, Africa is demanding significant reduction of U.S. and European agricultural subsidies and tariffs in return for agreement on a new round of worldwide trade improvements. Teaming up with India, Brazil, and other third world countries, Africa has essentially brought the negotiations of the so-called Doha Round to a standstill pending movement on these issues.

Africa is also rising in importance in the war on terror. Al-Qaeda terrorists bombed the American embassies in Kenya and Tanzania in 1998 and attacked Israeli facilities in Kenya in 2001. These acts revealed an extensive network of terrorist cells along the east African seaboard. The threat became apparent once again when an Islamic movement captured control of Somalia's capital, Mogadishu, in 2006 and seemed headed toward confrontation with America's ally, Ethiopia, and to be taking steps hostile to American objectives, e.g., protecting terrorists known to be associated with the 1998 embassy bombings.

In a lightning military move in December 2006, Ethiopia displaced the Islamists from Mogadishu and drove the leadership out of the country or into hiding. But the continuing weak government, clan warfare, and humanitarian disasters make Somalia vulnerable to future infiltration and sources of trouble for the United States. Elsewhere on the continent, the United States has initiated a training and intelligence-gathering program throughout northwest Africa, called the Trans Sahara Counter Terrorism Initiative, and sought to jump-start regional security efforts in the oil-rich Gulf of Guinea. In 2008, the United States will establish a single Africa Command to coordinate and amplify these programs.

Finally, Africa is at the center of worldwide concerns over global health. Africa is the epicenter of the AIDS pandemic, with 28 million of the 40 million worldwide infected with HIV. Africa suffers the most deaths from malaria, one million per year. And most recently, Africa has been recognized as one of the most vulnerable sources for the potential spread of avian flu, because of weak infrastructure, monitoring capacity, and control mechanisms. Led by the United States, annual worldwide expenditures on AIDS have risen from less than $1 billion in 2000 to $8 billion in 2006, and the United States has begun a major malaria initiative. But estimates are that as much as $22 billion will be needed annually in the next few years for AIDS alone. Whether these costs can be met, or met without subtracting from other forms of aid for education, agriculture, etc., is very uncertain. Meanwhile, investments in health and agricultural infrastructure for control of a potential avian flu pandemic are only on the drawing board.

Africa is well aware of both its challenges and potential. In recent years African countries have taken several steps to strengthen electoral democracy, economic policies, good governance, and the reduction of conflict. Nearly two-thirds of African governments today are elected, and the African Union (AU)—the continent's political body—will not seat a government that comes to power through nonconstitutional means. Under a program called the New Partnership for Africa's Development (NEPAD), Africa has set forth principles of governance, human rights, and economic management and instituted a peer review mechanism to help hold governments to these principles. With all the rightful attention to the ongoing violence in Darfur and the recent civil war in Congo, many international observers have not focused on the significant decline of conflict on the continent. Civil wars in Angola, Mozambique, Liberia, and Sierra Leone have been brought to a close, often with active African leadership in the negotiations and the contribution of peacekeepers. A near repeat of the Rwanda-type genocide in neighboring Burundi has been averted by a strong African diplomatic initiative that helped shape an elected national unity government and by the African Union providing a timely presence of peacekeepers. Even in Darfur the AU has so far provided the only peacekeepers, though well below the numbers and capabilities needed to control the situation.

Africa's democratic trend is nevertheless fragile. In Uganda, President Yoweri Museveni spurned international pleas and obtained parliamentary approval to run and be elected yet again after twenty years in power. In Ethiopia, elections in 2005 led to charges of rigging, violence, and the jailing of leading opposition politicians. In Zimbabwe, President Robert Mugabe continues to rule autocratically, cracking down on dissent, the media, judges, and even religious leaders while the once-promising economy plunges into ruin.

Nigeria may be the bellwether of Africa's democratic future. Nigeria is Africa's most populous nation, with as many as 130 million people. Nigeria's president over the past eight years, Olusegun Obasanjo, has been a leader in the formation of NEPAD and personally led the return to civilian rule in Nigeria with his election in 1999. In the spring of 2007, Nigeria faced a major milestone. After decades of largely military rule and two terms of Obasanjo's elected presidency, Nigeria for the first time had the opportunity to experience a democratic transfer of power from one civilian administration to another. But the election was deeply flawed through poor preparation, extensive legal battles over who could be on the ballot, violence, and considerable ballot stuffing and other irregularities. The newly elected president, Umaru Yar'Adua, will be seriously challenged to build credibility and the capacity to govern in the wake of the deep disillusionment and disputes about the electoral process. Much of Africa's future support for democracy will depend on the outcome of events in Nigeria.

Introduction

At the center of all Africa's issues and challenges lies the persistence of poverty. Africa is by far the poorest continent, poorer even than other developing regions, and marginal in the global trading system. Poverty adds to the potential for conflict, the vulnerability to terrorist influence, the pressures of illegal migration, the spread of disease, and it constitutes a drain on worldwide aid resources. Thus, the humanitarian problems return to center stage in contemplating U.S. policy. But they cannot be treated as objects of charity, nor be satisfied with emergency aid for relief and postconflict emergencies, which have comprised much of America's recent increases in assistance. The growing importance of Africa, in so many ways, demands a much more focused, long-term, and carefully directed program of economic assistance and trade reform. The Bush administration has begun in that direction with the Millennium Challenge Account, and Congress has contributed with the African Growth and Opportunity Act, which opens the U.S. market to African exports. But much more needs to be done.

The United States also lacks the personnel to develop and manage a truly comprehensive policy toward Africa, one that would address the full panoply of issues described above. As Congressman Frank Wolf (R-VA) recently said, "the bench is thin" when it comes to the State Department dealing with crises in Sudan, Somalia, and elsewhere. It is all the more shorthanded for developing long-term policies addressing oil-producing states or programmatic support for democracy. Only when Africa is recognized for the growing importance it has for America will these shortcomings be overcome. That is the theme and purpose of this publication.

The Council on Foreign Relations has had a strong program on Africa for several years. In 2003, it established the Ralph Bunche Chair on Africa Policy Studies, the first endowed Africa policy chair of any think tank in the United States. The holder of the chair has organized regular reviews of current developments in Africa, directed numerous studies, and published many articles and reports. In addition, the Council maintains on its website, CFR.org, a regular stream of updates and analyses on African issues. This book offers a selection of those reports and publications, designed to provide a picture of the broad range of African issues of importance to the United States and some recommendations for U.S. policy. If the book helps generate greater attention and understanding of Africa by both the public and policymakers, it will have served its purpose.

Princeton N. Lyman

Map of Africa

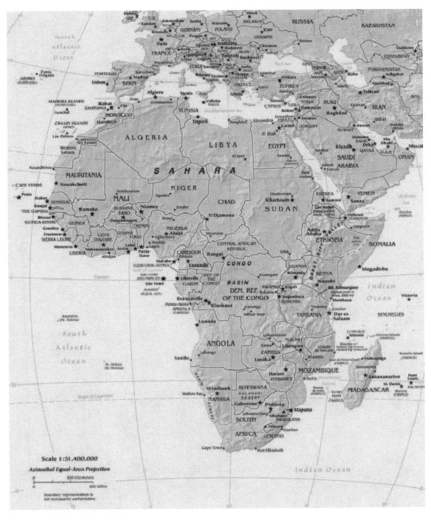

Source: CIA World Factbook.

I

Under the Radar

In 2006, the Council on Foreign Relations published a report of an Independent Task Force on U.S. policy toward Africa, cochaired by Anthony Lake and Christine Todd Whitman. The Task Force report, *More Than Humanitarianism: A Strategic U.S. Approach Toward Africa,* identified several factors that make Africa of increasing strategic importance to the United States, including some trends that had not yet captured public, or in some cases, policy analysts', attention.

In this section, "Under the Radar," the Council calls attention to the fact that, as one observer has noted, "Africa is in play." With the rapid growth in the economies of Asia and in some countries of Latin America, Africa has become the focus of investment, trade, and political outreach from a host of countries not previously so active on the continent. China stands out in this regard. As China moved from self-sufficiency in energy to a major importing country, it has reached out across the world for access to energy resources through a combination of investments, aid, high-level political attention, and promises of future largesse. In Africa, Angola recently passed Saudi Arabia as China's major source of imported oil. Sudan provides China with about 7 percent of its oil imports. India, South Korea, Malaysia, Brazil, and other countries are following China's lead in Africa, using the same mechanisms and pursuing many of the same resources.

China poses a challenge to the United States' objectives in Africa because China pursues its aid and investment programs without attention to issues of governance, human rights, or the environment. It uses competitive practices not available to the United States or American companies. But China and the other newly active countries also offer Africa a welcome new source of investment and trade. The challenge is to create a new consensus on how these opportunities can be harnessed to benefit Africa in sustainable ways, not as South Africa's President Thabo Mbeki warned, leading to a new "colonialism."

The Independent Commission report on Angola and Robert I. Rotberg's Special Report on Nigeria pick up on the theme of Africa's growing importance as a supplier of oil. The reports focus attention on how the United States needs to respond to countries in Africa that are of increasing importance to the world's energy supply but that are subject to civil strife, poor governance, and deep poverty in spite of record levels of oil earnings. In the case of Angola, traditional sources of leverage and influence, such as foreign aid, are of limited value, for oil wealth makes Angola independent of not only aid but of the influence of such institutions as the International Monetary Fund (IMF). Angola is not only important as a source of oil, however—it is also important to stability in central and southern Africa. Largely neglected in U.S. foreign policy since the end of the civil war in that country, Angola is an important case study in how the United States needs to develop a productive and mutually beneficial relationship to not only Angola but other oil-producing countries with similar characteristics in Africa and elsewhere.

Much of the public's attention on Africa focuses on conflict and humanitarian emergencies. But just as important are the emerging trends toward democracy and better governance over the past twenty years that are transforming many African countries. Nigeria is Africa's largest oil producer, and the fifth-largest source of U.S. imported oil; it is in many ways the bellwether of these trends. The report on Nigeria provides insights into the struggle for democracy, development, and stability taking place there. After returning to civilian elected rule in 1999, Nigeria undertook significant reforms in managing the economy, fighting corruption, and eliminating its debt. The elections of 2007 were a critically important test of whether Nigeria's democracy could then make the important transition from one elected administration to another. The elections were not well conducted, leaving a pall over the country. But other problems face the newly elected government as well. Rotberg's insights into the election dynamics of 2007 and the challenges facing Nigeria provide a valuable look at how strong and sustainable the positive trends of the past few years may be.

A different scenario is playing out in South Africa, the scene of one of the most dramatic stories of the twentieth century. In 1994, after decades of apartheid and much violence, longtime political prisoner and freedom fighter Nelson Mandela was elected president and a new and strong constitutional democracy was born. Today, South Africa is the strongest economy on the continent and a leader in African diplomacy, peacekeeping, and development. In his retrospective, Princeton N. Lyman, who was U.S. ambassador to South Africa during the transition to democracy, looks at how well the institutions of democracy, good governance, and the economy have performed and the problems that South Africa still faces.

Africa's strategic importance and future will also be shaped by a curious phenomenon that demographers call a youth bulge. In the final piece of this section, Council International Affairs Fellow Michelle D. Gavin provides a close look at the political engagement and political agendas of the youth in sub-Saharan Africa, arguing that the demographic power of young Africans is bound to have political consequences, and exploring the ways in which youths' quest for empowerment can make them significant catalysts for positive change.

U.S. Interest in Democracy And Human Rights Promotion

THE GROWTH OF DEMOCRACY in Africa is one of the most hopeful signs of change on the continent. Democratic African leaders are in the forefront of upholding the principle of constitutional rule, resolving conflict, advocating good governance, and developing sound economic policies. The development of democratic institutions and practices will serve first and foremost the interests of Africans. But partnering with African democracies and giving strong assistance and support to emerging institutions that promote democracy and protect human rights will help in all the areas of U.S. interest in Africa as well. Democratic states will be more stable over the long term, more attuned to the needs of their citizens, share more of America's values, and become better partners to the United States in trade, development, and countering crime and terrorism.

In the 2005 State of the Union Address, President Bush stated, "America will stand with the allies of freedom to support democratic movements in the Middle East and beyond, with the ultimate goal of ending tyranny in our world." Secretary of State Condoleezza Rice cited the spread of democracy as one of the specific outcomes expected from U.S. economic, trade, and peace programs in Africa.

This article is excerpted from the Independent Task Force report *More Than Humanitarianism: A Strategic U.S. Approach Toward Africa*. Anthony Lake and Christine Todd Whitman, chairs; Princeton N. Lyman and J. Stephen Morrison, project directors (New York: Council on Foreign Relations Press, 2006).

[5]

There is already a commitment to democracy from the AU and a positive trend throughout the continent. The United States should continue to encourage this trend through public diplomacy and with incentives in the Millennium Challenge Account (MCA), debt relief programs, and other instruments. However, U.S. support for democracy, while generally advocated and encouraged, should be strategically focused in countries that carry much influence and reputation in Africa and whose progress on the road to democracy, or steps backward, will have a major impact on the strength of democracy across the continent. Major challenges loom in Nigeria, Ethiopia, Uganda, and Sudan. Success in these countries will be telling for the AU's continuing commitment to democratization. The United States needs also to prepare for a possible collapse or significant unrest in Zimbabwe, which Secretary Rice has specifically condemned for its oppressive political regime. A collapse or widespread unrest would have ripple effects throughout southern Africa.

A POSITIVE, BUT FRAGILE TREND

DEMOCRACY HAS TAKEN ROOT in Africa. More than two-thirds of African nations have undergone elections, and the recently established AU has decreed that it will not recognize governments that come to power through unconstitutional means. In response to recent coups in Togo, Guinea-Bissau, and Mauritania, the AU issued forceful condemnations and engineered plans for a return to elected government.

However, African institutions are still fragile. Elections have come faster than the development of responsible and effective political parties, independent electoral systems, fully functioning legislatures, and independent judiciaries. Further, the media are increasingly vibrant, but often poorly funded and subject to bribery and intimidation. Civil society is flourishing as never before, but sometimes lacks the skills or the political support of elites necessary for lasting influence. And some African states remain resistant to democracy, defying both their neighbors and the international community.

Africa has also been the scene of horrific human rights violations. The 1994 genocide in Rwanda, the brutality of civil war in Sierra Leone from 1997 to 1999, and the ongoing rapes and mass atrocities in the Democratic Republic of the Congo (DRC) and Darfur are testimonies to the challenges still ahead to make Africa safe for all Africans. Such conflicts open a space for exploitation by rapacious criminal and terrorist organizations, further undermining economic development. In addition to the human costs, the United States and other donors pay billions of dollars in emergency and humanitarian aid nearly every year.

DISAGGREGATING PERFORMANCE

In this realm, as in others, there is not "one Africa." In its *Freedom in the World 2005* survey, Freedom House rated eleven countries in sub-Saharan Africa as free. It rated twenty-one others as partially free. It also classified twenty countries as electoral democracies—each boasting competitive, multiparty political systems, voting by secret ballot, and universal suffrage. The majority of African states are now at what scholars have called the "consolidation stage" of their democratic development. For states, such as South Africa, Botswana, Tanzania, Kenya, Senegal, Benin, Ghana, Mali, Namibia, Malawi, and Zambia, the process of institutionalizing democratic practices is well under way. But countries like Ivory Coast, Sierra Leone, Mauritania, Guinea-Bissau, the DRC, Central African Republic, Rwanda, and Burundi all went from elections to civil war or coups (and in some cases both) and have struggled to get back on the path of democracy.

A number of African countries are also what might be called "pseudo-democracies"—governments that have been elected, but are essentially autocratic. Eritrea, Equatorial Guinea, Gabon, Togo, and Mauritania (under its former president) are examples.

There are serious backsliders too. Zimbabwe stands out as a country that once had great promise and a democratic structure. However, democracy has virtually collapsed after twenty-five years of rule under President Robert Mugabe. Violence, repression, intimidation, disregard for the rule of law, suppression of the media, and continued land seizures have become routine. The economy is near collapse. Leading African states, which have condemned coups and reversed them elsewhere on the continent, have been disappointingly silent on Zimbabwe. Mugabe retains a certain cachet among Africans as a former liberation leader and one who is willing to pull the "lion's [British] tail." Zimbabwe has become the greatest point of contention between Africa and the West on the issue of democracy. It also reveals the limitations on Western leverage and influence if decoupled from African leadership and where there is a willingness to engage bad actors. This situation is, however, now reaching a possible climax that will demand close cooperation between African states and attention by international partners.

INSTITUTIONAL FACTORS

Political Parties

In many countries, political parties are highly personalized, weak, and lack a solid base of funding. Opposition parties in some countries are highly restricted or even illegal, as in Swaziland. Moreover, where multiparty elections occur, a single party often dominates, despite the abundance of competitors. South Africa has as many as 140 parties and is one of the continent's strongest democracies, yet the African National Congress (ANC) so dominates the political scene that the country has no opposition with a credible chance of winning power. Fortunately, the strength of the courts, the press, and civil society preclude South Africa and the ANC from acting as a one-party state with no checks and balances. Elections in Tanzania and Mozambique in 2004, judged by international observers to be free and fair, have once again returned to power political parties that have ruled since independence.

Party finances also distort the political landscape. A June 2005 study of party finance reform in Africa by the National Democratic Institute for International Affairs (NDI) found that problems stem from "undemocratic, secretive, and unprofessional party organizing practices" that both "undermine public confidence" and "engender governments more susceptible to corruption."

[8]

Legislatures and the Judiciary

African parliaments, in general, are also wracked by poor performance. Most parliamentarians lack training and are not supported by competent, professional staff. In Ethiopia, less than a quarter of parliamentarians have a high school education or advanced degrees. Few African countries have independent judiciaries. Lack of confidence in the judicial system and the rule of law not only undermines human rights, but also discourages foreign and local investment.

Civil Society

African civil society, by contrast, has improved dramatically. Civil society has often been the mobilizing force for political change, accountability, and the protest of human rights violations. Today, a rich array of organizations—religion-based, human rights–focused, women's groups, international NGOs, and a host of others—are bringing about changes never experienced in the immediate post-independence decades. Add to this mix a vibrant, if sometimes irresponsible, media and the existence of a growing, engaged, and vocal middle class.

The growth of religious institutions and religious fervor, in particular, is a major phenomenon throughout Africa. The full implications are hard to predict. Especially notable is the growth of independent Christian churches; their banners can be seen in every Nigerian city, and in those of East Africa as well. They seem to provide an escape from the burdens of poverty and loss of confidence in government, and to hold out hope for miraculous cures for diseases like AIDS. Similarly significant are the rise of Protestant evangelical movements (with support from the West, particularly U.S.-based groups), the awakening of mainline Christian churches to social justice and governance issues, and the spread of both radicalized and moderate Islam (with support from Muslim states).

Civil society can play a positive or negative role. Some groups that have sprung up are self-serving, seeking cooperation with autocratic regimes, while others exacerbate religious or ethnic tensions and provoke violence. On the whole, however, the growth of civil society is a positive trend, lending support to democratization, good governance, and peace.

GOVERNANCE

Good governance—the responsible management of government affairs, services, and finances—is one of the objectives of democratization. Improved governance has become a major criterion for African governments to gain access to new sources of assistance such as the MCA, debt relief, and private investment. Across Africa, many countries are making strides in this area, especially in macroeconomic management. In 2004, the continent experienced an average economic growth rate of 5 percent—an eight-year high. The average fiscal deficit declined to almost zero. Botswana, Mauritius, Mozambique, and South Africa are among the best economic performers and have adopted sound macroeconomic management frameworks and policies.

African governments have made good governance a top priority in their own development agenda. The New Partnership for Africa's Development (NEPAD) established the African Peer Review Mechanism (APRM), which monitors whether participating states' policies and practices accord with agreed political, economic, and corporate governance norms and standards. A total of twenty-three countries have signed up for peer review. Two of the APRM's most innovative features are a self-administered internal review process that each country conducts to determine its own weaknesses, followed by an outside assessment and preparation of a plan for corrective measures. Once complete, a final report is submitted to the participating heads of state and the government.

MAJOR CHALLENGES FOR THE UNITED STATES

THERE ARE SEVERAL COUNTRIES of special importance to the United States that are undergoing critical transitions in the next two years. The outcome in these countries could spell success or failure for U.S. hopes and interests in much of Africa.

NIGERIA

Nigeria, with 130 million people, is Africa's most populous country. It is also the continent's largest oil producer and a magnet for U.S. private investment. Under President Olusegun Obasanjo, Nigeria has closely allied itself with the United States in the war on terrorism and has been a leader in ending the civil wars in Liberia and Sierra Leone. It has also provided peacekeepers to several conflict situations, including Darfur, and has instituted a significant economic reform program in a country notorious for corruption and mismanagement.

Nigeria has been under military rule for most of its postcolonial history. But in 1999, the military, vastly unpopular after years of corruption and economic decline, yielded to civilian rule. President Obasanjo, himself a former military ruler who was once jailed for his opposition to continuing military rule, was elected president in 1999 and reelected in 2003. The constitution limits a president to two terms. The 2007 election therefore represents a true test of the strength of Nigeria's democratic system, specifically its ability to manage a successful electoral transition, which would be the first in its history.

Unfortunately, the previous two elections were marred by serious irregularities and there have been few systemic improvements since. Nigeria is almost evenly divided between Muslims and Christians, and the political tension within the country as a whole during the coming election is palpable and potentially explosive. President Obasanjo is a born-again Christian. There is suspicion among northern Muslim Nigerians that the president, perhaps with American encouragement (for which there is no evidence), will seek to change the constitution and run again or extend his term.

An election in 2007 that lacks credibility with significant parts of the population, or that is seen as unconstitutional, would spark tremendous unrest. It would jeopardize the economic reforms that President Obasanjo has instituted. There is an urgent need for electoral reform, clarifying rules for presidential succession, and building a strong system of civil society election monitoring. Yet, the United States has cut back sharply on its democratization support funds in Nigeria at this critical juncture.

ETHIOPIA

Ethiopia is an important partner with the United States in efforts to stem the supply of money, arms, and recruits to terrorist cells along the east coast of Africa and in the Horn. With seventy million people, Ethiopia is also a major country in the fight against HIV/AIDS. Ethiopia remains in a serious border dispute with Eritrea that was the focus of a devastating war in the late 1990s and could potentially turn violent again.

Ethiopia is in the process of a tentative, if stumbling, transition to democracy. Its outcome will significantly affect future stability in the Horn. Recently, Ethiopia conducted its second ever multiparty elections. The opposition parties made significant gains. However, there were charges of major irregularities, including harassment of opposition leaders and party officials, especially in rural areas, unbalanced access to the media, and rigging of ballots. Opposition parties staged demonstrations that turned violent. The EU issued a strongly worded critique of the election that strained its relations with Ethiopia. The United States has been more restrained in its criticism and has urged all sides to remain peaceful as they sort out the situation.

The situation has recently taken an even more negative turn. The Ethiopian government has arrested opposition leaders and charged them with treason. The possibilities for a resolution of the impasse (e.g., the formation of a coalition government, a new general or partial election, or an agreement for the opposition to take its seats in the parliament) now seem less likely. What was at first a promising step toward democracy has turned into the threat of increased military-backed rule and further instability. So far, there is little evidence of concerted international influence on the government. At the same time, Ethiopia and Eritrea are locked in a tense border dispute that could once again break into open warfare.

SUDAN

Sudan's success or failure will have more than regional significance. Sudan is roughly half Arab, half African, and largely Muslim, but with a significant Christian population in the south. It is, therefore, an important test of the U.S. goal of bringing democracy to Arab, Muslim populations.

Sudan is emerging from more than twenty years of civil wars between the north and south. The complex peace agreement calls for a major restructuring of the central government to include representation not only from the south but also from opposition parties in the north and, eventually, from previously underrepresented regions of the east and west. Elections are scheduled for 2007. However, the initial assignment of portfolios in the new government does not appear to provide a significant broader role for northern political parties or address the representation of either Darfur or the eastern region. Meanwhile, conflict and major human rights violations continue in the western Darfur region, and there is growing unrest in the east. The death of southern leader John Garang has added to the uncertainty. Extraordinary international attention will be needed to keep the north-south peace process on track and to resolve the ongoing conflict in Darfur.

UGANDA

Uganda is an important player in East and Central Africa, and in the Horn. It has been engaged in both conflict and peace processes in the region. It has also received praise from the United States, the UN, and other countries for its successful efforts to combat HIV/AIDS and to overcome a history of misrule, civil war, and mass atrocities. Under President Yoweri Museveni, Uganda has enjoyed increased stability, steady economic growth, and a greatly improved overall human rights situation. President Museveni, who came to power by force, has since been elected more than once. However, he has only in 2005 permitted multiparty elections. Furthermore, if Museveni chooses to continue his presidency for yet another term, after more than twenty years in power, it could indicate a step backward in the development of multiparty democracy, the processes for succession, and strong sustainable democratic institutions. A worst-case scenario sees a post–Museveni Uganda falling back into internal strife.

ZIMBABWE

The situation in Zimbabwe, which the secretary of state has rightly singled out as a tyrannical reversal of democracy, may be reaching a climax. Up to now, international criticisms and sanctions have failed to sway the government. African countries have been reluctant until recently to criticize the vaunted liberation leader, Robert Mugabe.

However, the collapsing economy, four million people in need of food aid, the migration to neighboring countries of as many as three million Zimbabweans, and the growing, if divided, internal resistance, all point to a potential collapse of the state or a forced change in leadership. Public criticism of the regime by the U.S. ambassador, in November 2005, added to the tension within the country and placed a public spotlight on the mismanagement of the regime that is causing so much human misery.

The United States needs to prepare for possible state collapse, which would have ripple effects throughout southern Africa. Cooperation with South Africa, which will have a major role in whatever regional responses have to be taken, and a contingency plan for U.S. and other donor assistance to bolster a possible, more responsible successor government should be put into place. It is right to have criticized sharply the Mugabe regime. It is also necessary to avoid the worst possible ramifications of a total collapse, the one thing South Africa has feared the most.

OTHER CONFLICT-RIDDEN EMERGING DEMOCRACIES

Several other African countries are emerging from conflict and are pinning their hopes on elections as the first step toward establishing, or in some cases reestablishing, democracy. Liberia, Ivory Coast, and the DRC are a few examples of such broken places. Establishing democracy in any of these countries will be a major challenge, and the results will be less than perfect. But the alternative could be more war, human rights violations, and the need for outside intervention and emergency aid.

The United States has a special historic relationship with Liberia and has already invested heavily in its reconstruction. The election in December 2005 of Ellen Johnson-Sirleaf as president offers the opportunity to restore both peace and development to this war-torn country. The United States should lead in formulating an international support program for Liberia. The DRC is one of Africa's richest countries in natural resources and its fate impacts on the stability of the whole center of the continent. The United States can look to France and the UN to lead in guiding the peace and reconstruction process in Ivory Coast, and to South Africa with AU support to mediate in Burundi in hopes of avoiding a repeat of the genocide that took place in neighboring Rwanda. But the United States should dedicate high-level attention to the DRC, where as many as four million people have died as a result of the conflict, and continuing conflict threatens the stability of the entire Central Africa region. It is most unfortunate that in October 2005, the United States opposed the UN secretary-general's recommendation to increase the UN peacekeeping operation in the DRC in advance of scheduled elections there.

U.S. SUPPORT FOR DEMOCRACY: MATCHING RHETORIC WITH ACTION

THE UNITED STATES has taken several steps to reinforce its support for democracy in Africa. Both the MCA and AGOA include elements of good governance in their qualifying criteria. The United States has insisted on similar criteria for debt relief. Democratization programs are supported by the U.S. Agency for International Development (USAID) in a number of countries.

Nevertheless, democratization funds for Africa have been cut back, especially funding for the strengthening of institutions that make democracy sustainable after elections. In Nigeria, this aid has been reduced from $20 million in FY 1999 to $3 million in FY 2005. Congress's curtailment of the president's FY 2006 request for the MCA by more than $1 billion also sets back U.S. support for democracy by reducing rewards for African states that are moving in the right direction. MCA funds could be used for a variety of institutional developments that would further encourage democratization. The president's 2006 request for the Transitional Initiative, directed at supporting democratization worldwide, singled out only two African states for attention, Sudan and Ethiopia, leaving out critically important transition countries, such as DRC and Nigeria.

The United States must dedicate more resources to building African institutional support for democracy. The value of negative leverage is in many cases reduced. The United States, the United Kingdom, and the EU have all placed sanctions on Zimbabwe, forced a cutback of multilateral institutions' programs there, and denounced the government's actions, to little effect. On the other hand, UN Secretary-General Kofi Annan's appointment of Anna Tibaijuka, executive director of the United Nations Human Settlements Programme, to investigate the recent destruction of thousands of urban homes and marketplaces by the Zimbabwe government, produced a crack in Africa's indifference. Tibaijuka issued a scathing report that increased outrage within the UN and finally prompted criticism of Zimbabwe from the members of the AU. South Africa, which perhaps has the most leverage in the situation, finally took a tougher line, attaching conditions of both political and economic reform to a loan requested by Zimbabwe. African leadership may be one of the most effective instruments that the United States can engage to further the democratization process in countries falling backwards or resisting the democratic trend.

In Uganda and Ethiopia, the demands on the United States are less for resources than for exerting influence on the processes of democracy. In those cases, however, even where both countries are major recipients of international assistance, negative leverage is limited. The leaders of these countries are strong willed and Ethiopia has already talked of reaching out to China to offset pressures from the EU and the United States on its electoral practices. The United States has not yet, however, assigned high-level diplomats to undertake special efforts with Ethiopia or to mobilize a consortium of countries, both African and others, to address the crisis there. In Uganda, perhaps the best path is for the United States to invest much more in the civil and political institutions that can survive yet another term of Museveni's presidency. In any case, the four countries highlighted deserve special attention if democracy is to flourish on the continent and the recent positive trends are to be sustained. Such a strategy is not yet evident.

U.S. SUPPORT FOR HUMAN RIGHTS: MAKING "NEVER AGAIN" A MEANINGFUL PROMISE

THE UNITED STATES has not hesitated in recent years to speak out on serious violations of human rights in Africa. The secretary of state has singled out Zimbabwe as "an outpost of tyranny" and condemned Sudan for deprivations in Darfur. The Department of State's annual human rights report is an important instrument, helping to focus U.S. leverage and urge African attention to human rights violations wherever they occur. Reports from USAID and from U.S.-based and international NGOs were critical in building support for U.S. leadership in the Darfur crisis. The United States is the only country to label the Darfur situation "genocide," and the United States has been the leading force in seeking strong UN condemnation and sanctions in response to the actions by the government of Sudan and its associated militia.

Despite these steps, Darfur remains in crisis. The AU has not been able to mobilize rapidly or effectively support its current force there, nor is it likely to be able to provide the 13,000-person peacekeeping mission it promised. International assistance to the AU, even through NATO and the EU, has not overcome this problem. A rapid mobilization of international force is necessary to protect the displaced and to send a strong message to the Sudanese government. Other steps to further the negotiating process, in particular with the rebel forces, are urgent. Finally, the United States and the EU should be prepared to break the UN logjam on approving sanctions against the Sudanese government, caused by Chinese and Russian objections, by stepping up their own sanctions and confronting China on its role in furthering a humanitarian disaster.

African leadership in human rights will be essential. However, in cases of mass atrocities, as the Darfur crisis shows, Africa must have the assistance and cooperation of the international community. The AU's human rights mechanisms are still not fully in place. AU peacekeepers are already stretched beyond their capacity. These are important areas for U.S. assistance. However, even with assistance to African institutions, none of the steps taken so far by the United States, the UN, or those contemplated in support of African capabilities ensure that in the event of another Darfur or Rwanda, the international response will be proactive, swift, and effective in preventing mass atrocities—not just reactive after lives are long lost. Such mass atrocities are devastating to every U.S. value and goal. Failure to react in Rwanda was not only a major moral failure, it also damaged the reputation of the United States and the UN in Africa for years afterwards. Further, the repercussions of that genocide are still felt today throughout Central Africa in the instability, fighting, and the episodic massacres that occur in eastern Congo and Burundi. Similarly, the continuing crisis in Darfur now threatens the implementation of the north-south peace process in Sudan in which the United States and others have invested so much. The fighting in Darfur is also spreading into Chad and perhaps farther.

The United States, with its power and its influential position in the UN Security Council, has a special role in strengthening the UN's ability to mobilize an international response to such mass atrocities. The United States should press for strengthening the UN secretary-general's role in identifying the early-warning signs of such atrocities and for recommending swift action by the UN Security Council. Where the Security Council is deadlocked from taking action, the United States should mobilize European and other countries' support for imposing sanction. Finally, the United States should build upon the recent decision of NATO to help the AU to plan for future contingencies for Darfur whereby NATO, the EU, and other countries outside Africa can speed African as well as UN and other international response in a far timelier manner than has been seen in the past.

China Ups the Ante in Africa

Princeton N. Lyman

IN NOVEMBER, CHINA hosted its largest diplomatic event ever, celebrating fifty years of Africa-China relations with a red carpet reception and conference for forty-eight African delegations. No fewer than thirty-five African heads of state attended. The meeting produced an action plan that covered not only extensive economic commitments, but a wide range of areas for political cooperation. Subjects included cooperation on UN reform, countering terrorism, promoting Africa as a nuclear weapons-free zone, combating illicit traffic in arms, and assistance in managing natural disasters.

But it was the economic agreements that have captured the most attention. The breadth of those agreements should cause Western observers to rethink some of their assumptions about China's motives and long-term objectives, which are more far-reaching than normally thought.

The breadth and vigor of Chinese activity has been breathtaking. Prior to the summit, China had been steadily increasing its economic role in Africa over several years. This included multibillion-dollar loans to Angola, pledges of billions of dollars in investments in Nigeria—in both cases related to acquiring oil exploration rights and, in the case of Angola, the loans were secured by oil deliveries. Hundreds of Chinese companies are involved across Africa in everything from agriculture, textiles, and telecommunications to the building of stadiums, public buildings, roads, and railroads. China's heavy investment in Sudan's oil industry, from which China obtains 7 percent of its oil imports, has been a source of

This article was part of a CSIS Online Africa Policy Forum, December 1, 2006. Reprinted by permission of the Center for Strategic and International Studies.

international criticism as has been China's investment and arms sales in Zimbabwe. But China's investments and aid have been well received in Africa, as has Chinese diplomacy. There have been repeated visits to Africa by China's president, prime minister, and other top officials, making the once or twice in a term visit by the American president seem paltry by comparison.

For Africa, China offers a new source of both capital and investment. China's engagement also comes with none of the conditionality that marks much Western and multilateral aid, in particular conditions on governance, human rights, and economic reform. China boasts that in its approach to Africa, "business is business, politics is politics," and that economic relations fall in the former category. From China's point of view, whether Africans choose to pursue democracy, protect human rights, liberalize their economic and trading systems, or open their books are all decisions for Africans to make and not the concern of China.

Until the recent summit, figures on China's economic involvement in Africa were difficult to determine. There were widely variant estimates of the sum of Chinese direct investment, the full extent of aid, and the conditions or terms of loans. How much Chinese private investment was being promoted and subsidized by the state was also not clear. There has been wild speculation on the number of Chinese citizens in Africa, including not only government and corporate officials, but also Chinese workers carrying out infrastructure projects and merchants selling low-cost Chinese consumer goods. Claims of as many as seventy thousand Chinese in Angola, and similar numbers elsewhere, have been common. Not all the details are yet clear, especially regarding the number of Chinese in Africa. But the breadth and extent of Chinese activity is becoming clearer, as are the sources of financing.

According to Chinese officials, Chinese investment in Africa has reached $6.27 billion, covering trade, manufacturing and processing, resource development, communications, and development. China also claims to have completed 720 projects in forty-nine African countries and launched another fifty-eight, all financed by preferential loans. China has canceled $1.3 billion in African debt and has promised to raise to 440 the number of products from least developed African countries that can enter China duty-free. China's trade with Africa has grown sharply, from $11 billion in 2000 to an estimated $50 billion in 2006. Most of the trade is in Africa's favor, through export of oil, minerals, and other natural resources. Nevertheless, African countries have complained that imports of Chinese consumer goods are undercutting local production and costing African jobs. China has agreed to voluntary restraints on textile exports to South Africa, and also to look into other ways to ameliorate the impact of Chinese exports to Africa generally.

At the November summit, China made extensive new economic commitments. Over the period 2007–2009, China will establish a $3 billion preferential loan package and a $2 billion preferential buyer's credit for Africans. It will double aid to Africa, and cancel all debts owed by African countries that came due in 2005. China will establish a $5 billion China-Africa Development Fund to provide start-up capital to Chinese companies investing in Africa. In addition, China, which claims to have already trained over 14,000 Africans, will train another 10,000 professionals and set up ten centers of agricultural excellence. Finally, China will establish five trade and economic zones in Africa to promote trade and investment.

What emerges from these figures and other Chinese actions is that the accepted wisdom about China in Africa—namely that China's interest is primarily to gain access to and in many cases ownership of vital oil and mineral resources to feed its fast-growing economy—is short of the mark. China sees in Africa not only an important source of raw materials, which clearly have been a major focus of Chinese attention, but also a growing market and possibly a source over the long run for food, manufacturing, and industrial goods. China's investments and aid thus range over the full spectrum of economic sectors, and are especially interesting in agriculture, long thought to be one of Africa's weaknesses, as well as in tourism in such unlikely spots as Sierra Leone and Zimbabwe.

Another exaggerated claim may be that China takes no interest in Africa in issues of stability and conflict. China may not yet pay much attention to transparency or form of government in choosing its partners—witness its strong positions in Sudan and Zimbabwe and the less than transparent terms of its loans to Angola and other countries. But China has recently played a constructive role in persuading Sudan's government to agree at least in principle to deployment of a UN peacekeeping force in Darfur. China also now provides over 1,600 peacekeepers to the UN, mostly in Africa, including troops in southern Sudan. China has even taken a role in the UN Security Council in trying to find a solution to the crisis in Somalia.

China's engagement thus presents extraordinary challenges and opportunities, both for Africa and the West. For Africa, the availability of new financial resources, coming not only from China but also from India, South Korea, Malaysia, and elsewhere in Africa, is accelerating growth and providing the opportunity to construct badly needed infrastructure. The opening of new markets in Asia is welcome as well. But if Africa uses alternative resources from Asia to push back on pressures for further and highly necessary economic reforms from the West, and regresses on transparency, its gains will only be short term. If these negative consequences can be avoided, China's rising engagement in Africa may come to be seen in the West as a welcome fresh source of capital, which the G8 has agreed Africa desperately needs, and as a complement to Western aid programs that have long eschewed basic infrastructure. China is demonstrating that Africa offers rich opportunities for investment across a broad range of sectors—and not just in oil and natural resources where Western investment is concentrated.

But China's ability to combine its state-owned company bids on resources with aid "sweeteners" presents a serious challenge to Western private companies that cannot work hand in glove with government aid programs in this way. China's rapid response capability on projects—no negotiation of conditionality and no environmental studies or other requirements—also presents a challenge both to Western contractors and to Western aid agencies. In sum, for the West, competition with China will demand new means of cooperation and perhaps less conditionality, but at the same time continuing encouragement of reform within Africa itself.

Toward an Angola Strategy: Prioritizing U.S.-Angola Relations

EXECUTIVE SUMMARY

OUTSIDE THE CONTINENT'S crisis areas, few African countries are more important to U.S. interests than Angola. The second-largest oil producer in Africa, Angola's success or failure in transitioning from nearly thirty years of war toward peace and democracy has implications for the stability of the U.S. oil supply as well as the stability of central and southern Africa. Consequently, the United States has an interest in helping Angola address its numerous and significant national challenges.

At the same time, the United States would not be true to its tradition of democratic values if it did not express concern about the development of democratic governance, protection of human rights, and the rule of law in Angola. Much progress has been made in public transparency and tolerance of dissent, but there is still a way to go. Angola's great wealth is still held by few, and the country continues to rank poorly in terms of human development and governance. Furthermore, an immense amount of physical reconstruction and psychological rehabilitation remains to be done. Angola must wisely use the wealth created by its abundance of natural resources by investing in education, training, and institutional capacity building. It will take years of commitment and

This piece is excerpted from the Independent Commission report *Toward an Angola Strategy: Prioritizing U.S.-Angola Relations,* sponsored by the Center for Preventive Action and the Council on Foreign Relations. Vincent A. Mai and Frank G. Wisner, commission chairs; William L. Nash, project director; Adam P. Frankel, deputy project director (New York: Council on Foreign Relations Press, April 2007).

[23]

determination for Angola to prove to its own people, its neighbors, and the world that it can meet the goals it has set for itself.

Given that U.S. policy toward Angola is a difficult issue for policymakers, businesspeople, and civil society, building a stronger relationship with Luanda will be the most effective means for the United States to help Angola make progress toward peace, democracy, and equitable development, while simultaneously looking after U.S. interests in the Gulf of Guinea region. As part of the U.S. efforts to develop both a broad energy policy and a strategic approach toward Africa, Angola deserves much greater attention in the formulation of U.S. foreign, national security, and economic policies.

Adopting a strategic vision for relations with Angola and strengthening U.S.-Angola relations requires sustained U.S. diplomatic attention and strategic resource allocation. It also involves building trust and strong lines of communication. To begin, the United States can associate itself with sensible Angolan priorities, take steps to advance shared, nonpolitical objectives, and commence regular bilateral discussions with a comprehensive agenda. Common objectives, such as education, public health, poverty alleviation, and institutional capacity building should be advanced through bilateral assistance and support for international organizations.

An integral part of this policy must also be for the United States, working in partnership with international and regional organizations like the United Nations (UN), World Bank, and African Union (AU), to support those individuals in Angola—political leaders, community activists, and civil society leaders—who are striving to build from within a democratic country in which good governance and a more equitable distribution of national wealth are regarded as national priorities. This can be done without undermining the development of a stronger bilateral partnership between the United States and Angola.

The United States must also develop a multilateral strategy to advance the goals of regional security, stability, and development. The Southern African Development Community's (SADC) SADC-U.S. Forum is one setting in which to discuss the political and security situation in the region, and to evaluate progress in areas of cooperation. It is important that the United States support and coordinate with international institutions, both behind the scenes and publicly, to help Angola achieve its development goals and build the infrastructure and human capacity it needs for sustained growth.

Greater levels of U.S. private sector investment in Angola depend more on action by the Angolan government than by the U.S. government. Investment will increase when the Angolan government takes steps to make its business climate more user-friendly and its overall economy less dependent on oil. That said, by sponsoring trade and investment missions, U.S. government departments can help fill information gaps for financiers and businesspeople in a range of sectors, perhaps ultimately building bridges to Angolan businesses and expanding commercial ties.

So deep and complex are Angola's problems, and so sensitive is the history of U.S.-Angola relations, that relatively modest goals must be set for the near and medium term and then achieved only incrementally. Without foregoing commitments to promoting democratic governance and the rule of law, the United States must show patience and forbearance—rebuilding a country after so much destruction, and creating a more equitable society in which Angola's leaders are politically accountable, will not be achieved quickly. Yet sustained attention is the best way to develop long-term partners who contribute to international stability and the best conflict-prevention strategy available.

To that end, the commission recommends:

BILATERAL

- The Bush administration launch a series of visits by congressional delegations and high-level administration officials, such as the undersecretary of state for economic affairs, to southern African states, including Angola, that are making progress in democratic and economic development.
- The assistant secretary of state for African affairs visit Luanda to discuss Angola's national elections, capacity needs, and

postconflict reconstruction and reconciliation process, as well as to compare assessments about developments in the Democratic Republic of Congo (DRC) and Zimbabwe.

- The U.S. Department of State facilitate a discussion with the Angolan government and representatives from the U.S. private sector, nonprofit community, and higher education to explore the possibility of public–private partnerships in capacity building and technical assistance.
- The U.S. government maintain the approximately $35 million of U.S. bilateral assistance to Angolan institutions currently anticipated for 2008. Such funds should continue to provide technical assistance for democratic institution building, civil society, education and professional training, financial and land reform, agricultural development, and public health. Specifically, the Department of State's nonproliferation, antiterrorism, de-mining, and related programs funding, which supports the development of Angola's de-mining capability and the management and destruction of small arms, should not fall below the current $6 million for the next five years. Funding for International Military Education and Training (IMET) programs aimed at developing apolitical and transparent defense institutions, such as training in civil-military relations, defense budgeting, and human rights, should be increased to $600,000 annually.
- The U.S. Embassy discuss with Angola the possibility of expanding current law enforcement training programs with the International Law Enforcement Academy (ILEA) and establishing police institutional development programs through the International Criminal Investigation Training Assistance Program (ICITAP). Programming should include community policing, election security and civil disturbance techniques, and academy development.
- The U.S. Department of Defense make building rapport with Angola a priority of the new U.S. Africa Command. Increased engagement with the Angolan Armed Forces (FAA), through contacts and briefings with FAA leadership, should focus on the progress of disarmament, demobilization, and reintegra-

tion of former combatants, developments in the DRC and Zimbabwe, and the role of the FAA in postconflict Angola. Furthermore, the Department's Africa Center for Strategic Studies initiative can work to hold some of its leadership and topical seminars in Angola.

MULTILATERAL

- The United States propose holding a SADC-U.S. Development Community Forum summit meeting in Luanda.
- The United States support an international investment and economic development conference for Angola, as recommended by the official representatives of donor countries in Luanda. This conference would be an opportunity for Angolan government and development stakeholders to discuss how to strengthen partnerships, prioritize development goals, and build the capacity Angola needs for sustained growth.
- The United States prepare to offer a technical assistance package that complements future cooperation between Angola and the International Monetary Fund (IMF).

PRIVATE SECTOR

- The United States articulate a free trade agreement (FTA) as a goal toward which the U.S. and Angolan governments can aspire, and set milestones for its completion, including an agreement on a Trade and Investment Framework Agreement (TIFA) to establish a consultative mechanism between the U.S. Trade Representative and the Angolan government.
- The United States continue the current practice of supplementing the funding for bilateral assistance programs by public–private agreements with private enterprises active in Angola.
- The U.S. Department of Commerce launch trade and investment missions, particularly for agricultural and agribusiness companies, and establish a permanent presence in the U.S. mission in Angola.

- American businesses in Angola, particularly oil companies, expand support for Angolan education institutions and support more advanced education and training opportunities for Angolan students.

Nigeria: Elections and Continuing Challenges

Robert I. Rotberg

AS NIGERIA GOES, SO GOES AFRICA

NIGERIA'S VITAL IMPORTANCE for Africa's political development, for U.S. and European interests, and for world order cannot be exaggerated. Nigeria's sheer aggregate numbers—possibly as many as 150 million of the full continent's 800 million—and its proportionate weight in sub-Saharan Africa's troubled affairs, make the country's continuing evolution from military dictatorship to stable, sustained democracy critical.

Moreover, four factors are salient. First, Nigeria's sizable production of petroleum, 3.22 percent of world output and 8.5 percent of all U.S. imports, emphasizes Washington's deep interest in sub-Saharan Africa's most populous country. Second, that Nigeria is a committed Muslim land as well as a fervently Christian polity raises questions about Islamism and potential sanctuaries for global terrorists. So far, however, even if northern Nigerians have expressed views favorable to Islam in public opinion surveys, there has been no known embrace of Islamist terror. Indeed, if encouraged and well led, Nigeria could become an effective example of Muslim–Christian cooperation within a plural nation. Third, from a health security vantage point, HIV/AIDS is ravaging Nigeria, as are malaria and tuberculosis. Avian influenza's reservoirs exist significantly in Nigeria and threaten other countries. Likewise,

This piece is excerpted from the Council Special Report *Nigeria: Elections and Continuing Challenges*, sponsored by the Center for Preventive Action and the Council on Foreign Relations (New York: Council on Foreign Relations Press, April 2007).

just as Nigeria's role in exporting polio and measles after failed inoculation campaigns demonstrated, borders no longer bar contagion. What infects Nigerians potentially endangers all of Africa and the world. Fourth, Nigeria has abundant economic potential beyond oil. It is the fastest-growing telecoms market in the world. Its stock market is thriving. Nigerians do not lack for entrepreneurial talent.

But despite oil wealth, despite its vast human capacity, despite its demonstrated heft in the African Union and its significant role in reversing coups in West Africa and helping to broker the Darfurian and other peace initiatives, Nigeria is still a poor, struggling country, even by the standards of its continent. In 2006, Nigeria's gross domestic product (GDP) per capita was $800. That modest figure, less than Mauritania, Côte d'Ivoire, and Senegal, but more than Benin and Ghana, camouflages vast disparities of wealth—Nigeria's Gini coefficient was 0.44 in 2003, among the least equal income spreads in Africa. The Economist Intelligence Unit reports that 70 percent of Nigerians live on less than $1 per day. Nor are Nigeria's social attainments commensurate with its oil and gas wealth. Although $500 billion of oil has been extracted since 1970, life expectancy at birth was only forty-three in 2006, a poor number even within Africa.

These numbers, and Nigeria's reputation as one of the world's most corrupt places, mask the reality that Nigeria, together with South Africa, remains the pivot of Africa. If Nigeria can harness its oil wealth for the good of all of its people, if it can banish (or at least reduce) poverty and squalor, if it can diminish the palpable sense that an overlord class is stripping the people of their rightful shares of prosperity, and if these changes can be funneled into a sustainable effort, then Nigeria can probably become more secure and more a strong leader for good in tomorrow's Africa.

Nigerians want that result. So does the rest of Africa and the international community. But there are severe hurdles to be overcome before Nigeria can begin to achieve its national potential—namely, holding free, fair, and credible (incident-free would be too much to hope for) national elections this April, institutionalizing the fledgling steps toward improved governance and transparency begun in the past eight years, and delivering a modicum of political goods to its citizens in all parts of the country. Good governance is just that: the provision of adequate qualities and quantities of the prime political goods of security, rule of law, political freedom, economic opportunity, and access to infrastructure, education, health, and an empowered civil society.

As Nigeria approaches these crucial elections and a series of decisions that may well alter the trajectory of democracy there and throughout Africa, it draws on a strong well of recent national political accomplishment. The woes of Nigerians may be many, but so are its achievements as a reconstructed nation-state since 1999, when President Olusegun Obasanjo led the nation back to democracy after decades of excessively corrupt military tyranny. Nigeria and Nigerians have been resilient. There is a large, expanding middle class that cherishes and demands more, rather than less, stability. The ranks of the hegemonic bourgeoisie are expanding; entrepreneurs less and less depend on the largesse of the state. The government's dominance of the economy is shrinking, giving space for Nigeria's numerous, skillful entrepreneurs to take the initiative within an increasingly participatory framework.

Most of all, Nigeria has demonstrated since 1999 that it can survive the kinds of major crises that would have derailed less secure, less mature polities. As a "secular" state, Nigeria has managed without too much dissonance to endure and embrace the introduction of sharia law into its north. Contentious as was that insertion of religious law, the nation itself never crumbled. The nation also survived another census, historically a source of competition and conflict. Last year's exercise was received with a little less opprobrium than its predecessors in 1962–63, 1973, and 1991, and was endorsed by the Council of State. It was, comparatively, a successful milestone despite ample cries of disdain in the press and from Lagos.

Similarly, Obasanjo's quest for a third presidential term, breaching constitutional provisions, could have rent the national fabric. Instead, the legislative branch of government diffused hostility and anger, denying Obasanjo what he wanted but without pushing the nation into violence. Shifts in political power from north to south and now, potentially, back again, seem to be accepted as normal—a potential affirmation of Nigeria's growing political maturity. Power sharing, in other words, has become a recognized norm.

The professionalism of the higher judiciary, especially the Supreme Court, has by and large been a force for good, and for moderation, at the national level. Important constitutional challenges have been debated and judged there rather than settled in the streets or by coups. Obasanjo's administration has managed to institute improved budgeting practices, begin reforming the banking system, and massively reduce Nigeria's foreign debt. Furthermore, probity in the petroleum sector has been enhanced thanks to the Nigerian Extractive Industries Transparency Initiative (NEITI). Outside of the government, Nigeria has a thriving civil society. Active nongovernmental organizations, and especially a vibrant media, mean that public accountability mechanisms function.

For policymakers everywhere, Nigeria should be *the* central African question. No country's fate is so decisive for the continent. No other country across a range of issues has the power so thoroughly to shape outcomes elsewhere in sub-Saharan Africa. If Nigeria works well, so might Africa. If the democratic experiment in Nigeria stalls, and development and governance stagnate, the rest of Africa suffers and loses hope. This report carefully examines Nigeria's abundant advances since 1999, discusses some of the constraints on further progress, and recommends a range of policy priorities for Abuja, Washington, Brussels, and London in 2007 and thereafter.

In urgent particular, this report argues that Washington should immediately turn policy eyes to Nigerian questions now, in time to help Nigerians to hold democratically confirming elections in April. A presidential-appointed mission or task force is required, together with high-level attention to many of the near-term and medium-term questions set out in this report and in the appended recommendations. A rapid injection of democracy and governance funding is indicated to assist the Nigerian government in strengthening civil society and accountability before, during, and after the election season. Longer term, the United States and other donors should find the means to offer enduring assistance to Nigeria across the range of governance problems specified throughout this report. A high-level forum—a U.S.-Nigeria commission modeled on the U.S.-China, U.S.-India, and U.S.-Brazil commission models— should be established by Congress to encourage regular dialogue between senior American and Nigerian officials and business-people.

GOOD GOVERNANCE

ACHIEVING GOOD GOVERNANCE requires that the Nigerian state provide adequate qualities and quantities of the prime political goods of security, rule of law, political freedom, economic opportunity, access to infrastructure, education, health, and empowered civil society.

SECURITY

Thus far (since Obasanjo became Nigeria's civilian president in 1999), Nigeria is remarkably less secure than when he took office. Its external borders are unchallenged, but nonstate actors and a variety of indigenous insurgent groups continue to attack (rather brazenly) either the nation-state or the governments of individual states. The nation-state cannot claim a monopoly on the sources of firepower or violence. Additionally, crime against persons, including murder, rape, and robbery, has grown in scale and viciousness. For instance, a survey conducted in 2005 revealed that 25 percent of respondents in Lagos had been victims of theft at some point in the past five years, 12 percent said they had been assaulted, and 9 percent of women admitted being victims of sexual violence.

The Niger Delta

Violence in the oil lands of the Niger Delta, in the Middle Belt between supposed "natives" and alleged "newcomers," and throughout the whole of the country between Muslims and Christians, continues to threaten Nigeria's national sense of itself and to undermine democracy and development. Oil has flowed from the Niger Delta region since 1970. In the six states of the Niger Delta, seven million Ijaw, Ogoni, Itsekiri, Andoni, Ibibio, and other communities have since about 1980 demanded a greater share of Nigeria's oil and gas wealth than that allotted to the relevant local states, now according to the revenue-sharing provisions of the Constitution of 1999.

The Delta region's energy assets provide about 75 percent of all government revenues from minerals. Under Obasanjo, who served as minister of petroleum resources until the end of 2006 as well as president, the nation talked of various ways to be more generous with regard to oil-derived revenues, and about 13 percent of all national revenues, more than ever before, now flow back to the Delta. Even so, those attempts to return additional monies to the relevant states, and new well-meant federal instruments of transparency and other initiatives, have been derided as too miserly and much too late. Certainly they little appease or deflect from militancy the several locally strong protest movements, the most significant of which nowadays is the umbrella Movement for the Emancipation of the Niger Delta (MEND).

In the Delta, insurgents are battling for local hegemony, for control over oil royalties, for autonomy, and for leverage over both the foreign and domestic petroleum-producing companies that exploit deep petroleum reservoirs onshore amid the creeks and tributaries of the mouth of the Niger River and under the Gulf of Guinea. MEND says that it is fighting for "total control" of the Delta's oil riches since the local people have not gained commensurately from "their" resources and from the despoiling of their domain. They also look around them in the Delta and elsewhere and wonder where Nigeria's ample oil and gas revenues have gone; most of the Delta, and much of the remainder of the vast country, is deeply impoverished, with little access to clean water, electric power, or even good, unpaved roads. Bayelsa State boasts only one multilane, paved road, naturally leading to the state capital. Within the Delta there are few decent hospitals or satisfactory schools and many lack staff, supplies, or equipment. The environmental insults have been damaging and numerous—oil spills, blowouts, fires, sulfuric acid spews, and acid rain—and wellhead natural gas flares that turn day into night as well as release 25 million tons of carbon dioxide and 12 million tons of methane into the air annually.

MEND claims to be a "union of all relevant militant groups in the Niger Delta," some of which are political and some of which are criminal. These groups, notably the criminal ones, finance their protest activities by the dangerous and destructive process of siphoning and selling oil from pipelines, extorting "protection" funds, and kidnapping foreigners for ransom. The criminal gangs have also become major arms importers into the Delta. Some of these gangs are allied to state governors or other politicized factions; the line between protest and criminality is too often blurred.

In late 2006, several sets of foreign oil workers were held for weeks and ransomed for substantial sums. More than one hundred foreign hostages were seized throughout all of 2006; a number of them, as well as others caught in cross fire, were killed. In early 2007, separate sets of Chinese, Korean, Filipino, Lebanese, and Italian workers were kidnapped. In late February 2007, seven hostages were still being held, twenty-four Filipinos having recently been released. Each attack on foreigners shuts down a pumping station, delaying production and accelerating global anxiety about Nigeria's reliability as an oil exporter. Car bombs planted by MEND in Port Harcourt also added to the general atmosphere of danger and malaise in late 2006. In January 2007, fifty machine-gun-firing MEND affiliates attacked the main police station in Port Harcourt, killing a passerby and freeing one of its notorious jailed leaders, a so-called gangster.

The actual number of barrels of oil exported falls each time extractive activities are disturbed by MEND or others. Although Nigeria exported 2.5 million barrels of oil in 2005, the violence of 2006 reduced that total by 25 percent. This year promises to be worse for petroleum production (and therefore for foreign importers), as little national leadership is being exerted to negotiate with the Delta movements or to contain them militarily.

The Delta is a mess, and the failures of state and local governments, plus massive peculation, are at least partially responsible for the destruction and despoliation of the environmental commons and for the mayhem that is among the major stories of the Delta.

[35]

The police cannot control events there. Military patrols will be essential. What could help address the root causes of unrest and violence would be international participation and independent oversight of a special international fund for the overhaul and uplift of the Delta—as discussed in the recommendations section of this report—plus the exercise of greater responsibility by oil producers. Equally critical at the local level would be the initiation of a viable dialogue between militants and representatives of civil society, and between local rulers (the local elections are apt to be rigged) and genuine representatives of "the people."

SECTARIANISM AND ETHNOLINGUISTIC FRACTIONALIZATION

Sectarian and communal strife in the Delta and throughout the entire nation stems from a lack of credible leadership in Abuja and in the states, and an overemphasis on the politics of personalist rule. The delegitimation of national and state institutions, the perceived absence of formal avenues for political participation by aggrieved groups at all levels, and a federal government that has failed to project power all contribute to the growth in violence.

Furthermore, no one trusts the poorly trained national Nigerian Police Force (NPF), or its local detachments, to provide effective human protection anywhere, whether in the Delta, in Lagos, or in the cities of the north. Minorities justly fear that they will be victimized or oppressed. Sometimes they accordingly react defensively and preemptively. Given the scarcity of alternatives, entities that rightly or wrongly consider themselves disadvantaged seek redress for grievances through local or regional mayhem. Protest surges, vigilante brigades, and intercommunal mayhem then results, more often than not within a cascade of tit-for-tat retribution.

Nigeria, after all, contains more than 250 ethnolinguistic groups and about seventy "nationalities." Hausa, Igbo, and Yoruba speakers account for about 60 percent of the total population according to the discredited existing censuses, but within each of the thirty-six states and one federal territory, even within the twelve sharia-observant northern states, there are long-resident and recently resident minorities, some ethnolinguistic, some religious, and some a combination of both such identities making and shaking concerns. From its origins as a nation, Nigeria has been unsure and confused about whether legal and administrative institutions of governance should recognize or mostly ignore those distinctions. Nigeria has attempted over its four-plus decades to honor self-determination within a governmental framework much more unitary than federal. Among the many critical issues now facing Obasanjo's successor is whether and how to deal with the continued upwellings of claims to self-determination, as in the Delta, and at the same time improve security for all Nigerians through the exercise of responsible central control.

During Obasanjo's time, Nigeria has been unable to protect its citizens equably. More than 12,000 people have been killed since 1999 in local clashes, and more than three million have been displaced from their homes. Jukun have fought Tiv in the Middle Belt, especially in Taraba State. Yoruba have battled Hausa in the southwest. Christians have fought Muslims in Kaduna, Yelwa, and elsewhere in Plateau State with great losses of life. Igbo have clashed with Hausa in the southeast. Jos, once an oasis of peace, has seen several bitter clashes between supposed indigenous and nonindigenous groups. There has been fighting in Langtang North and South, in Wase, Bardi Ladi, Riyom, and in many other places. Each clash has a specific local cause and a possible local solution. But nearly all of the ongoing conflicts, real or perceived, are over resources. Trading privileges, employment possibilities, welfare payments, water access, and land rights are continually contested.

In the absence of any belief in the legitimacy—and fair dealing—of governmental authority, and given deep skepticism everywhere over local and national rule of law regimes, these intercommunal disputes—and their violent settling—will hardly diminish. A new president and his government could do well to foster a climate of tolerance and equitable resolution, but that might mean rebuilding the NPF and judicial systems from scratch.

Obasanjo could well argue that the governance problem is in the states, not in the nation. After all, the states collectively receive half of Nigeria's oil revenues, and spend those revenues inconsistently and without much accountability. Many of the decisions that affect aggrieved communities adversely are indeed taken at the state level, especially by autocratic governors. When state civil services overwhelmingly employ the members of one ethnolinguistic group over another, confidence is very hard to engender, especially in those states where heterogeneity is the rule. Preferential admission to secondary schools and local universities creates additional grievances. Land ownership is contested. Access to political opportunity may also be limited or circumscribed. Above all, the heavy corruption and partiality of state governors and governments hardly boosts confidence in the overall system among those in the minority or out of favor. Reform of state governance is therefore overdue, but April's election is unlikely to produce a president or legislators capable of restructuring the nation in this manner. Some of the candidates for president in April may or may not transcend their sectional roots and appeal effectively to the Nigerian nation, but most Nigerians will be skeptical and distrustful regardless.

RULE OF LAW

Another obstacle to national unity, for whoever is elected president, is a judicial system that is seen to be ponderous (in both its criminal and civil procedures), partial, prejudiced, and incompletely independent. The country's formal justice system fails to ensure personal safety or secure personal or corporate property. It rarely settles disputes quickly and fairly, compelling too many Nigerians to conclude disputes by force. Arbitrary arrests are common. So is prolonged incarceration without trial—pretrial detainees comprise at least 70 percent of persons held in prisons. The customary and area courts (south and north, respectively) hear most Nigerian cases. They are as characterized by delay as are the formal courts. They often lack due process, are noted for arbitrariness, and are presumed to be corrupt. Rule-of-law breaches are responsible for the rise of vigilantism or private law enforcement.

The failures of the justice system (despite acknowledged successes in the constitutional realm) are also blamed for serious and systematic human rights abuses. Too few ethnolinguistic conflicts have been effectively justiciable in recent years. Indeed, Bronwen Manby concludes that "impunity for the use of violence for political and personal ends has . . . been a major contributor to the escalation of ethnic violence." Moreover, justice at all rungs below the federal appellate level is widely believed to be purchasable. Hence, an initial enthusiasm in 2000 and 2001 for the introduction of more certain, more swift codes of justice; Nigeria's twelve northern, Muslim states adopted the sharia one after the other, despite the "secular" provisions of the national constitution. Even there, however, palpably fair and objective justice has largely remained an ideal. Rule of law, the second most critical political good, particularly in developing societies, continues to be more of an aspiration than a Nigerian reality.

ECONOMIC OPPORTUNITY AND CORRUPTION

Good governance includes the provision of the political good of economic opportunity—the creation of an environment conducive to the maximizing of personal entrepreneurial instincts within an effectively regulated macroeconomic framework. Because Nigeria under Obasanjo has become more open, with inflation held in check in 2006 at 11 percent, an estimated budget deficit of 1.4 percent of GDP in 2007, and GDP growth rates reaching 5 percent in 2005 but falling in 2006 to 4.3 percent, the Nigerian government can be regarded as successful in delivering a more adequate amount of this political good than its misguided predecessors.

But oil and gas are everything, still providing 20 percent of GDP, 65 percent of budgetary revenues, and 95 percent of foreign exchange earnings. In 2005, Nigeria exported $47 billion worth of petroleum and gas.[1] Agricultural and non-oil mineral exports contribute little to Nigeria's GDP, especially when compared to the 1970s. Once a large exporter of food crops, Nigeria must now import most of its food and most of its refined petroleum products. Manufacturing also constitutes much less of the national economy than at independence.

Because it suffers from a weak rule of law performance, Nigeria also often lacks the ability to enforce contracts without resorting to violence. In the late 1990s, Nigeria's effective "tax effort" was among the poorest on the continent. Nigeria's entrepreneurial culture essentially runs wild, still benefiting individual Nigerians but not Nigeria as a whole. Overall, 70 percent of all Nigerians were deemed "poor" in 2004, more than twice as many as in 1981.

Admittedly, the country's long period of military rule still drags down the economy. Obasanjo's first civilian administration tried in some respects to recover ground, but its economic performance was lethargic. Peter M. Lewis suggests that "policy initiatives or institutional reforms that might have shifted the country's trajectory were wanting."[2] During the second administration, particularly during the thirty-six months that Ngozi Okonjo-Iweala was finance minister, deficits were reduced, statist remnants were removed, and accountability was enhanced. But Nigeria, with so much annual oil and gas revenue, still underperforms its democratic peers on the continent.

Corruption distorts economic priorities and, as a result, greatly diminishes performance and encourages wave after wave of cynicism and emulation. Levels of venal and lubricating corruption are higher than most places in the world. Corruption is a way of life, especially concerning the government; few such acts are not infused with bribe giving and taking. Governors, judges, bureaucrats, police officials, soldiers, and many citizens enrich themselves whenever possible. No road, bridge, or building is built without officials benefiting. Thus, priorities are endlessly distorted, politicians enriched, and the nation consequently impoverished. In 2006, Transparency International's Corruption Perception Index ranked Nigeria 142 of 163 countries, an improvement over previous years, but still lamentable and probably an understatement of reality.

Obasanjo promised in 1999 to clean house. He appointed an anticorruption commission and later created a serious crimes commission. But he made too few public examples of corrupt cabinet ministers, governors, or others. He also seemed to tilt toward the need for party electoral funds and in favor of corrupt cronies when he pushed aside Finance Minister Okonjo-Iweala in 2006. Yet, in 2006, during the run-up to the next election, there were several prosecutions of prominent miscreants, including several governors, and many threats to expose the corrupt activities of persons opposed to Obasanjo and the PDP. For various reasons, Obasanjo seemed finally to regard combating corruption as an area where he could lead by example.

Yar'Adua may be significantly less corrupt than alternative candidates, especially if his press can be believed, but many of his associates in Katsina are immensely wealthy and his family businesses have always benefited from a gubernatorial connection. He would have to be an extremely strong candidate to run for the presidency with few commitments to wealthy power brokers. He would be unusual for a Nigerian politician if he ran an austere campaign or failed to protect himself from being outspent by his opponents. [Goodluck Ebele] Jonathan also seems potentially tainted, as well as being undistinguished. The PDP team thus enters the final weeks of the electoral season with few claims to unusual integrity and precious little national appeal.

SPREADING THE WEALTH AND COMBATING HIV/AIDS

Historically, Nigeria's wealth has benefited the few, mostly military officers from the north, and their clients. Sticky fingers appropriated billions of dollars; only a matter of millions has been reclaimed from Swiss banks despite determined efforts by the Nigerian and European authorities.

The erosion, and personal appropriation, of state revenues and royalties from oil must explain Nigeria's appalling ranking on every international official and unofficial human development indicator. The 2006 Human Development Index (HDI) prepared by the UNDP ranks Nigeria 159 of 177 countries, after Eritrea and Rwanda, and before Guinea and Angola.[3]

Life expectancy has fallen to forty-three from recent levels in the fifties. Infant mortality rates, for example, are listed as more than ninety-seven per one thousand live births. For comparison, South Africa's rate is fifty-four, Tunisia's is twenty-one, Singapore's is three, Finland's is three, and the U.S. rate is seven. The maternal mortality ratio per one hundred thousand live births in 2000 was eight hundred, among the highest in Africa. About 30 percent of all children under five were underweight for age or height in 2003, an average result for Africa but high compared to Asia or Europe. For instance, countries classified by the World Bank as "middle income" had a malnutrition prevalence of 19 percent height-for-age and 11 percent weight-for-age.

In 2004, there were twenty-seven physicians per one hundred thousand people. In 2001, Nigeria spent an amount equal to 2.6 percent of its GDP on health care, both public and private. Those modest numbers mask a massive drain of medical professionals and infrastructural weaknesses that are common to Africa and Nigeria and that work against the new, welcome, external, high-profile assistance available to attack the causes of Nigeria's penetrating health problems and virulent diseases.

Neither the national nor the state governments has managed effectively to catch up with and manage the country's very serious HIV/AIDS epidemic. After India and South Africa, Nigeria has the greatest number of HIV/AIDS sufferers in the world. Although its 6 percent adult prevalence rate is far less than the prevalence rate throughout southern and eastern Africa, Nigeria's large population means that at least eight million must be infected in 2007. A few years ago, Daniel J. Smith reported that 170,000 Nigerians died each year from AIDS or AIDS-related diseases.[4] That number reached 220,000 deaths in 2005. Cumulatively, 1.7 million people or so have died since the scourge of HIV/AIDS appeared in 1986, and more than 1.5 million children have been orphaned.

For the country's 2007–2011 government, the projections are dire: The adult prevalence rate will reach as high as 26 percent and up to fifteen million people will be infected. By 2011, possibly ten million Nigerians will have died from AIDS. Sometime between now and 2011, Nigeria will overtake South Africa as the continent's most AIDS-devastated nation. Nothing will stanch the trajectory of the disease before 2011, but a fuller distribution of antiretroviral cocktails will enable many sufferers to live longer, and an existing health infrastructure more robust than today's could provide welcome palliative care. But the big challenge is slowing the spread of HIV/AIDS. The Obasanjo government did less than it might have to create governmental programs to combat AIDS and prevent future generations from succumbing.

The U.S. President's Emergency Plan for AIDS Relief (PEPFAR)'s several grants to Nigerian agencies may help to stem the tide of disease, and Nigerians are much more aware now than they were earlier in this century about the spread of AIDS and its economic and social consequences for the nation. But the new Nigerian administration will want to do even more, and to devote increasing proportions of its oil revenues to a massive attack on the disease. The increase in funding should be focused on prevention efforts. Malaria, tuberculosis, infantile paralysis, and a host of other diseases, including measles and meningococcal fevers, are also rife. The new government, with its northern credibility, needs to do more than the Obasanjo regime did in this general area to explain the necessity of vaccination and other broad spectrum campaigns against such scourges. More of Nigeria's resources, with appropriate help from outside, should be devoted to the ongoing battle against dangers to the health of the nation, the continent, and the globe.

Terrible numbers testify to vast unmet public health needs. In 2003, there were 2,608,479 reported malaria cases and 5,343 reported malaria deaths in Nigeria. In 2004, Nigeria had the world's fourth-largest tuberculosis burden, with nearly 374,000 estimated new cases annually.[5] Of the new and old cases, about 105,000 die annually; the in-country case detection and treatment success rates were among the lowest of nations with high tuberculosis case numbers. In 2004, two-thirds of all polio cases worldwide occurred in Nigeria (760 out of 1,170 total). Between January and August 2004, at least 35,856 children in Nigeria became infected with measles. However, in 2005, Nigeria completed Africa's largest measles campaign, vaccinating thirty million children. In 1996, a meningitis epidemic swept the country, infecting over one hundred thousand people. In 2003, there were 3,508 reported cases, with 428 deaths.

In three countries in the world—Nigeria, Egypt, and Indonesia—the lethal H5N1 avian influenza is officially, by World Health Organization standards, "out of control." A woman (and possibly her relatives) died in crowded Lagos in early 2007 from this flu, demonstrating an alarming human susceptibility. Evidence of the flu in birds has been found in nineteen of Nigeria's thirty-six states, according to the Food and Agriculture Organization. Although Nigeria has already culled about seven hundred thousand domestic chickens and ducks, the president of the national Animal Science Association said that bans on the movement of poultry and the killing of infected birds were not being enforced. Chicken parts, guinea fowl, ducks, and turkeys from northern Nigeria were easily available in southern Nigerian markets in February 2007. Nigeria also exports poultry to all of West Africa. Experts worry that the avian flu could combine with human influenza strains in Nigeria. If so, a pandemic of alarming proportions could follow. Nigeria's new government needs to attend to these dangers as well as to strengthen its existing inadequate public health infrastructure.

Although 68 percent of Nigerians are literate, the net primary enrollment ratio was only 67 percent in 2003. The net secondary enrollment ratio, an even more important statistic, was 29 percent in the same year. In Africa, those are below-average attainments. So are all of the comparisons between women and men, with the former considerably lower than men on all measures.

All Nigerians complain about their roads, and access to them. On a universal pothole index, Nigeria's arteries would rate among the worst maintained. For a country the size of two Californias, there are only 60,000 kilometers (km) of nominally paved roads and another 134,000 km of unpaved roads and tracks. California, for comparison, has 169,906 miles (273,437 km) of public roads. Nigerians would welcome attention to their insufficient network of roads, but there are many other critical infrastructural deficits, each of which limits economic growth and democratic achievement.

South Africa in Retrospect

Princeton N. Lyman

THERE ARE SEVERAL ways by which to measure South Africa's progress and prospects. One is of course to compare its achievements against the contemporary performance of other countries, using such indexes as that of Freedom House, the United Nations' Millennium Development Goals (MDGs), or the performance of other "emerging markets." In this regard, South Africa does rather well: rated "free" by Freedom House (one of only eleven states so rated in Africa), having a steady if not spectacular growth rate and having avoided the financial and banking crises of several other emerging markets, and ahead of many other developing countries in reaching the MDGs. Another is to measure South Africa against the challenges the country faces, for example, whether the rate of growth is sufficient to cut into the high rate of unemployment, whether the programs to combat HIV/AIDS are equal to the magnitude of the problem, etc. In this regard, the country fares less well. Growth rates have stayed within the range of 3–5 percent at best, whereas most estimates are that rates of at least 6 percent are needed to make inroads into the unemployment problem. South Africa provides antiretroviral drugs to more HIV/AIDS victims than almost any other affected country outside the industrialized world, but most observers fault the government for obtuseness and denial in reacting to one of the highest rates and largest number of HIV/AIDS-affected people in the world.

Another way, however, and the one adopted in this paper, is to measure South Africa's performance against the expectations of

---

This paper was presented to the conference, "Africa and Prospects for Hope," University of Oklahoma, International Programs Center, September 14, 2006.

the period when it was on the brink of emergence from the apartheid period. What did experts and informed observers predict for South Africa, given its history, its plethora of problems, and the challenges it faced? In this respect, South Africa's record is in some senses extraordinary if flawed.

PEACEFUL OR VIOLENT CHANGE

IN THE 1980s, whether looking at the fiction of writers like Nadine Gordimer and Mongane Wally Serote, or indeed much of the political writings of the time, the prospects if not the outright prediction was that South Africa would eventually undergo a bloody and perhaps devastating civil war. The war would bring about an end to apartheid but also perhaps a black dictatorship with dangerous prospects for the white minority. A distinguished panel of American experts warned in 1985 that "time was running out" for peaceful change.[1] A liberal white writer, acknowledging the bankruptcy of the apartheid dream and philosophy, nevertheless feared the worst for both blacks and whites.

> The townships are hellholes because everyone is afraid . . . Garbage collectors are afraid. Rent collectors won't go near the townships. Repairmen are afraid. Residents are afraid. . . . The black townships are a mass approaching criticality. Everyone searches for a way of defusing them: the Afrikaners, the other whites, the moderate black leaders—even the less moderate black leaders have cause for fear. No one yet knows if a way will be found.[2]

Not everyone was so dire. Already Nelson Mandela was sending signals that a post–apartheid South Africa would not tolerate black oppression any more than white. The armed attacks of the ANC were in fact relatively limited and rarely aimed at civilians or large-scale loss of life—a far cry from some of the tactics of other movements in our time. There was also movement within the apartheid government, seeking a new vision and disposition, leaders whom the Afrikaner writer quoted above described as having "hearts large enough to make the dramatic leap."

In the 1990s, the predictions of chaos and mayhem gradually lessened as the process of negotiation proceeded and the leadership of Nelson Mandela and his entourage became manifest. But they did not disappear. Right up to the final days before the 1994 election, the resistance to the election from Chief Mangosuthu Buthelezi's Inkhata Freedom Party created the prospect of civil war after the elections, not dissimilar from Robert Mugabe's brutal attack on Matabeleland in Zimbabwe with repercussions that last to this day. That threat in South Africa was averted in an almost bizarre series of events that brought Buthelezi into the electoral process at the last moment.

Still, fears were evident. On the eve of the election of 1994, whites emptied the stores of paraffin, canned goods, and other emergency supplies. There were warnings that all services would collapse on the day after the election, that blacks might storm white neighborhoods and take over homes. On the part of the blacks there were fears, right up to the day of the election, that it might all come to naught. Bombs at the Johannesburg airport on the morning of the first day of voting sent chills into many observers (including this one). However, the security forces acted quickly to apprehend the bombers, the elections proceeded peacefully, and majority rule was established. Whites were soon relieved. In the days afterward, and indeed the years afterward, life went on remarkably as it had before. (The emergency supplies fortuitously were donated to Rwanda relief.)

In the aftermath of the elections, the political violence that had wracked South Africa during the negotiations virtually disappeared. Buthelezi went on to serve in the national government as a minister for more than a decade and at times served as acting president. The military underwent a gradual transformation, without ever threatening a coup or overt political activity. Other problems arose or persisted, but there was no bloody civil war and whites would continue to enjoy not only freedom but continued economic superiority. Today these things are taken for granted. In the 1980s almost no one would have predicted them.

THE PROSPECTS FOR DEMOCRACY

ONCE THE QUESTIONS of chaos and mayhem were put aside, the issues that took prominence were of what kind of rule could be expected from the new government. And equally important, what would be its economic policies? Even with the relatively peaceful transition and a constitution filled with guarantees of civil and human rights and various forms of citizen protection, there were worries that South Africa would follow the path of so many other African countries where one-party rule turned increasingly into political autocracy, oppression, and even brutality. Even as fervent a supporter of the antiapartheid movement as Trevor Huddleston voiced this concern.

> It will also become obvious that the transitional period will be a struggle for political power, which history shows to be full of ethical and moral dangers. African countries (like all other countries seeking national identity) since achieving political independence from their colonial masters, have all seen just how dangerous power can be. South Africa will not be the exception.[3]

The longer-term viability of democracy was debated extensively among many scholars as well as pundits in the run-up to the transition. Some democracy analysts like Donald Horowitz were pessimistic. Horowitz argued in his 1991 book, *A Democratic South Africa?*, that the intrinsic nature of liberation movements as well as the inevitable role of ethnicity would lead the ANC, once in power, toward autocracy. Only strong institutional arrangements, such as federalism, would constrain it. Others were more optimistic. Stephen Stedman, Robert Price, and others argued that the very use of ethnicity to divide people during the apartheid regime had discredited ethnicity and promoted a sense of national identity among black South Africans. They also pointed to the emerging capacity for negotiation and compromise in the ANC, and the strength of civil society in South Africa as important forces in support of democracy.[4] Fears that South Africa would follow the history of other African countries down the path of autocracy and ethnic domination of one group over others have in fact proved unduly pessimistic.

One of the key determinants of how matters would progress came in the agreement during the transition period to establish a set of principles that would guide all future constitutions and governments. These principles would be monitored and enforced by a Constitutional Court. The test, however, was what would happen once the ANC was in power.

The immediate cause for concern was if the ANC received a two-thirds majority in the parliament, the number needed to amend the constitution. Would it then undo many of the most protective provisions of the constitution? Indeed, the number required for amending was one of the most contentious issues in the transition negotiations, leading in large part to the breakdown of negotiations in 1992 (de Klerk had pressed for 75 percent). In what most analysts believe was a behind-the-scenes deal between Mandela and other leaders in the wake of muddled electoral returns, the ANC was awarded 62 percent, alleviating these fears. But these fears have also been put to rest for the longer term—at least so far. The issue arose again, when the ANC in 1999 specifically urged its supporters to give it a two-thirds majority. However, the ANC promised at the same time to consider only "technical changes" to the constitution. The ANC received more than the two-thirds majority needed in the 1999 election and again in 2004. But as promised, it has made no move to amend the constitution in any major way.

Other tests of the viability of the democratic provisions of the constitution have been passed. Twice AIDS activists have taken the government to court over the provision of antiretroviral drugs. In both cases, and in other cases before the Constitutional Court, the government lost. Unlike in Zimbabwe where, after losing a case, the government forced the resignation of the chief justice, and has since basically emasculated the judiciary, South Africa's government bowed to the courts' judgment (if not altogether gracefully or with enthusiasm). Justice Edwin Cameron, a champion of the provision of treatment and other programs for those with HIV/AIDS, began a recent address to an American audience by reminding them that, "The first thing I want to emphasize is that South Africa is a democracy. Because it is a democracy we could take our case for treatment to court and win, and today treatment is being provided."

While the government often bristles over press criticism, and raises worries by occasionally playing the "race card" in pointing to continued white ownership of major newspapers, the press remains free. Civil society also remains vibrant, though receiving far less foreign support than it did during the antiapartheid period.

What is most worrisome for the long run is the utter failure of any other parties than the ANC to capture support among the black population. The National Party had totally unrealistic dreams of eventually playing that role and has now virtually collapsed into the ANC! But the once-liberal Democratic Party has also failed, in part because it has chosen to position itself as a sharp critic of the ANC (and therefore in the minds of black voters critical of the liberation movement) and in part because of the ANC's continuing claim on black South Africans' loyalty. Efforts by black politicians, like Bantu Holomisa, or leaders of the Pan African Congress, have been similarly unsuccessful. The result is that South Africa is governed as almost a one-party state. Only a serious split within the ANC would produce anything like a serious competition for power. And how such a split would come about, and whether it would engender efforts to constrain the political process by those resisting the split, is one of the remaining concerns.

In the meanwhile, the ability of the ANC to dominate the parliament's agenda, and often its investigatory process, through its majority and sometimes strict enforcement of party loyalty, reduces the checks and balances that are desirable. In particular parliamentary investigations of government corruption and competence are inhibited. Much of the most serious debate over government policy and performance thus comes from within the ANC, a desirable process in itself but not sufficient for a truly open democratic system.

ECONOMIC POLICY

THE SECOND MAJOR source of concern in the 1990s was over economic policy. Many believed that the ANC's history of anticapitalist rhetoric, coupled with enormous expectations on the part of the black majority for post-apartheid benefits, would lead the ANC to resort to deficit spending, government control of the economy, and distributive policies that had proved ruinous in other African countries. R.W. Johnson, one of the most consistently negative commentators on South Africa during this period (and beyond), stated it this way:

> There is almost no power on earth which will prevent politicians (and certainly not ANC politicians) from taking large bags of money if their constituency is frantic for houses and jobs and the money is on offer. There will, in other words, be almost inexorably a debt-led boom, with money poured into black housing, education, and welfare, into an increased public sector and, of course, into politicians' bank accounts.[5]

Even more sympathetic observers thought the pressures on the ANC were irresistible. Jeffrey Herbst wrote:

> Once in power, the ANC will probably try to retain most of its constituency by widely distributing increases in government spending even at the cost of incurring a high deficit. The historical pattern of trying to gain maximum popular support is so deeply ingrained in the ANC that it will have great difficulty shedding certain groups to avoid deficit spending.[6]

The prognosis proved incorrect. To the surprise of many, and indeed to the consternation of some of the ANC's most important constituencies, e.g., the labor movement, the ANC-led government proved almost paranoid in its fear of debt and determined to avoid the mistakes of other African countries it had witnessed during its long period in exile. It resisted the earnest courting of the World Bank, eager to lend, taking full advantage of the Bank's grant-funded technical analyses but fending off any loans for years. It similarly refused the seemingly generous (but high interest rate) offer of credits from Japan in the wake of the transition. Instead, it pursued a policy that put stabilization at the heart of its fiscal policies and met its dedication to increased social services through savings. Thus in the first five years after Mandela's election, the ANC administration reduced short-term foreign debt by 80 percent, reduced inflation by an average of 15 percent to little more than 6 percent, and by 2001 achieved perhaps the first budget surplus in decades. At the same time, more than nine million people were given access to clean water, and 1.5 million people gained electricity. One million houses were built through subsidies and support of new mortgage systems, rather than direct government expenditure. Free lunches were provided to all schoolchildren, and free medical care to mothers and children.[7]

Unfortunately, these policies—applauded by the World Bank, the IMF, and most economists—failed to generate the level of growth or investment that had been expected. A widely publicized set of economic scenarios produced during the transition period had predicted that while a burst of deficit spending would produce a short-term boom, it would lead to a later economic downturn, while such policies as the ANC adopted would in a few years produce growth rates of 6 to 7 percent. Throughout the balance of the 1990s, however, growth averaged no better than 3 percent. In the formal sector a half million jobs were lost. Foreign direct investment was only one-third to one-tenth that in other emerging markets. South Africa learned that profuse congratulations on the relatively peaceful end to apartheid, and promises of great post-apartheid support, did not in fact translate into positive decisions by the foreign business community. At a conference of the leaders of the European Union in 1998, Nelson Mandela was urged to take advantage of all the praise being expressed to ask the leaders to open their checkbooks. With a wry smile, Mandela replied, "They have no ink in their pens."[8]

Nevertheless, despite deepening criticism within the ANC and a growing demand for more expansive economic policies, the ANC has remained committed to the same basic economic policies. A recent assessment by the IMF noted that inflation was now being held between 3 and 6 percent, the South African Reserve Bank was maintaining a flexible exchange-rate system while continuing to build up international reserves, external debt had declined, and the fiscal deficit had fallen to 0.3 percent of GDP. The conclusions of the IMF assessment sum up South Africa's achievements and the predicaments of such policies quite well:

> Supported by well-designed macroeconomic policies and structural reforms, growth in recent years has been strong, inflation had

remained within the target band, and employment has increased. The public finances are sound, and international reserves have been rebuilt. Directors noted also that South Africa continues to face important challenges over the medium term, including reducing high unemployment [the IMF noted that the rate of unemployment had remained unchanged], inequality and poverty, and staunching the HIV/AIDS epidemic. . . . Directors considered the economic outlook for South Africa is broadly positive. Continued solid policy implementation and favorable external conditions should establish the foundations for sustained growth.[9]

It cannot go unnoted here that in 1994, the representatives of the IMF were among the most openly critical and pessimistic about South Africa's future economic policies and prospects under an ANC regime.

There is no doubt that the conservative economic policies followed by the government are now the most divisive issue within the ANC. They form the core (at least substantively) of the competition between President Mbeki and the supporters of his erstwhile Deputy President Jacob Zuma. Some of the implications of this debate will be discussed below. But first it is important to note that these relatively conservative policies have not kept the government from greatly increasing spending on social services and the poor. To the contrary, such expenditures have been significant, but financed by reduced debt and better tax collection. For example, in 1998, 24 percent of tax revenue went for debt servicing, in 2005 it was 14 percent, and by 2009 it is predicted to drop to 10 percent.

In the meanwhile, there have been significant achievements since 1994. Electricity has been extended to 3.5 million homes, water supply infrastructure now reaches 90 percent of the population, 3.9 million poor households now receive free water, and free basic electricity reaches 2.9 million homes. More than 1,300 clinics have been built and 2,300 upgraded, and health services now receive 101 million patient visits a year. School fees will be phased out in low-income communities in 2006.[10] Problems surely remain, and on a large scale, but the amount of progress, within conservative fiscal policies, is admirable.

But perhaps most significant, for maintaining minimal incomes and perhaps even more for stability, is the provision of direct social security and social assistance grants to vulnerable households. Alone among developing countries, South Africa provides a "safety net" for the poorest. These grants have been the fastest-growing category of government expenditure since 2001 and now amount to R70 billion (around $10 billion) a year, or 3.4 percent of GDP. They reach more than ten million beneficiaries, nearly one-quarter of the population. Social grants account for more than half the income of the poorest 20 percent of households.[11] Added to these grants are the pensions that go to every retired schoolteacher, nurse, or other government worker, on which many households depend (pensions between whites and blacks, unequal in the apartheid period, were equalized as one of the first acts of the ANC regime).

STABILITY

THESE SOCIAL PROGRAMS have undoubtedly contributed to the surprisingly extended "window" of opportunity for the government to address what it has not yet been able to address sufficiently: the high rate of unemployment, the deep levels of absolute poverty, and the continuing and glaring inequality between the incomes and economic ownership of whites versus blacks.

If widespread economic benefits were slow to come, some analysts had in 1994 predicted that the country could become unstable in a matter of a few years. The population, they said, would grow disillusioned with the ANC. The proliferation of arms in the region would be further cause of concern.

> The nature of a significant portion of the ANC's constituency suggests that it will have a relatively short grace period before it is under extreme pressure to deliver the political goods. . . . South Africa's population is highly politicized and there are already numerous politicians and groupings around which aggrieved urban residents can coalesce. . . . A further aggravating factor, in contrast to most other African countries at independence, machine guns, mortars, and land mines are readily available in South Africa because

of the long armed struggle, the regional arms markets that developed from the conflicts in Mozambique and Angola, and the greater local capacity to produce weapons. Thus, a future South African government will face a much more demanding population that is more concentrated, easier to organize, and better armed than was the case in the rest of the continent.[12]

The material changes for most black South Africans did not in fact improve dramatically in the first several years of Mandela's presidency and for many they are still dire today. But the fears of instability and disillusionment also proved unnecessarily dire.

During the run-up to the election, most people spoke of black expectations and white fears, i.e., black expectations that there would be immediate gratification in terms of houses, jobs, and other material benefits, and white fears that this would cause attacks on white privileges and even physical attacks on their person and possessions. But an astute observer of South Africa at the time voiced a different concern, of white expectations and black fears: white expectations that nothing would change and black fears that they were right. That has turned out to be closer to the truth. Ten years after the transition, whites continue to enjoy wages and benefits far greater than blacks, hardly any diminution in their standard of living, and indeed continue to own the vast majority of the nation's wealth. South Africa's growing array of modern shopping malls and luxury hotels are largely filled with white South Africans and tourists. While there is a steady growth in the black middle class, the vast majority of black South Africans continue to live in substandard housing, suffer unemployment at rates between 27 and 40 percent, and barely crack the senior levels of management outside the government.

However, the predictions that this would cause unrest, or at least a turning away from the ANC, have proved wrong. Polls and surveys have continued to show that black South Africans have a remarkably sophisticated view of how long it takes to alter such basic social and economic conditions while basking in the new freedoms and absence of oppression that the transition has brought about.

In some ways the polls defied the analysts looking at them. Writing a preface to the description of polls and focus groups conducted from 1992–98, Padraig O'Malley—not an unsympathetic observer—wrote:

> Not that things were falling apart. For that to happen they would have to have been together in some way, and in South Africa they never were. Once the repression that held the country together was removed, once the glue that held the separate bits of separate peoples together, they had gone their separate ways, each committed to the pursuit of its individuals, with little sense of a common cohesiveness, other than a generalized selfishness in the face of the needs of others.[13]

Yet the polls showed something quite different, and constantly defied the pundits. In 1992, the surveys suggested the vast majority of blacks would not flock to the polls in the first truly democratic election. Yet in 1994 the turnout was overwhelming. Six months after the election, another survey found that the fashionable belief among "many politicians, journalists, business people and academics" that the new government would be unable to meet or manage popular aspirations was unfounded. Instead, the survey conducted at that time found that while people were disappointed with the pace of change, there was not widespread discontent with the government. "Rather the findings suggest that the public is considerably more aware of the limits facing the new government, more realistic in its expectations than conventional wisdom holds."[14]

In 1996, a survey found that general satisfaction with political developments had dropped from 76 percent to 45 percent. For economic matters, the drop was from 51 percent to 34 percent. The pundits were quick to see the worst:

> As a result, the mood on the ground is gradually becoming more adversarial, more impatient with the slow delivery of the most basic needs (water, sanitation, housing), the government's failure to support community development initiatives, and the continued day-to-day experience of unemployment and poverty.[15]

However, a closer look at the data revealed that pessimism was higher among the whites, whose income and lifestyle was more vulnerable to market forces such as rising interest rates and market instability. For the vast majority of the population, these factors did not touch their lives. Not surprisingly, the same survey found that while white consumer confidence dropped in this period, black consumer confidence did not. Moreover, none of this changed voter attitudes toward the various parties. While responses indicated a drop in favor of the ANC, attitudes toward other parties did not change and the ANC continued to reap an undiminished share of the vote.

Differences in perception among whites, Asians, and blacks continued through the 1990s. The political gains since 1994 dominated the overall positive view of black South Africans while issues such as crime were at the top of white and Indian concerns. For blacks, the issue of jobs came to dominate, but it did not generate a negative view toward the government as a whole. For all parts of the population, the country had settled into relatively normal politics. Focus groups in 1998 expressed the following:

On the one hand, voters protest the insufficient level of change to their lives. On the other hand, they have settled into the business of elections and democratic representation. They often have highly critical assessments of government, but cherish the notions of elections and the electoral power afforded to them.

Voters protest the fact that "so little has changed in their lives." Yet all participants in these groups, especially black South Africans, acknowledge the value of human rights, human dignity, and political power. These are the victories they hope to consolidate. Elections and voting are the means through which they envisage the consolidation will happen.[16]

Predictions that disappointing economic performance might turn people away from the government, especially disillusion blacks from the ANC, continued to be proved wrong. The issue of jobs did rise steadily as the No. 1 issue among blacks as formal employment declined and few inroads were made on overall unemployment. There was also growing despair by the end of the 1990s. Especially at the community level, people complained that they still lacked basic services, that where such services were installed they lacked the jobs to pay for them. Church leaders complained of the collapse of moral fabric. "Something has gone terribly wrong," said one judge. "It seems there has been a collapse of moral fibre. Maybe the new freedom is being interpreted in the wrong way."[17]

Despite these complaints about the pace of change, and especially the lack of jobs, the population continued to show remarkable patience and understanding:

> They criticize but their criticisms are tinged with an understanding that the demands on government are enormous, that government needs more time, and the inexperience in office often contributes to mistakes being made.
>
> Despite their disappointments that democracy did not deliver more, faster, the voters continued in their dreams for a "better life." They commonly agree that a second chance should be given to the existing government to accomplish the better life that they are still dreaming about. There is hardly any perception that government is not trying. The catch phrase is that government should be trying even harder.[18]

No armed resistance to the government rose either. Violent crime, ignored by the apartheid era's security forces, did burst its bounds from the segregated townships into the major cities, often abetted by corrupt police officers—the first two senior police officers assigned after 1994 to combat carjacking in Johannesburg were found to be in collusion with the hijackers. While whites expressed far more concern over crime than blacks, blacks were in fact the primary victims of it. Despite the fact that the Constitutional Court had ruled capital punishment illegal under the constitution, a large majority of South Africans—black and white—now favor it.

But, with the exception of some white right diehards and an extreme Muslim group, none of the violence in South Africa after 1994 was politically motivated or connected. Populist leaders who did challenge the ANC on its lack of progress in social and economic matters—Winnie Mandela, Bantu Holomisa, the Pan African Congress—never undertook to form armed followings. A serious problem with political overtones was drug trafficking. This did give rise—or rather excuse—to an extreme Muslim group named PAGAD to engage in a form of vigilantism to combat drug traffickers in the Cape flats. Later the group was accused of bombings of several nightclubs in Cape Town, and its leaders were arrested. Its motives were, however, unrelated to general economic conditions and in no way linked to the majority population.

The economic debate has most recently surfaced into a major competition within the ANC and threatens at least some mass protests and possible violence. At heart is the battle over succession to Mbeki in 2009 and the control of the ANC. Rallying around Jacob Zuma, who had been dismissed from his position as deputy president on corruption charges, the unions and the Communist Party within the ANC are demanding much more expansive fiscal policies, with more government spending on public works, social programs, and the like, backtracking on privatization (on which the government has not been very fast in any case), and generally a more populist set of policies and programs. It is too early to know the outcome of this competition. But it is unlikely to destabilize the country, only perhaps lead closer to what many believe is inevitable, a split within the ANC into a more moderate/conservative business-oriented wing and a left-leaning populist one.

ANGST: THE BLACK MIDDLE CLASS, THE BLACK WEALTHY, AND THE SOUL OF THE ANC

ONE ASPECT OF THIS GROWING debate over economic policies is whether the policies and programs followed by the government have produced real transformation in the heritage of inequality of apartheid or instead simply profited a small well-connected elite of blacks, some of whom are now billionaires (in rand terms) and others who are part of a growing but still seemingly elite black middle class. The recently enunciated policy of Black Economic Empowerment (BEE) is designed to extend the transformation that has taken place up to now to an ever-broader number of blacks. It requires every business sector to meet targets over the next ten or more years for equity, management, general employment, and other facets of both opportunity and ownership for blacks.

BEE is a political response to the criticism over earlier affirmative action programs, which seemed to have benefited most of all a small elite. But it is also recognition that, over time, much broader equalization of ownership and opportunity for the majority black population is essential both for stability and long-term economic growth. Today, black-owned businesses account for but 3.3 percent of the capitalization of the Johannesburg Stock Exchange. Unemployment, concentrated among blacks, continues to hover between 26 and 41 percent.

This paper does not attempt to assess the specific policies and processes of BEE. But behind the debate over BEE is a deeper one within the ANC, one that will affect the future of economic policy and perhaps political direction of future administrations. And ironically, one can most easily examine this debate within the policies and the psyche of President Thabo Mebki.

Some years ago, in the annual Oliver Thambo lecture, Mbeki shocked some business leaders with an attack on the "black bourgeoisie." He accused the up-and-coming black business community of selling its soul to white capitalistic ethics and principles rather than retaining a more singular racial identity and more socially oriented outlook. A few weeks later Mbeki made amends to the business community, assuring it that the speech did not herald a shift in the economic policies of the administration.

The irony is that Mbeki's policies have been directed precisely to helping build a black middle class and black entrepreneurs. Large amounts of government funds, together with government-supported bank loans, went into "empowerment" deals that shifted corporate control over several companies to black owners. The government's explanation of BEE defends the policy. Acknowledging the criticism and shortcomings of these efforts, the government nevertheless contends:

> We have also seen a black middle class emerging, which is a necessity for the success of government's overall goal of achieving transformation of our economy. This black middle class has been credited for

being the key driver of growth in some of the sectors of our economy such as the monumental increase in car sales, property sales, and the much talked about consumer boom currently being experienced.[19]

Yet deep within Mbeki's mind there is something dangerous in the very policies he has so assiduously followed. In the Nelson Mandela Memorial Lecture he delivered on July 29, 2006, he returned to his earlier concerns. This time he railed at the very heart of capitalism as the cause of the distortion of values among the newly enriched South Africans.

The new order [in South Africa], born of the victory in 1994, inherited a well-entrenched value system that placed individual acquisition of wealth at the very center of the value system of our society as a whole. . . . Society assumed a tolerant or permissive attitude towards such crimes as theft, corruption, especially these related to public property. The phenomenon we are describing, which we considered as particularly South Africa, was in fact symptomatic of the capitalistic system in all countries.

Quoting Karl Polanyi, Mbeki went on:

The capitalistic market destroys relations of kinship, neighborhood, profession and creed, replacing these with the pursuit of personal wealth by citizens who have become atomistic and individualistic.

And then he concludes in this portion of his speech:

Thus, everyday, and during every hour of our time beyond sleep, the demons embedded in our society, that stalk us at every minute, seem always to beckon each one of us towards a realizable dream and nightmare. With every passing second, they advise, with rhythmic and hypnotic regularity—get rich! get rich! get rich!

But here is the irony, the dilemma that faces this and every future South African government that seeks to retain its more radical, or at least populist, roots. After this long and emotional attack on capitalism, Mbeki refers to "the undoubtedly correct economic objectives our nation has set itself." South Africans will continue to have to wrestle, within their souls, like Mbeki, and within their policy decisions, with the dynamic tension between what are undoubtedly sound, business-oriented economic policies, and the deep desire for something new and more dramatic than the ways of middle-class and even richer folks who will direct the economy those policies produce.

AIDS

THE AIDS CRISIS was not unknown in the 1990s. Indeed by 1994, the handwriting was on the wall. While estimates at the time were probably low—550,000 infected—the rate of increase was not: a doubling of infections every thirteen months. The U.S. Centers for Disease Control predicted that if unchecked, the number of persons infected by 2000 would be more than five million. The prediction was close to the mark—the UNAIDS estimate in 2000 was just over four million.

At the beginning of the Mandela administration there was optimism that the issue would be addressed. In 1992, Nelson Mandela had opened the first conference of the National AIDS Committee of South Africa (NACOSA), a government and civil society body that was charged with coming up with a national program. In 1994, Mandela appointed Nkosazana Zuma as minister of health. Dr. Zuma had headed one of the NGOs dedicated to addressing the HIV/AIDS crisis and was chair of NACOSA. An AIDS newsletter wrote at the time:

> The commitment of Dr. Zuma, the new South African Minister of Health, and her staff to the fight against HIV is beyond question. She has announced a multi-million rand program against AIDS and we expect she will get most if not all of it.[20]

Alas, these early hopes were to be disappointed. Dr. Zuma's program became bogged down in a controversy over funding for an anti-AIDS musical. President Mandela did not return to the issue for the rest of his term. A national program was begun but with limited funding and little widespread participation. By the end of the decade, the whole issue had become embroiled in controversy. In 1999, President Thabo Mbeki questioned the scientific basis of the link between HIV and AIDS and suggested that Western countries were pressing governments on the issue in order to make countries like South Africa dependent on Western pharmaceuticals that they could ill afford. Mbeki saw the emphasis being placed on HIV/AIDS as a diversion from the basic need for poverty alleviation, and at a minimum from the need for basic health services, which the vast majority still lacked.

While Mbeki was raising important issues relevant to the connection between poverty and susceptibility to AIDS, and the importance of linking HIV/AIDS programs to the wider need for basic health services and development—points since accepted in international circles—his stance created conflicts and confusion within the government's own programs. As noted, the issue pitted activist HIV/AIDS NGOs against the government and resulted in court cases regarding the availability of antiretroviral drugs. It remains one of the most controversial issues in South Africa and in South Africa's international relations.

The irony is that today South Africa budgets more for HIV/AIDS than most affected countries in the world. It has placed more people under treatment for AIDS, 175,000, than any other developing country. One commentator has even suggested that the slow, cautionary approach the government has taken to introducing treatment—now available in 192 hospitals and clinics—will avoid the development of drug-resistant strains and other mishaps that are taking place in countries that rushed into treatment with inadequate infrastructure and poor oversight.

But the face of South Africa's AIDS policies, the minister of health, has constantly discredited herself and her country by touting unproven "natural" remedies, downplaying the very crisis she is charged with addressing, and continuing thereby to send mixed messages to a population that has yet been engaged sufficiently to change its practices and outlooks that underlie the pandemic. One of the principal aspects of this is the treatment of women. Only recently, on the occasion of the fiftieth anniversary of the 1956 women's march on government, has President Mbeki recognized that South Africa has largely neglected the degree of violence and intimidation and desperation that mark the lives of many of South Africa's women. In 2003, there were 52,425 official reported rapes, a third of the estimated actual number. Forty percent of the victims were eighteen years or younger. The conviction rate for rape was 7 percent.[21]

SOUTH AFRICA AND THE WORLD

THERE WAS LITTLE QUESTION that South Africa, once free of apartheid, and with an economy far greater than much of Africa put together (South Africa produces 60 percent of the continent's electricity) would play a major role on the continent and beyond. Vice President Al Gore, at Mandela's inauguration, warned the new president that he would be called upon around the world and should be careful to husband his energies for the immediate tasks at home. But the United States was one of the first to make that appeal, in 1995 asking for South Africa to send security forces to Haiti, and the rest of the world was not far behind.

Mandela resisted getting too heavily involved, lending his moral authority more than South Africa's resources to far-flung conflicts and demands. But from the beginning, South Africa assumed a major role in the region, joining the Southern Africa Development Community (SADC) and helping transform it from an economic entity to one that addressed political and security issues as well. South Africa soon learned, however, that prestige alone would not enable it to control such alliances. In 1998, Robert Mugabe hijacked SADC's incipient security organ to commit, on behalf of SADC, military forces into Congo, against Mandela's wishes. Mandela was forced to endorse the intervention as a means to regaining leverage over SADC and the Congo situation.

If South Africa moved cautiously at first in asserting itself across the continent, by the end of the 1990s, South Africa was embarked on a series of engagements that would put it at the center of almost every peace and security issue on the African continent and soon at the center of Africa's political and economic policies. The spread of South Africa's governmental influence was accompanied and abetted by the expanding role of South African business. By the first decade of the twenty-first century, South Africa had emerged as the largest foreign investor elsewhere on the continent.

Not long after the transition, South Africa became the chair of SADC, the chair of the nonaligned movement (NAM), the leader of the G77, a member of the UN Security Council, and host to numerous international conferences. Nelson Mandela would become the chief arbiter of the Burundi peace process, and Thabo Mbeki would emerge as a major figure in bringing about an end to conflicts in Congo, Liberia, and Cote d'Ivoire.

Once engaged well beyond its borders, economic power was one asset for South Africa, but military power was also essential. Two issues were of concern in the 1990s about South Africa's military capacity. One was how well the South Africa Defense Force (SADF) would be integrated with the liberation forces—most writers concerned themselves with the MK (the ANC's armed wing), but in fact the first black leader of the army would come from APLA, the armed wing of the PAC—and the impact on internal stability. Would a new defense force be free of "Third Force" elements that had carried out covert actions against anti-apartheid leaders and sought throughout the transition negotiations to instigate violent conflict between the ANC and the Inkatha Freedom Party?

A related question was whether South Africa would pose a security threat to its neighbors. Laurie Nathan, one of South Africa's most astute security analysts, expressed concern that without a change of culture the South African military force, dominated by the old SADF leadership, would alarm neighboring countries.

> In [Nathan's] analysis, continued SADF control of the new defense force could mean the continuance of the military's potential to destabilize and disrupt; a low level of legitimacy in the perception of the masses; and feelings of suspicion and insecurity in Southern Africa as a whole, particularly among Frontline States. Countries like Mozambique and Angola that have had to divert vast resources to defense may be inhibited from substantially reducing force levels and military spending.[22]

These fears were perhaps exaggerated with regard to neighboring states. But the integration of the military did not go entirely smoothly. Mandela made the decision to keep de Klerk's chief of the SADF, General Meiring, in his post and disciplined ANC members who resisted direction from their white officers. But Mandela eventually dismissed Meiring over a confusing report of a coup attempt and step-by-step the new South Africa National Defense Force (SANDF) has come into being. Its legitimacy at home has not been a serious problem. Third Force elements appear to have been removed. The ANC further mollified military leaders with a huge purchase of military equipment that has on the other hand caused much controversy, not only over the expense but because of charges of corruption.

The original assumption was that South Africa could safely reduce its military expenses. But that assumption did not take into account the growing demand for South Africa's political role on the continent and a concomitant demand for participation in peace-keeping. By the late 1990s, UN and related peacekeeping on the African continent was exploding. New international peacekeeping forces were being deployed in Sierra Leone, the Central African Republic, along the Ethiopia-Eritrea border, and eventually in Liberia, Burundi, Congo, and Sudan. At the same time, South Africa's political role on the continent and the world was expanding. Soon South Africa was called upon to play a major military role as well.

An abortive intervention in Lesotho, under SADC auspices, demonstrated that the SANDF was neither as strong nor as well trained for interventions or peacekeeping operations as some had assumed. But in subsequent years, South Africa has deployed peacekeepers to Burundi, Congo, Darfur, and elsewhere. On the whole, these deployments have been very effective. But the growing number of SANDF members with HIV/AIDS poses a serious limitation on South Africa's ability to maintain this role. One estimate is that South Africa cannot deploy more than three thousand personnel abroad because of the prevalence of HIV/AIDS. A second problem is the recent charges of misconduct (rape, prostitution) affecting South African along with other contingents in the UN peacekeeping force in Congo. Older cultures seem to have lingered within the SANDF, with reports that South African officers summarily rejected any cooperation with the UN investigating the charges.

CONCLUSION

THE ANC GOVERNMENT has defied nearly every prediction in instituting economic policies that were at heart conservative: reducing rather than taking on debt, bringing down inflation, lowering rather than raising taxes, eschewing any forms of nationalization, and even instituting some programs of privatization. All the while expenditures—on health and education, on support of housing, electricity, and clean water—were able to rise. The policies produced stability and even helped South Africa weather the worst of the Asian financial crisis of the late 1990s. But they failed to make even a dent in unemployment. They did not result in anywhere near the levels of foreign direct investment that some had hoped. Growth moved along for a long time at no more than 2 to 3 percent, more recently 4 to 5 percent, rather than the 6 percent or more that most analysts believed was necessary.

Pessimists about the strength of democracy have also been proven wrong. Democracy has been institutionalized, with no signs of either ethnic divisiveness nor any trend toward oppressive government. A new constitution after the 1994 elections retained the basic principles of the interim constitution, established various instruments to protect human rights, and an independent Constitutional Court whose decisions have been respected. A second election went smoothly in 1999, a third in 2004. The ANC has emerged even more strongly as the dominant party, raising a serious concern over the lack of a credible opposition, and limiting somewhat the independence of the parliament in which the ANC is dominant. The relatively incomplete investigation into possible corruption in relation to arms purchases was an example. Nevertheless, the press remains free and lively debate continues to characterize South African politics.

South Africa has become almost inevitably a major player on the continent. As its political role expanded, so too did its economic reach and its military role. Whether South Africa can retain or rebuild enough military capacity to maintain this degree of involvement and influence is not yet clear.

On the negative side, problems of crime, drugs, and above all AIDS ran rampant in the first ten years of freedom—partly because they were more than a new government could handle, partly because the government failed to act sufficiently. AIDS has become one of the most divisive and challenging issues of the next century. The lingering problems of inequality in wealth distribution between whites and blacks, the slow progress in reforming the dysfunctional education system, and joblessness will put steadily more pressure on the government in the decade ahead, posing challenges to both government and the private sector.

As one observer commented in 1999, contemplating the end of Mandela's presidency:

> When he retires from office in June 1999, Mandela will leave a South Africa full of contradictions, with enormous social and political challenges to overcome, a South Africa still in the process of transformation, a South Africa not yet out of the woods, not yet one in which democracy has fully taken root, although the vine is ripening.[23]

Africa's Restless Youth

Michelle D. Gavin

SCANNING THE HORIZON for insight as to what will influence the future of sub-Saharan Africa, one can immediately point to several broad baskets of important indicators. Obviously contributing to the picture are economic growth (or the lack thereof), insecure borders, increasing resource scarcity, the HIV/AIDS pandemic, and the balance of power within nations among ethnic and regional groups. However, a close look at the political engagement and political agendas of youth should also be included in the mix. Young Africans' quest for empowerment will make them significant catalysts for change.

Africa is currently in the midst of what demographers call a youth bulge. A youth bulge typically occurs when less-developed countries, with both high fertility and high mortality rates, begin to bring infant and child mortality rates down. Eventually, development gains tend to bring fertility rates down as well. But in the lag time before this occurs, a population boom of children who survive to adulthood reshapes the demographic landscape.

In Africa today, this dynamic translates into some startling figures. More than 70 percent of all Zimbabweans, for example, are now under 30; the same is true in Kenya, Uganda, Ethiopia, Liberia, and Nigeria, among other countries. Over one-third of the entire population of Zimbabwe, and over 56 percent of the adult (over 15) population, is between 15 and 29 years old. In fact, young adults (aged 15 to 29) make up 40 percent or more of the total adult population in the vast majority of sub-Saharan countries;

---

in roughly 30 African countries, they constitute more than half of the adult population. In contrast, approximately 40 percent of the population in the United States is under 30, and young adults constitute less than 30 percent of the adult population as a whole.

Any discussion of the youth bulge in Africa risks veering into the land of breathless alarmism—*young men and street gangs and guns, oh my!*—or overcorrecting and wandering into the territory of commencement-speech clichés about how the children are indeed the future. But there is room for a closer examination of African youth that emphasizes their political role, and this should be a priority in future research. The young are more inclined to take risks, but vast youthful populations are not going to engage in violence simply for its own sake. On the other hand, violence may be a symptom of clashing political agendas.

In a region where the state has been the source of most power and economic opportunity, but governing institutions are often weak, the desires and grievances of youth are very likely to have political implications. Governments and international actors probably cannot control the degree to which youth bulges shape societies for good or for ill, but they can at least influence outcomes. Focusing too narrowly on violence and conflict rather than on underlying political tensions tends to yield a fairly sickly crop of policy prescriptions, all variations on the theme of "brace yourself." By seeking to understand youth political engagement more clearly, policy makers may be able to create conditions conducive to youth movements that do not leave a legacy of trauma and dysfunction in their wake.

FOREVER YOUNG?

FOR THE PURPOSES of this article, I am defining youth as anyone from 15 to 29 years old. However, definitions of youth are tricky and often culturally specific. They are also subject to revision and even manipulation. Sierra Leone's National Youth Policy, for instance, targets citizens ages 15 to 35, and Sierra Leoneans sometimes use the term "youth" to describe people in their 40s—this in a country where average life expectancy for males is about 38. Last November, Zimbabwe's *Financial Gazette* questioned the youth credentials of Absolom Sikhosana, the ruling party's Youth League Secretary, suggesting that he was masquerading as a member of the 35-and-under set and that he might in fact be "past his sell-by date." In 2002, South Africa's National Youth Development Policy Framework included a youth definition of 15 to 28, but the National Youth Policy adopted in 1997 had targeted the 14-to-35 range. In any case, according to the International Council on National Youth Policy, various South African government departments use different definitions, which rarely correspond to either of the official policies.

These variable and amorphous definitions point to an interesting phenomenon: in some African countries it is getting increasingly difficult to make the transition from youth to adulthood. Inadequate education systems combine with stratospheric unemployment rates to foreclose the possibility of securing a job that could provide financial security. This in turn makes it unfeasible to marry and start one's own family. Meanwhile, population growth has contributed to a land squeeze, and as desirable land has been divided many times over to accommodate heirs, younger siblings in particular are cut off from the prospect of inheriting workable plots.

Youths are pushed into the continent's urban centers seeking a pathway to a viable future, only to find themselves among the unemployed and alienated masses of young people already looking for the same thing. Here, they are increasingly exposed to many of the same media images of material success that bombard young people in the most developed countries—messages often crafted by marketers to explicitly target the youth demographic. The contrast between these images and their own circumstances and prospects is hard to ignore, amplifying a sense of relative deprivation.

Some young people continue their quest for opportunity by leaving their country and even the continent altogether, risking their lives by placing themselves in the hands of sophisticated and dangerous human smuggling networks that profit from the vast divide between the prospects for African and European youth. But practical and legal constraints ensure that this pathway, like the others, is often blocked. In these situations, many of Africa's youth are caught in a Peter Pan scenario gone terribly wrong. Try as they might, they cannot seem to become adults.

Many African cultures place an extremely high premium on respect for elders. Young people are expected to know their place and to abide by the wisdom of those rich in life experience. Yet, if youth are trapped—indefinitely—in some sort of preparatory state, awaiting the time when they are accorded the respect, responsibility, and opportunity associated with being full-fledged adults in their society, it seems unreasonable to assume that they will wait patiently for a day that is nowhere in sight.

Youths have something to prove, and given opportunity, they will assert themselves. Just how violently or constructively that might happen depends on a range of factors, including the existence and nature of manipulation from older elites, the amount of political space available for civic action, and the capacity of the state and the private sector to hear and understand youth aspirations and to deliver opportunities in a relatively timely fashion.

Of course, no country's youth is monolithic. Ethnic, religious, and regional schisms can split demographic cohorts just as they can split a population at large. Also, it is often hard to discern where young women fit into the picture. This is so in part because many become mothers during this period of life, culturally moving into adulthood and a lifetime of domestic responsibility. In addition, young women's leadership and civic engagement opportunities, even within the context of youth movements, often are limited on the basis of gender alone.

Even among young men, agitation for power and respect—be it peaceful or violent—will not be the preoccupation of all youth in any setting. Nevertheless, a vocal, visible, organized segment of the youth population, particularly if it is concentrated in Africa's urban centers, can make for a movement with profound political consequences, and these political actors will be on the stage for many years to come.

CHANGE AGENTS

IN AFRICA'S INDEPENDENCE movements and struggles against colonial powers, young people played an important role in case after case. The party that governed Somalia on independence was even called the Somali Youth League. More recently, youth were pivotal in the anti-apartheid struggle in South Africa. Nelson Mandela was 26 when he and other young leaders came together to form the African National Congress Youth League in 1944; their work transformed the ANC. Later, in 1968, 22-year-old Steve Biko led the newly formed and highly influential South African Students Organization. The Soweto uprising of 1976 was grounded in secondary school students' resistance to apartheid policies, and students mobilized en masse to demand change throughout the rest of the struggle.

But today, when their demographic weight is much greater relative to older Africans' than it has been in the past, young people are most often cast in the role of a diffusely destabilizing threat, rather than as potential agents of political and social transformation. The strain of analysis that sees the youth bulge as a fundamentally threatening phenomenon often points to research that suggests a strong relationship between the likelihood of civil conflict and the existence of an urbanized youth bulge. In 2001, the U.S. Central Intelligence Agency released a report on global demographic trends, saying of the projected youth bulges in Africa and parts of the Middle East that:

"The failure to adequately integrate youth populations is likely to perpetuate the cycle of political instability, ethnic wars, revolutions, and anti-regime activities. . . . Increases in youth populations will aggravate problems with trade, terrorism, anti-regime activities, warfare, and crime and add to the many existing factors that already are making the region's problems increasingly difficult to surmount."

In an influential 2003 report titled *The Security Demographic*, researchers with the nongovernmental organization Population Action International found that countries experiencing a youth bulge were more than twice as likely as other countries to experience civil strife. The numbers are compelling, and so are the recent histories of devastating conflict in states like Liberia and Sierra Leone, where youth were both perpetrators and victims of appalling violence on a massive scale. It is easy to develop a generalized sense that "youth bulge" is code for marauding, angry young men.

Certainly it is not hard to understand why many African youths might have a highly developed sense of grievance. In addition to the frustrating struggle for adult status, shocking numbers of young Africans have at some point in their short lives fallen into one or more of the following unhappy categories: combatants, victims of atrocities, refugees, internally displaced persons, forced laborers, or street children.

AIDS orphans are expected to number 18 million in sub-Saharan Africa in 2010. In the worst-affected areas, their numbers are already overwhelming the capacity of extended family networks to care for them, and alternative support structures are weak or non-existent. According to UNAIDS, 6.2 million Africans 15 to 24 years old are already HIV positive, and half of all new infections in the region occur in this age group.

The vast majority of Africa's young people have an intimate knowledge of poverty. Even elite youths are faced with a shortage of jobs in which to apply the skills they may have acquired at tremendously overcrowded, underfunded universities. Overall, according to the International Labor Organization (ILO), there are more than 17.4 million unemployed 15- to 24-year-olds in Africa, leading to a regional youth unemployment rate of 18 percent. And even the young people who do have jobs are hardly financially secure: the ILO notes that over 57 percent of African youth are working at the $1-per-day level. One can easily imagine that this cohort as a whole would be quick to blame someone or something—a governing regime or an ethnic group—for a rough past and an uncertain future.

The relationship between youth bulges and violence is important, but it speaks to just one manifestation of youth frustrations and desires. Other avenues for affecting the future include partisan political action, participation in civil society organizations, student activism, and engagement in transnational religious movements. Regardless of whether these manifold forms of expression are accompanied by violent tactics, in light of youths' demographic dominance, all of them will affect the region's future. In one way or another, young Africans are in the market for alternatives to the status quo.

This could mean significant change. In many African countries, the actors dominating the political scene have been on stage (if not in power) for quite some time. President Mwai Kibaki of Kenya is over 75 years old. President Abdoulaye Wade of Senegal is over 80. President Robert Mugabe of Zimbabwe is 83. Most existing state structures, such as party youth wings, do not actually function as entry points to party leadership. The nearly ubiquitous ministries of "youth and sports" are marginal and marginalizing institutions. They are ill-equipped to function as sustainable mechanisms for accommodating and responding to the size and potential strength of youth political activism. When voters under 29 constitute 40 percent of all registered voters, as they did in the last Liberian election, their issues and demands cry out to be mainstream priorities, not sideshows.

TOOLS OF THE ELITE

BUILDING A CAPACITY to respond to youth demands for empowerment, rather than simply trying to keep a lid on unrest, starts with understanding the dynamics of contemporary youth's political engagement. African youth in the market for alternatives to their current situation will either generate their own vision, or adopt ones supplied by others.

Instances in which youth are manipulated and mobilized to serve an elite agenda are all too easy to come by. Military movements throughout the continent have recruited children and youth on a massive scale. Vast numbers of young Rwandans complied with the most hideous instructions during the 1994 genocide. In Zimbabwe, the ruling party established brutal camps to indoctrinate young people in the party's ideology and to train the party's youth militia.

The camps were organized in 2001 under the auspices of the National Youth Service Training Program, an initiative ostensibly aimed at improving job skills and awareness of civic responsibility. In fact, young Zimbabweans were coerced into attending training camps that taught torture techniques and exposed them to beatings and rapes in the course of molding them into new party loyalists. As the main opposition force in the country, the Movement for Democratic Change, has faltered and split, factions of it, too, have deployed young thugs to intimidate rivals. Meanwhile, the outlook for young Zimbabweans grows increasingly dim, as the national unemployment rate soars to an estimated 80 percent and the economy continues to shrink.

In 2004, disturbing reports emerged from the city of Mbuji-Mayi in the Democratic Republic of Congo. Street children and youths eager for any kind of employment had been mobilized by political elites to demonstrate in rallies and protests and to intimidate opposition figures and supporters in exchange for payment. But these young people went from being political militants for hire to becoming the victims of a massacre. Angry mobs, fed up with the crimes being committed by young people who felt empowered by their political patrons, rampaged through the city, beating and in many instances killing street children and youths.

These horrifying incidents speak to the time-honored tradition of rounding up young people and, by offering short-term opportunity (payment, license to loot, and so forth) and some proximity to power, convincing them to act as violent, visible backers of a given political power. Youth often are enlisted to support political repression and to occupy political space so as to deny it to others. From Kenya to Cameroon, the recruitment of young people to reinforce ethnic divisions, intimidate voices of dissent, and send signals about who possesses strength and power—whatever is most useful for the elites doing the recruiting—has been a regular feature of Africa's political landscape. In some cases, the formation of militant party youth wings is explicit. In other cases, direct ties to the party are less formal, perhaps protecting the party from being held accountable for disruptive youth action.

IN THE DRIVER'S SEAT

BUT INSTANCES IN WHICH youth pursue their own agendas can be found as well, and the nature of these efforts ranges from nonthreatening to extremely confrontational. The sub-Saharan region is rich in dynamic, creative youth groups with a public service focus, from theater troupes dramatizing HIV/AIDS prevention techniques in Uganda to peace-building programs sustained by Tutsi and Hutu youth in Burundi. Some student groups are clearly co-opted by elites. But others, like the Kenyan University Students Organization that existed in the mid-1990s to demand democratic change, challenge the ruling class and operate as independent civil society actors.

Consider the action of some Sierra Leonean youths, including ex-combatants, in the wake of that country's devastating civil war. These youths wanted power, but rather than focusing exclusively on personal enrichment, the Movement of Concerned Kono Youth, or MOCKY, tried to stand in for what its members perceived to be an absent or ineffective law enforcement presence. As the country's civil war wound down, MOCKY tried to fill roles one would normally associate with government—conducting patrols, monitoring mining activity, and attempting to negotiate with a multinational mining company operating in the region in an effort to secure community development commitments. Dissatisfied by what the state had to offer and longing to assert themselves in positions of leadership and authority, these youths tried to organize an alternative.

Some youth-dominated armed groups in the Niger Delta claim to have a similar agenda. Interestingly, former Nigerian dictator Sani Abacha's "two million man march" in 1998 was a turning point for youth activism. A group calling itself Youths Earnestly Ask for Abacha ostensibly organized this display of support for the regime, although the government clearly directed the entire affair. Young people from around the country were bussed to the gleaming capital city of Abuja to participate, where they saw state-of-the-art infrastructure and facilities presumably financed with Nigeria's oil wealth. The contrast between the wealth on display in Abuja and the desperately poor oil-producing communities in the Niger Delta helped to radicalize a generation.

Being used as Abacha's instruments drove the young people to develop and pursue their own agenda. No longer content to let local chiefs negotiate with the government or oil companies on behalf of communities, youth formed pressure groups and, in many cases, armed militias. Some groups remain available for hire to politicians around election time, but it is clear that these armed youth movements cannot be controlled by the state. Today, media-savvy, youth-dominated militant groups like the Movement for the Emancipation of the Niger Delta (MEND) engage in operations ranging from kidnapping foreign oil workers to hosting CNN correspondents. Their actions have consequences not only for local security, but also for international oil markets.

THE CASE OF IVORY COAST

THE DISTINCTION BETWEEN youth acting as instruments and youth acting as agents is not always clear, and power between elites and youth leaders can ebb and flow. Perhaps nowhere are the lines as blurry today as they are in Ivory Coast. Once a proud island of stability and economic growth, over the past decade the country has descended into a toxic mix of civil conflict, violent xenophobia, and political stalemate—with youth as major actors throughout.

When longtime President Felix Houphouet-Boigny died in 1993, he was replaced by Henri Konan Bedie, who sought to consolidate his power by marginalizing his primary political rival, Alassane Ouattara. Bedie's method was to promote *"ivoirité"*—an ultra-nationalist vision of the country's identity that excluded many of the migrant workers from Burkina Faso, Mali, and Guinea who had long labored in Ivory Coast's northern agricultural fields. Not coincidentally, it also excluded Ouattara, whose main base of support was in the north, because of complicated questions about where his parents were born.

Bedie was soon overthrown in a coup, but his formula for neutralizing any political threat from Ouattara was later embraced by the current president, Laurent Gbagbo, who came to power in 2000 in a dubious election in which the two major parties' candidates were prevented from participating. A rebellion broke out in 2002, eventually splitting the country into two parts—the north and west controlled by rebels known as the *Forces Nouvelles*, and the south and east under the control of the Gbagbo government, state security forces, and their militia allies. Notably, both sides' ranks were strengthened by former combatants hardened by youth-dominated conflict in Liberia and Sierra Leone. These roving soldiers-for-hire are a new part of the regional youth landscape.

While these political machinations and the resulting conflict unfolded, global economic conditions that had been squeezing the Ivorian economy throughout the 1980s and 1990s—particularly falling prices for coffee and cocoa—began to bite ferociously. *Ivoirité* fed many elite youths' hunger for someone to blame for the scarcity of jobs, land, and opportunities. Meanwhile, northern youth became increasingly agitated about the prospect of being systematically excluded from the few opportunities available within the country. Both youth groups acted on their anxieties, led by young men who had risen to prominence as students in Ivory Coast's highly political university setting.

In fact, Guillaume Soro, the leader of the *Forces Nouvelles*, and Charles Ble Goude, leader of the pro-Gbagbo Young Patriots militia, were consecutive secretaries general of the Student Federation of Ivory Coast (FESCI) in the period from 1995 to 2001. Other militia leaders also have backgrounds as FESCI officers. FESCI was founded in the early 1990s to advocate for improved conditions at increasingly overcrowded and under-resourced university campuses; it was a movement of youth resisting the shrinking opportunities presented to them and protesting favoritism in the distribution of scholarship funds. In those early days, FESCI's dissatisfaction with government policies aligned it with the movement that advocated for multiparty politics—a movement in which the political party founded by Gbagbo (a former university lecturer himself) played an important part.

Today, the Young Patriots and allied youth militias are among the primary enforcement arms of Gbagbo's state. They can mobilize masses of youth with astonishing speed, and their activities range from the conventionally political (collecting signatures on petitions calling for the *Forces Nouvelles* to be disarmed) to the clearly repressive (prohibiting the distribution of newspapers deemed insufficiently loyal to the ruling party) to the extremely violent (brutally beating opposition supporters or simply those who appear to be of Burkinabe or Malian descent).

The International Crisis Group has documented how rural youth, some of whom had left the city after finding no employment despite having attained university degrees, have been inspired by intense state-controlled media coverage of the Young Patriots' activities to take actions that give them their own social and economic power. They set up barricades to monitor movement in and out of villages, enabling them to collect fees and attempt to reform the land tenure system according to the dictates of *ivoirité*. For their part, the *Forces Nouvelles* act as a de facto government in the territory they control, and profit from trade in cotton and arms, maintaining their own trans-boundary economic networks.

Meanwhile, FESCI lives on, allied to the Young Patriots and the Gbagbo regime. It dominates campus life by controlling access to housing, extorting money and goods, and intimidating students and professors who do not toe the ruling party line. A student organization once devoted to holding government more accountable to youth has become a zealous pro-government force. Those who have tried to form an alternative student organization have been attacked and even killed.

Thus, many youths in Ivory Coast have maneuvered through a complex political environment to establish leadership positions and sources of income for themselves in an arrangement that suits the needs and desires of the ruling political class. Others have abandoned the state structure entirely through rebellion. The country has a long history of student activism, but whereas student leaders used to graduate and move on to senior posts in government or the private sector, students more recently have constructed entirely new spaces to occupy—quite literally, in the case of the *Forces Nouvelles*.

While the ruling party and its youth enforcers are unquestionably linked, it is no longer plain that the power of the youth militias depends on patronage from the state. Political elites may be just as much hostage to the desires of the militia leaders as the other way around. Youth violence features in the case of Ivory Coast primarily as a tool married to youth leaders' own political and economic agendas. The latest peace agreement, under which Soro will serve as prime minister, offers hope of reuniting the country. But until now the country has been in a stalemate in part because the impasse benefits old and young elites in both sectors of the country, despite the fact that Ivory Coast as a whole is growing poorer.

APPEALS TO A HIGHER POWER

ELSEWHERE IN AFRICA, increasingly influential transnational religious movements, both Christian and Muslim, are largely fueled by African youth's enthusiastic response to alternative paths to empowerment. Faith can provide surrogate social structures and supports for those who have been through traumatic experiences and have lost other moorings. In some cases, it can also provide a form of education, which may not be available from any other source. Religious movements offer prescriptions for how to improve one's life and transform society, and in Africa today, these prescriptions have explicit political significance.

Revivalist Christian movements are thriving in much of Africa. From Malawi to Ghana, Pentecostal churches are encouraging youths to reject the "old ways" that led to poverty and despair and to embrace a faith that promises social networking opportunities, promotes links to fellow worshippers around the world, uses mass media to impressive effect, and embraces the quest for prosperity. The renewal inherent in being "born again" also speaks to the desire for an alternative to the status quo. Prominent figures within these churches can be very young themselves, exemplifying how African youth can attain respect and prominence despite the limited opportunities they may be confronted with. Moreover, unlike university-based movements, religious youth movements are accessible to non-elites.

These religious networks are not divorced from politics. A recent survey by the Pew Forum on Religion and Public Life found that 83 percent of renewalists in Kenya and 75 percent in Nigeria believe that religious groups should express views on social and political questions. And they have put this belief into action—for example, when Christians organized to help defeat a referendum on a new constitution in Kenya in 2005.

At the same time, Muslim youths may find in an Islamic revival movement a vehicle for their rejection of the status quo and desire for an alternative. In a 2005 article in the *Journal of the Royal Anthropological Institute*, Adeline Masquelier described how unemployed young men in Niger embrace a Muslim movement that condemns extravagant customs surrounding marriage (a helpful point that brings the prospect of marriage closer to their modest reach). Foreign Muslim clerics, often from Pakistan or the Middle East, have established a notable presence in the Sahel, drawing in young people to be educated in an ideology that advocates enforcing Islamic law and abandoning the secular state.

Long-standing local movements may move in new directions as young members try to effect radical change, sometimes taking cues from abroad, as with the Al Sunna Wal Jamma group of students in Nigeria that staged attacks in several northern towns in 2004. They claimed to be inspired by Afghanistan's Taliban, and apparently wished to create an Islamic state. In countries where both Christian and Muslim movements are operating, tension is inevitable. It comes as no surprise, for example, that youth have been primary players in the religiously charged communal conflicts that have plagued Nigeria in recent years.

WHAT NEXT?

PEOPLE INTERESTED IN Africa's future ought to concern themselves not just with potential conflict, but also potential political change. Youth populations are at the heart of these possibilities. There is a strong temptation to write off a "lost generation" in the most battle-scarred, traumatized countries, but there is no avoiding the fact that those currently holding power will not be able to wield it forever. Even those who aim to cope with vast, dissatisfied youth populations by pressing young people into the service of the ruling elite may find that, in time, their youthful foot soldiers cease to answer to their elders. Today's young people will, sooner or later, play a dominant role in society.

For policy makers, job creation clearly must be an urgent priority. A focus on educating and socializing children so that they are prepared to play a positive civic role should be another priority, particularly since so many African countries are still at an early phase of their demographic transition. In addition, by understanding youth as political actors rather than simply drivers of conflict, policy makers can aim to manage the challenge to existing orders posed by youth rather than, unrealistically, try to avoid it entirely. A viable way forward involves a thorough understanding of the various youth dynamics on the ground, and also involves a serious effort to give youth the tools, opportunities, and political space in which to pursue their interests and aspirations.

More needs to be done to shed light on how specific variables affect the capacity of youth movements to engage, reshape, and even strengthen the state. What can be done to give Africa's young people reason to believe in governing institutions or to trust that peaceful civic action can effectively address their grievances? How might a closing of the digital divide empower African youth to form new networks for change? The answers will undoubtedly vary from country to country, but the significance of the questions, and the importance of youth political engagement, will remain constant for quite some time to come.

II

Trouble Spots

Conflicts in Africa are sources not only of humanitarian concern. They effect important U.S. security objectives as well as the achievement of international norms of conduct that are vital to America's moral values. In this section, "Trouble Spots," we deal with several conflicts that touch on these various interests and the difficulties in addressing them.

Zimbabwe is a tragic country. Over the past decade, President Robert Mugabe has steadily destroyed the commercial farming economy of the country, stripped away the protection of law by undermining and intimidating the judiciary, closed down much of the independent press, rigged elections, and ruthlessly crushed opposition. The result is a country nearly in "free fall." Inflation exceeds 2,000 percent, unemployment in some estimates is as high as 80 percent, millions of Zimbabweans have fled the country, and those remaining rely heavily on the support of international humanitarian agencies and the remittances of their relatives abroad. Yet somehow, neither the surrounding states, the African Union, nor the international community as a whole has been able to alter these developments. In his article on "The Limits of Influence," Princeton N. Lyman explains how such happenings in a country cannot only go on without being stopped, but also how the international community is perforce an enabler in Mugabe's continuing authoritarian rule. Only Mugabe's recent excesses of brutality, and uneasiness within his own party, may portend an end to this situation.

[85]

Darfur, the western region of Sudan, has on the other hand captured the world's attention. With at least 200,000 people dead, 2.5 million displaced, and continuing harassment and violence against the survivors, Darfur has challenged the world's commitment of "never again," i.e., to prevent genocide such as happened in World War II and again in Rwanda in 1984. In this situation, unlike Zimbabwe, the United States and the United Nations have been actively involved, seeking to end the conflict that began in 2003, to bring an international peace force into the region to protect the displaced, and to punish those accused of the most egregious offenses. The Africa Union has been similarly engaged, providing the only peacekeepers in the region so far, but at levels and equipment woefully below what is needed. For all these efforts, the situation remains nearly as bad today as it has been for the past four years. Lee Feinstein has put this conflict into the context of the commitment, made at the UN's Millennium summit, that it is the responsibility of the international community to protect those in any nation whose government cannot or will not protect them from widespread violations of their human rights and threats to their very survival. Feinstein demonstrates the difficulties that face nations and institutions in carrying out this commitment in Darfur and provides clear and practical recommendations not only for the immediate crisis in Darfur but for similar situations in the future.

Eben Kaplan's article traces the development of the terrorist infiltration in Somalia, and the complexities of how to address it. For fourteen years, the conditions within Somalia simmered below the surface of American attention. Burned by the debacle of U.S military intervention in 1992–93, when eighteen U.S. servicemen were killed and some dragged through the streets of Mogadishu, the United States largely stayed out of the many subsequent but largely ineffective efforts by neighboring African states to bring some kind of order and centralized government to the country. America's interest, especially after 9/11, focused almost exclusively on trying to capture alleged terrorists who had taken refuge there. But in 2006, America's interests were seriously challenged when an Islamic movement, similar in its initial strategy to the Taliban in Afghanistan, swept to power in Mogadishu, providing for the first time in decades order, the protection of commerce, and the potential for national government. The movement was, however, also determined to impose a strict Islamic system of laws and culture on the country, and was led by some who were on the U.S. and the UN's terrorist lists. Ethiopia, whose interests were similarly challenged by this movement, swept the new government out of power in a lightning military attack in December 2006. But the result has been a guerrilla war, pitting insurgents against both the Ethiopian military and the fledging Somalian government it protects. An Africa Union peacekeeping force, barely mobilized, faces similar opposition. Mogadishu has thus once again become the scene of daily fighting, mortars, and casualties. Hundreds of thousands have fled the capital, creating a major humanitarian crisis. The United States faces a more difficult challenge than ever in trying to address the dangers of this failing state.

Somalia brings into relief the larger security threats that exist in the Horn of Africa. Professor Terrence Lyons examines these in his report. The Ethiopian-Eritrean conflict, which he addresses, has the potential to spill over into the larger region of the Horn of Africa. Sudan, Somalia, Uganda and Kenya are all drawn into the complexities of the Horn's conflicts. For the United States, there is the special dilemma of dealing with an Ethiopian regime that is its most valuable ally in the war on terror in this region, but that has stepped back from the promising opening toward democracy of two years ago and that faces internal threats of its own. Not surprisingly, the U.S. Senate has been calling for the Bush administration to develop a comprehensive policy toward the Horn. John Prendergast and Colin Thomas-Jensen offer one approach to developing such a policy.

Zimbabwe:
The Limits of Influence

Princeton N. Lyman

THE DILEMMA

THE UNITED STATES SECRETARY of State has labeled Zimbabwe an "outpost of tyranny." President Bush has cited it in his State of the Union message as one of the undemocratic regimes targeted in U.S. democratization policy. Zimbabwe has been driven out of the Commonwealth.[1] Most donors have suspended all but humanitarian assistance. Both UN and African institutions have denounced its human rights practices. The economy has all but collapsed.

The net political effect, however, has been zero. President Mugabe remains firmly in charge, the opposition is cowed and divided, civil society is all but decimated, and the government continues on its same policies and practices. In the meanwhile, the international community now feeds half the population, lifting the most difficult burden of a failed economy from the shoulders of the government.

What does this tell us about international influence on individual regimes? What does it say about the democratization process in Africa? Above all, what does it say about Zimbabwe?

THE CASE AGAINST ZIMBABWE

ZIMBABWE WAS ONCE seen as one of the most promising and vibrant of African states. Possessed of a relatively advanced educa-

---

This article was originally published in *African Renaissance*, Vol. 3, No. 1, Jan/ Feb 2006, pp. 8–16. Reprinted with permission from *African Renaissance*.

tion system, a functioning bureaucracy, considerable mineral wealth, rich agricultural land, and a significant industrial base, Zimbabwe appeared capable of addressing its inherited burdens— a distorted land situation where a minority of farmers owned much of the best land, a history of segregation and racial oppression, a brutal civil war of independence, and a crowded black agricultural sector—with the resources and skills that could achieve both growth and equity without major unrest or further racial confrontation. Mugabe indeed began his presidency with a commitment to reconciliation and, despite a strong rhetorical loyalty to socialism, placed the economy in the hands of a skilled and pragmatic Minister of Finance, Robert Chidzero.

But the bloom was fairly quickly off the rose. Shortly after independence, Mugabe waged a brutalizing war against the supporters of his main political rival, Joshua Nkomo, killing perhaps 20,000 in Matabeleland and forced a demoralized and politically castrated Nkomo to fold his party, the Patriotic Front, into that of Mugabe's, creating in essence a one-party state under the banner of ZANU-PF. For years thereafter, Mugabe flirted with land reform, but largely as a political issue around election time, while allowing the issue to lapse in between.[2] Only when Mugabe lost a critical referendum in February 2000 on constitutional changes, and faced a growing opposition, did Mugabe launch a land grab that in the next few years forced most white farmers off their land without compensation, and displaced thousands of black farm workers, all in the name of justice and anti-colonialism. But by giving out the land in large part to political cronies and even for those small farmers who received land providing no agricultural services or support, the policy hardly dented the basic land problem or benefited many black farmers, while destroying the commercial agricultural sector.

The political situation deteriorated at the same pace. Faced with a significant new opposition party, the Movement for Democratic Change (MDC), Mugabe deployed thugs, police, intelligence services, and various militias to break up MDC rallies, jail and sometimes beat up MDC leaders and officials, and intimidate voters.

The independent press was curtailed to the point where almost all media is now in government hands. Elections after 2000 were marked by suspect voter rolls, intimidation, no-go areas for opposition campaigners and often for international election observers, and contested vote counts. When challenged for his land reform or political practices by the courts, Mugabe forced the resignation of high court judges and virtually crippled the independence of the judiciary. By 2004, democracy in Zimbabwe had been all but wiped out.[3]

To add insult to injury, in the summer of 2005, Mugabe initiated "Operation Murambatsvina," which displaced some 700,000 residents of Harare. The operation destroyed markets, homes, and support systems for these urban dwellers, under the ruse of cleaning up illegal marketing and immigration. It was a human rights and humanitarian disaster. The operation resulted in some of the first serious criticism of the Mugabe government from prominent African leaders and the UN. But once again, the international community is left to help cover the costs, while the Zimbabwe government remains unrepentant about the whole operation.

The economy has fared no better. According to a study by the Center for Global Development, the Mugabe regime has wiped out 52 years of income growth, throwing the per capita income back to that of 1953. The decline exceeds that of countries that have suffered devastating civil war such as Côte d'Ivoire, Congo, and Sierra Leone.

The economy has contracted in real terms in each of the past five years, inflation is in triple digits, the local currency has lost 99% of its value and almost half the country faces food shortages. . . . Manufacturing has shrunk 97% since 1997 and exports have fallen by half in the past four years.[4]

ZIMBABWE'S RESPONSE

Zimbabwe rejects any responsibility for these calamitous results. Mugabe has denounced international criticism as a form of neocolonialism. He has been particularly harsh in his reactions to British criticism, including personal attacks on Prime Minister Tony Blair.[5] Regarding land reform, Mugabe regularly claims that the crisis is due to the failure of the international community, especially the United Kingdom, to live up to its commitments to finance a more orderly and compensated land reform program. The fact that early efforts to finance such programs came a cropper due to questionable assignment of land by the Mugabe government goes unrecognized. Other efforts, by the IBRD, the UNDP, and other governments to put together a meaningful land reform program have similarly fallen apart in negotiations with the government (African governments tried with UNDP help to put together a program financed by Arab governments, but the idea was ultimately rejected by Mugabe). Nevertheless, Mugabe's line on this subject has resonated with Africans, including neighboring South Africa, where apologists for Mugabe repeatedly point to the unresolved land issue as a legitimate source of unrest and needed reform.

Similarly, Mugabe blames the international community for much of the country's economic collapse. There has been a sharp decline in aid to Zimbabwe over the past five years, depriving it of hundreds of millions of dollars. Mugabe's government sees this decline as part of a deliberate conspiracy against Zimbabwe, rather than as a result of the Zimbabwe government's actions. The Zimbabwe government also points to drought in the region as the cause of agricultural decline, rather than the land reform it has carried out. At one point, a pro-government newspaper in Harare claimed the United States controlled the weather at the United Kingdom's behest to produce the recent drought.[6]

The Center for Global Development has analyzed these various arguments and concluded that while reductions in aid and drought do have some impact on the economy they do not explain the dire dimensions of Zimbabwe's collapse. By comparing the impact of drought in neighboring countries, and examining domestic spending patterns of the Zimbabwe government in respect to foreign aid, the study concludes that misgovernance is the principal culprit in this decline. The study predicts little change. "Regardless of rain clouds or imaginary foreign scheming economic misrule will continue to cost Zimbabweans not only their children's opportunities for a better life but, for many, any life at all."[7]

THE INTERNATIONAL RESPONSE

IF ZIMBABWE HAS GONE so far down the path of autocracy and economic ruin, the international response has been far more rhetorical than forceful. There has been a sharp decline in foreign assistance, and some mild sanctions placed on some of Zimbabwe's ruling elite. But much of the responsibility for addressing the crisis has been left to the Africans.

That is not surprising. The United Kingdom has found that its highly vocal criticism of the Mugabe regime has only served to give Mugabe a platform for attacking the former colonial ruler to the enjoyment of many Africans. The United States has neither the degree of influence in Zimbabwe nor sufficient strategic interest for doing more than criticize the situation and place some mild sanctions on the regime. Zimbabwe is indeed a sad backslider in Africa's general trend toward democracy and as such runs contrary to the hopes and ambitions of the U.S. emphasis on building a worldwide community of democracies. But U.S. focus in Africa is much more on Ethiopia, Nigeria, Uganda, and of course South Africa itself, than on this former British colony that offers little opening for dialogue or reform.

Thus when President Bush visited South Africa in 2003, he emphasized that the United States looked to South Africa as the lead in addressing the Zimbabwe crisis. Bush said he thought Mbeki could be an "honest broker" in the Zimbabwean crisis, and urged Mbeki to "continue to work for the return of democracy" there.[8] There is a logic to that position. South Africa after all is the closest neighbor, provides Zimbabwe much of its power, and has the strongest economy in the region. However, South Africa's response, particularly that of President Thabo Mbeki, has been muted, focused on "quiet diplomacy" and promises of progress that alas never materialize. Much of the rest of Africa has followed suit.

South Africa's rather cautious approach is shaped by several factors. First, Thabo Mbeki has little personal influence over

[93]

Mugabe. Indeed, Mugabe treats Mbeki as a junior, as having far less prestige than Mugabe sees himself enjoying. Second, South Africa fears that a total collapse of the Zimbabwean economy would fall on South Africa, with millions of refugees and unrest that could spread into South Africa itself. Third, Mbeki—and this has been true of Nigeria's Obasanjo who also has taken a hand in addressing the crisis—has little respect for the Zimbabwean opposition, the MDC. Mbeki sees it at worst a tool of white farmers, at best an unsophisticated and divided party not capable of ruling. Thus Mbeki has focused primarily on engineering a ZANU succession to Mugabe, not a wholesale change in government or even a serious coalition one. Since Mugabe rejects any real coalition, and there seems little chance in the near future for Mugabe to retire or be retired by his ZANU party, South Africa's policy seems to promise no more than a long-term solution.

South Africa of course pays a price in this regard. Foreign investors are uneasy, especially those whose CEOs have only a passing knowledge of Africa. They see in Zimbabwe the collapse of the rule of law and the uncompensated appropriation of land that could be repeated in South Africa. Mbeki's failure to denounce clearly Mugabe's land policies, even while denying that South Africa would do the same, adds to investors' unease. Second, South Africa already has several million Zimbabweans in the country, swelling the immigration numbers and causing some internal concern. Third, there is considerable dissension within South Africa over the government's Zimbabwe policy. Within the government's coalition, the labor movement, COSATU, is much more sympathetic to the MDC in Zimbabwe because the latter has a labor base. COSATU has criticized government policy accordingly. Press criticism of Mbeki's Zimbabwe policy is almost relentless.

Nevertheless, there may be a bit of *schadenfreude* as South Africa's elite watches the crumbling of Zimbabwe's economy. Mugabe was never a close ally of Mandela and was jealous of Mandela's hero status throughout the world. Mugabe dragged the Southern Africa Development Community (SADC) into the Congo civil war against Mandela's wishes. As noted, Mugabe treats Mbeki with even less respect. Zimbabwe also offered the only serious economic rivalry to South Africa in the region and to South Africa's leadership of the SADC. Once Zimbabwe collapses totally, and Mugabe departs the scene, South Africa may be in the best position to pick up the pieces.

Elsewhere in Africa, there has been only a slowly gathering criticism of Mugabe's regime. Mugabe enjoys still widespread popularity as a liberation leader. His ranting against the United Kingdom and the west in general resonates with Africans who still feel the weight of colonialism's history and who believe there is neocolonial control still of the global economy and Africa's access to it. African governments have been careful not to go against this feeling. Indeed, there is a lingering respect throughout Africa for liberation leaders, even when they have out lived their value as leaders or veered into autocratic rule.

The first real break in this reluctance came in the wake of Operation Murambatsvina. The human cost, and the crassness of the government's handling of it, provoked outrage throughout international circles. UN Secretary-General Kofi Annan wisely selected an Africa leader, Anna Tibaijuka, Director of Habitat, to investigate the situation. Her report was damning, breaking the African silence over the deepening crisis in the country.[9] Then in December 2005, the African Union Commission on Human Rights issued a sharply critical report on Zimbabwe. It found "continuing violations and the deterioration of the human rights situation, the lack of respect for the rule of law, and [a] growing culture of impunity."[10]

Yet nothing has really changed in Zimbabwe. Mugabe's regime has even thwarted an effort to suspend it from the International Monetary Fund (IMF) for failure to repay its loans. At first Mugabe seemed on the ropes, seeking a loan from South Africa or further help from China. When South Africa insisted on some reform conditions on the loan, Mugabe balked. China did little. But Mugabe trumped his critics by finding the foreign exchange to pay a first tranche on the debt and has pledged recently a further $15 million. Taking a superior tone, a pro-government paper warned Zimbabwe's Central Bank governor not to try to please the IMF, which sent a team to examine the situation, for they are "insincere partners."[11]

THE OPPOSITION ONCE LOOKED formidable in Zimbabwe. It led the fight against Mugabe's constitutional referendum, then scored big in subsequent parliamentary elections. But Mugabe has struck back and left the opposition divided, stumbling, and uncertain of its future.

A series of recent electoral defeats, engineered by Mugabe's repressive tactics and electoral machinations, has left the MDC divided as to whether to contest elections further, whether to participate at all in the parliament. Initially the MDC took its charges of electoral fraud to the courts, but lost, not surprisingly given Mugabe's packing of the courts. It sought an "orange revolution" by bringing large crowds into the streets. But ruthless suppression of demonstrations and arrests of MDC cadres eventually defeated this strategy. Now the MDC has to worry whether further demonstrations will only endanger its supporters. The divisions that have emerged over strategy have left the opposition weaker than ever.

One should not be too hard on the MDC however. Any opposition to an autocratic or occupational ruler has to have either room to maneuver within the country, or a base of outside support to which it can retreat and from which it can draw resources. The MDC has neither. Mugabe has been exceptionally successful in undermining the operations not only of the MDC but of civil society in general. The government has placed restrictions on outside funding, closed down the independent press, and harassed critics. There has been little effective counter support from abroad. The question then arises why, as the economic situation worsens as well, the population does not rise up in protest, and create serious unrest. There are two reasons.

The MDC has long eschewed undertaking an armed resistance. That is morally commendable in many ways, but it is also practical. To undertake an armed insurgency in Zimbabwe the MDC would need to have support bases across the borders and active if tacit support from one or more of the neighboring countries. That was true of the liberation struggle in Zimbabwe and of the long struggle against apartheid. (Recall the apartheid government's frequent raids into neighboring countries.) None of Zimbabwe's neighbors is prepared to provide such support or even to tolerate a resistance movement operating in the shadows. No outside government is prepared to finance and provide arms to an insurgency in Zimbabwe. No western country, as noted above, has sufficient interest to do so. China is a strong supporter of the Mugabe regime and sells it arms, so there is no support from that quarter. An armed insurgency is not really possible.

A second reason is that at least one-third of Zimbabwe's population has left the country. These include some of the best educated of the country, people who might provide the intellectual foundation, the organizational skills, and the determination needed for an effective uprising. Instead, these emigrants have concentrated on finding jobs in neighboring countries and sending funds home to their families to help them cope with the dire economic situation there. Thus Mugabe has succeeded in having some of the pressure taken off by people leaving while getting the benefit of remittances flowing back to the country.

WHAT IS LEFT TO DO

LITTLE BY LITTLE, both the internal opposition and the international critics are coming to the conclusion that their only hope is to wait until Mugabe leaves the scene and then to pick up from there. The internal opposition no longer believes that western or even the increasing international, including African, criticism of the regime is going to produce any real pressure on the Mugabe regime, or that outsiders will come to their rescue.

A recent article by Todd Morse and Stewart Patrick, two scholars who have looked closely at the options for addressing the situation, recommends that the international community turn attention less to seeking change in the current circumstances and focus instead on developing strategies for after Mugabe has left the scene. They recommend the United States assemble a coalition of interested nations to plot out a recovery scenario. The Mugabe government, they write, "appears impervious to international pressure to reform or even to moderate political repression and disastrous economic policies."[12]

As long as the Mugabe regime persists, the international community, through the World Food Program, is left feeding half of Zimbabwe's population, further relieving the pressure on the government that would result from the economic collapse. The world is caught in a classic Catch-22 situation. To walk away entirely from Zimbabwe would mean allowing mass starvation or malnutrition, producing perhaps a collapse of the regime but at terrible human cost. Or, the international community can continue, with meager means of keeping the food from becoming a political prop for the regime, alleviating the suffering and doing the "right thing."

The conclusion is unavoidable that those who have been shocked, upset, outraged, or otherwise concerned with the decline of one of Africa's most promising countries into dictatorship and economic ruin have not found the means to reverse that process. A combination of limited interests, conflicting objectives, and lack of pressure points have left Zimbabwe largely untouched by the international community. Rhetoric alone, even from the strongest nation in the world, does not move either the Zimbabwe regime nor its neighbors. Without either more leverage or the willingness to take much more drastic action—which would have its own risks—the United States, and its allies in this cause, are left without any results of their singling out Zimbabwe among the outposts of tyranny.

Recognizing these limits should lead policy makers to look long and hard at democratization strategies in Africa and elsewhere. First and foremost, the international community needs to act early in a declining situation, lending support to the institutions of democracy and building coalitions of pressure long before the situation has hardened into one that pits a determined regime against a divided international community. Second, it is important to recognize that the strength of the democratization process in

Africa must come primarily from within Africa itself. Outside powers cannot force such trends, only encourage and support them where they are maturing. Third, it is time indeed to begin planning for the post-Mugabe regime. But it will not be easy. Once that regime begins to change, South Africa's interests, those of China, and those of the various factions within, will not cede easily to any coalition put together by the United States or even the United Nations. A long decline, as has occurred in Zimbabwe, will mean a long road back.

Darfur and Beyond: What Is Needed to Prevent Mass Atrocities

Lee Feinstein

THE KILLING AND DESTRUCTION of national, ethnic, racial, or religious groups is a historical reality. So, too, is the dependable failure of the rest of the world to do much about it.

Slow-motion ethnic cleansing in western Sudan is the most recent case of a state supporting mass atrocity and the rest of the world avoiding efforts to end the killing. Preventing and stopping such mass atrocities faces four reinforcing problems.

First and most fundamentally, states of different cultures and economic circumstances continue to pursue ethnic cleansing as a national security strategy. Second, prevailing international rules and practices have been a bar to international action, and an excuse not to respond in cases where states do not believe their national interests are at stake. Third, international capacity to act, especially regional capacity, is limited and ad hoc, a function of poor planning and deliberate political choices. Finally, public support to take action to prevent mass atrocities is episodic or nonexistent, the result and product of a historic lack of political leadership around the world, including in the United States.

The profound changes in international security of the last few years, and the related changes in how and what states view as security dangers, have the potential to erode some of these barriers.

This piece is excerpted from the Council Special Report *Darfur and Beyond: What Is Needed to Prevent Mass Atrocities* (New York: Council on Foreign Relations Press, January 2007).

One year ago the 191 members of the United Nations formally endorsed a principle known as the "responsibility to protect." The responsibility to protect is the idea that mass atrocities that take place in one state are the concern of all states. The universal adoption of this principle at the United Nations World Summit in 2005 went relatively unnoticed. Yet the adoption of the responsibility to protect is a turning point in how states define their rights and responsibilities, and removes some of the classic excuses for doing nothing.

The UN's role in averting mass atrocities is also being examined, as part of a broader rethink of the UN's purposes triggered by the Security Council crisis over Iraq in 2003. This reexamination has generated reports and investigations, and some improvement. The new secretary-general, Ban Ki-moon, needs to connect management reform to a set of clear mandates for the organization that corresponds to the world's expectations for the institution. Management reform detached from a clear assessment of the purposes of the UN is destined to sputter and fail. The new secretary-general should build a reform program that is designed to implement the responsibility to protect to begin to translate the principle into practice. Doing so would also fortify the overall push for reforms, which has faltered.

The United States and other capable states and organizations have given a degree of rhetorical support to the atrocity prevention mission. Yet, Washington and others have not enacted a policy to support their moral claims or to advance the overlapping security interest in preventing state failure, which can create the conditions that make genocide and other atrocities more likely.

Addressing the lack of political leadership in the United States and internationally is a complex and difficult issue. Public support to take action in Darfur, for example, spans a broad ideological spectrum in the United States. Yet most Americans, embittered by the Iraq experience and wary of humanitarian intervention, are skeptical that international action of any kind can be effective. That said, the public seems to support playing a more active role in Darfur, including military action and support by NATO.[1]

Overcoming these structural impediments to action requires balancing effectiveness against expense. Genocide is a historical fact and a present danger. It is possible to identify with a degree of accuracy *where* it might occur and in general terms *that* it is going to occur. But it is not possible to say exactly *when* it will happen or what will precipitate a genuine emergency. For example, there was a thirty-five-year backdrop to the 1994 slaughter of Tutsis by Hutus in and around Rwanda. This history alerted the world to the chronic danger of genocide in the region. It also dulled it to the acuity of the crisis in the weeks leading up to the killings in April 1994.

The failure to intervene militarily in Rwanda and the frustration over inaction to stop the mass killing in Darfur has had the unhelpful effect of framing the issue of preventing atrocities around the question of whether to "send in the Marines." Forcible humanitarian intervention cannot be ruled out. Nor can it be held out only as a last resort. Yet, the inherent risks of military interventions should limit invasion and occupation to extreme cases. In most instances, political, diplomatic, and a range of military options short of war are preferable and more effective.

THE RESPONSIBILITY TO PROTECT AND DARFUR

IF DARFUR IS THE FIRST "test case" of the responsibility to protect, there is no point in denying that the world has failed the entry exam.[2]

BACKGROUND TO THE CONFLICT

The current conflict in Darfur began in February 2003, when the Sudan Liberation Movement, a newly formed rebel group, joined the Justice and Equality Movement in a series of attacks on government military posts. The government of Sudan responded to the provocation by mobilizing proxy militias, the Janjaweed, drawn from Darfur's indigenous Arabs. The first wave of killings began in 2003. The Sudanese army and Janjaweed developed a pattern of close counterinsurgency cooperation. Improvised bombs of "explosives and metallic debris" dumped out of the doors of Russian transport aircraft were followed closely by successive raids by attack helicopters and fighter-bombers. Janjaweed militia on camel and horseback, sometimes assisted by army units, swept in to finish the job, by burning villages, killing principally young men, and forcing survivors to flee. The displaced fled to areas sometimes protected by Sudanese police. Janjaweed patrolled the perimeters, however, attacking women and girls who left.[3] By early 2004, as many as 80,000 people had been killed as a result of the conflict, and more than 1 million displaced, including 100,000 in refugee camps outside the country.[4]

Washington and others were initially slow to recognize the carnage; the Sudanese government had begun cooperating with Washington after 9/11, and Khartoum succumbed to U.S. pressure to sign the North-South peace agreement, which ended a decades-long civil war in Sudan that claimed the lives of 2 million people. It was not until September 2004 that then-U.S. Secretary of State Colin Powell described the conflict in Darfur as genocide and not until January 2005 that the International Commission of Inquiry, which investigated the mass killings on behalf of the United Nations, reached the softer conclusion that the Sudanese government and associated Janjaweed militias were responsible for "serious violations of international human rights and humanitarian law."

By the end of 2006, an estimated 250,000 people had died as a result of the conflict, and nearly 3 million out of a total population of 6 million Darfuris were displaced. The UN estimates that 40 percent of Darfuris now depend on outside assistance for their survival. The military situation remains precarious, despite the announcement in January 2007 of a sixty-day cease-fire. Rebels have regrouped and renamed themselves the National Redemption Front, and have renewed attacks against the Sudanese Army. Khartoum launched an offensive against rebel groups last November, accompanied by a surge in Janjaweed activity. Two major relief organizations have halted operations out of concern for the security of their staff. The UN's humanitarian chief, Jan Egeland, noted a "dramatic deterioration" in the humanitarian situation in November, saying the region has teetered "closer to the abyss than I have witnessed since my first visit in 2004."[5]

The conflict in Darfur also continues to spill into neighboring Chad, where some 200,000 refugees from the conflict have joined the 90,000 internally displaced persons uprooted by Chad's civil war. Both Chad and Sudan have accused each other of supporting rebellions in their countries.

TURNING POINT

The Darfur conflict is now at a turning point, similar to Bosnia in 1995. A pallid military force, United Nations Protection Force (UNPROFOR), did not prevent the first wave of ethnic cleansing against Muslims that began in 1992, including the massacre of 7,000 Bosnian Muslims under formal UN protection at Srebrenica. The failure of the UN effort eventually convinced the Clinton administration to lead a NATO bombing campaign to prevent further killing. The intervention of the United States, plus ground gains by Muslim and Croat forces, proved to be the punch in the nose that got then President of Serbia Slobodan Milosevic to back down and negotiate in Dayton.

There is no guarantee that early action by the United States and others would have moderated or prevented the Darfur conflict. Yet, the regime made concessions to Washington in the past. Khartoum forced Osama bin Laden out of Sudan in 1996 under pressure from the Clinton administration. It responded to Bush administration warnings after 9/11, and agreed to provide Washington with intelligence information about its former friends. In January 2005, Khartoum concluded the Comprehensive Peace Agreement, mediated by Washington, agreeing to accept the presence of UN peacekeepers in southern Sudan. Implementation of penalties or pressure authorized in Security Council resolutions dating back to July 2004 would have sent a determined message to the government of Sudan. International support to the African Union Mission in Sudan, which has never reached its authorized troop strength, would have signaled regional commitment to the humanitarian principles of the AU Charter. Concerted U.S. diplomacy rather than deference to Beijing would have also frustrated Khartoum's efforts to expose rifts within the Security Council. Having pursued this range of options, the international community would at least have laid the basis for a stronger response down the road.

The questions for Darfur now are what kind of action is needed to prevent a potential second genocidal wave; what, if any, action could get a confident Bashir government to relent; and what are the obstacles to mustering international will to carry out an effective political-military strategy?

The responsibility to protect outlines a range of options to achieve the first two of these objectives. As discussed earlier, the responsibility to protect calls for an international response that can stop mass atrocities, war crimes, and crimes against humanity, including genocide. Responses can be political, diplomatic, economic, and military. Military responses can span the range of options from cooperative assistance to the extreme case of forcible intervention against the will of a government. The overriding theme is the priority to protect the rights of people over protecting the right of states to do as they please.

In Darfur, the immediate goal is to provide protection for the civilian population, including 2 million people dispersed in 200 refugee camps in the country, and in twelve refugee camps in eastern Chad.

The present focus, supported by the United States, is on regional diplomacy to win Khartoum's agreement for a hybrid AU-UN force, whose mission would be to protect civilians and deter destabilizing rebel attacks. UN officials say that a credible force must have "sufficient military power to deter or defeat spoilers," including surveillance and reconnaissance, a command-and-control capability, and air and ground reaction forces.[6]

Diplomatic efforts to get Sudan's agreement to an international force have failed so far, and show little prospect for success. In Addis Ababa in early November, representatives of the Khartoum government accepted a hybrid force "in principle." But Khartoum hinged its consent on reaching agreement about the size and command of the force. Despite the government of Sudan's agreement to a sixty-day cease-fire in January, Khartoum continues to say that deploying a UN force would signal a return to "colonialism," and has insisted that the force be all African with only technical support from outside. The limitations the Khartoum government wants to place on an international force would make it impossible to provide a real measure of security for the people of Darfur. Even if Khartoum consented to a credible operation, the United Nations has said it will take months to field a small advance force.

The Darfur problem is an immensely difficult one. No solution is guaranteed to work. The facts will never line up one hundred to zero. Any policy will be messy. Setting policy requires a frank understanding of the risks and choices on the basis of those risks. Freedom isn't free, and neither is protection. The hard truth is that enforcing the responsibility to protect entails risks. If the prevailing policy is zero tolerance for casualties, then enforcement of the responsibility to protect is an empty promise.

The goal then must be to craft an effective policy that carries the lowest possible costs to the people who need protection, to the regional forces that bear the brunt of the risk, and to U.S. and European forces acting behind the scenes. The risk of a terrorist response in the United States, Europe, or elsewhere also cannot be ruled out. Any policy also needs to weigh the risks to broader U.S. foreign policy goals, including in the Arab world, where another Western-supported military operation in the Muslim world will be viewed with disdain, whatever the facts of the Muslim-against-Muslim killing in Darfur.

Getting Khartoum's formal support for a capable peacekeeping force should remain an international goal. The linchpin to getting Sudan's agreement to a peacekeeping force may be gaining wider adherence to the Darfur Peace Agreement (DPA), which has been signed by only one of the eight splintering rebel factions. (That signatory has since been co-opted by the Bashir government, and its leader, now living in Khartoum, depends on Khartoum for protection.) There is dispute about whether an agreement is possible soon. A Western adviser to the DPA negotiations says agreement is "not a distant hope: the political differences are small." If and when there is a peace to keep, introduction of UN peacekeepers or a hybrid force "will follow."[7]

Yet, the list of broken commitments by the Bashir government is long. There are questions about whether Khartoum will accept a minimally capable international force unless there is a cost for refusing to do so. In the meantime, delaying deployment of peacekeepers prolongs the insecurity of Darfuris, who remain vulnerable to Janjaweed and government attacks.

Nothing short of a major deployment of competent troops can provide a reasonable guarantee of security, but three interim steps would improve the situation now, and would also send an overdue message of seriousness to the Bashir government.

RECOMMENDATIONS

Immediately Strengthen the African Union Mission in Sudan

The African Union agreed on November 30 to extend its mandate for six months until June 2007. The African Union has a mandated troop strength of 11,000 troops, yet it has fielded only 7,200 troops since early 2005. Rwanda now has 1,800 troops in the African Union Mission in Darfur, and Nigeria has 2,000. Each could increase its contributions significantly. African troops currently serving in the UN mission in southern Sudan can also be transferred to Darfur at acceptable risk to the 2005 North-South accord.

The United Nations, the United States, and Europe can also improve the capacity, caliber, and morale of the African Union force. A place to start is to ensure that AU troops receive a paycheck; they were unpaid for two months last summer. Among the areas where Western states could play a role is equipping reinforcements. The United States, for example, has already armed and trained Nigerian troops, and trained Senegalese and Rwandan forces. NATO has also been ferrying African Union troops inside Darfur, but the support has been ad hoc and limited. A more dedicated effort would improve the AU's responsiveness, enabling a smaller number of troops to be more effective.

NATO and the African Union have been engaged in a years-long routine of "After You, Alphonse." NATO defers to the perceived pride of the African Union. The African Union does not request outside support because it fears the political consequences while using NATO's reticence as the formal excuse. The United

States must get an unambiguous NATO commitment to provide consistent support for the African Union, and Washington and others should press the African Union, on that basis, to accept assistance.

Ready an International Force Now

The United Nations, supported by the five permanent members of the Security Council, should intensify efforts to identify peace-keeping troops for a prospective international operation. So far, only Bangladesh, Nigeria, and Tanzania have volunteered to put troops on the ground. Norway and Sweden have offered a small joint engineering battalion. Within Africa, capable states are waiting to see who makes the first move. Western states with available military capacity are waiting for Africans to volunteer, and also want a clearer indication from the African Union that outside support is wanted. China has been participating much more widely in UN peacekeeping operations. Pledges by China to participate in a mission in Darfur would provide some political cover to the Sudanese government to accept an international force and pressure Khartoum to do so. Beijing has privately signaled it is considering contributing troops to a blue-helmeted force.

The absence of military capacity reinforces an absence of political will. If no ready sources for a peacekeeping operation are apparent, there is no impetus to push for fast deployment. The Bashir government interprets the lack of peacekeeping forces as an expression of international division and indifference, which it exploits and uses to its own purposes.

UN peacekeeping operations are at a historical peak. NATO and the United States are pinned down in Afghanistan and Iraq. Yet if there is a sense of crisis, states find the resources to shake loose, as they did in response to the conflict in southern Lebanon last summer.[8]

Enforce the UN and DPA Flight Bans

The Security Council authorized a ban on "offensive military flights" in 2005. The Security Council has not enforced that ban. The Darfur Peace Agreement also committed the Sudanese government in 2006 to end hostile military flights, and established a still-born cease-fire commission with responsibility for enforcement and monitoring. Yet, Khartoum has continued its bombing campaign in the eight months since the agreement was concluded.

The Security Council, backed by the African Union, the United States, and the European Union, should take action to enforce the bans it authorized and Khartoum accepted. Sudan should be warned that indiscriminate air attacks against Darfuri villages or refugee camps, or attacks on rebels that create disproportionate collateral damage, will be treated as possible war crimes for referral to The Hague. Rebel groups operating in Darfur or in neighboring refugee camps would also be warned to refrain from attacks.

The warning should be issued by the widest possible group of states, preferably including the Security Council and the African Union. A diplomatic strategy would be built around the prospect of issuing the warning, including more intensive diplomacy with the African Union, the Arab League, and China. One observer has proposed a meeting of P-5 and AU ministers in Khartoum to send a much more focused signal of international concern.[9] An intensified diplomatic push should also be supported by acceleration of economic pressure on the Bashir government, including sanctions on private firms held by the Khartoum leadership.[10]

A direct way to enforce flight bans would be to destroy or disable aircraft on the ground (rather than attempting to shoot aircraft in mid-flight), relying primarily on reinforcements to the AU force, which would secure the principal air bases used by the Sudanese air force. In the event of a flight confirmed to violate the bans, forces on the ground could shut down a runway, disable, or, if necessary, destroy aircraft. Because Sudan's fleet of improvised bombers (Antonov An-12 transports), fighters, and helicopters cannot travel long distances, the number of airfields to be secured would be small. El Fashir is Sudan's main air base in Darfur. There is already a Western presence at El Fashir, which also serves as the staging area for humanitarian flights by the United Nations and others.[11]

Another option is establishing a no-fly zone over Darfur. Carrying out a no-fly zone effectively would be a difficult and costly round-the-clock operation. Stringent rules of engagement would be needed to reduce the risk of shooting down the wrong target. Even with precautions, however, it would be impossible to eliminate those risks, as past efforts over Iraq and Yugoslavia illustrate. A no-fly zone would also require reliable, probably NATO, ground troops, to identify targets and direct attacks. A no-fly zone is also likely to interrupt humanitarian flights, which are the principal lines of support to remote refugee camps inaccessible by ground. Neither of these options is without risks, but both are preferable to leaving the current population at risk. Either decision would represent a significant escalation of Western involvement and a direct challenge to Khartoum, which should only be pursued if there is the stomach in Washington and Europe for a fight.

POLITICAL WILL

Summoning the political will to take risks is the main obstacle to converting the responsibility to protect into a program of action. Although the responsibility for atrocities against the African minority in western Sudan rests with the Khartoum government, the failure to stop the killing is a collective one.

Some have blamed the United Nations, and the presence of non-democracies on the Security Council, including veto-holding members, for the failure to apply the responsibility to protect in Darfur.[12]

The United Nations has failed to take strong action in the first instance because China has adopted the role of Sudan's protector on the Security Council. In an indication of broader hostility to an international effort in Darfur, the Human Rights Council in November narrowly rejected an EU-Canadian resolution calling on the Sudanese government to prosecute those responsible for atrocities in Darfur.

Nonetheless, the Security Council has succeeded in producing a series of resolutions on Darfur since 2003, including resolution 1706, passed August 31, 2006, which specifically connects the responsibility to protect to Darfur—the first time the Security Council invoked the principle in relation to a particular conflict. The Security Council has also authorized a ban on Sudanese military flights, referred indicted war criminals to the International Criminal Court in March 2005, and created a pathway for sanctions on certain financial interests of the Sudanese leadership.

Criticism of the United Nations is a form of self-criticism. The United Nations system was designed by its American framers not to be able to act decisively without great power consensus. Structural sloth is a built-in protection against a UN that acts without the consent of its most prominent members. These structural impediments both frustrate and serve larger U.S. interests.

Neither the United States nor the other democracies on the Council is pressing to carry out the unenforced Security Council resolutions. In the case of Darfur, the world's militarily capable and prosperous states, generally democracies, have been unwilling to take risks for a humanitarian principle that does not touch their vital national security interests. As Newt Gingrich and George Mitchell wrote, recently, "On stopping genocide, all too often 'the United Nations failed' should actually read 'members of the United Nations blocked or undermined action by the United Nations.'"[13]

The lack of Security Council agreement on Darfur is not a legal bar to action. Even if China were now to balk, Security Council resolution 1591 gives Chapter VII authority to enforce a flight ban over Darfur, and resolutions 1672 and 1679 authorize further action on economic and political sanctions. Given the existing authority, there is no need to apply the Kosovo precedent, where the relevant regional organization, NATO, was justifiably prepared to act without express Security Council approval. In any case, the Kosovo example, reinforced by the approval of the responsibility to protect in 2005, provides a compelling precedent for action outside the UN when exigency demands. As Kofi Annan said, "The choice . . . must not be between Council unity and inaction in the face of genocide, as in the case of Rwanda, on the one hand; and Council division, and regional action, as in the case of Kosovo, on the other." The problem in the response to Darfur is not a lack of legal authority, but a lack of will.

The evidence of the past three years is that the world is not prepared to use force or even concerted pressure to force the government of Sudan to end its military campaign in western Sudan. In the absence of international will, Khartoum will retain the capability to act with impunity, opening the possibility of further war crimes in Darfur, and deepening the possibility that a conflict that is seeping across borders will engulf the region. The weak international response to date is discouraging. The question is whether the prospect of a second wave of atrocities will compel governments to act.

CONCLUSION

IN ADOPTING THE RESPONSIBILITY to protect last year, the United Nations accepted the principle that mass atrocities that take place in one state are the concern of all states. The new secretary-general should begin to bridge the gap between these words and the institution's deeds by taking the General Assembly's endorsement of the responsibility to protect as a mandate and a mission statement. Economic and militarily capable states and organizations including the United States must also take steps to bolster UN action, and to be available when the UN is not.

Darfur illustrates the difficulties in converting the principle of the responsibility to protect into a program of action. The difficulty is acute when, as in this case, the international response is slow and inadequate. The failure to demonstrate seriousness to Khartoum early has left the world with a Hobson's choice. Focusing on diplomacy now will be read by Khartoum as a permission slip to do as it pleases. Military action may be the only way to get Sudan to relent, yet it is dangerous, not guaranteed to succeed, and, as a consequence, unlikely to receive broad international political support.

The long-term goal is to avoid the stark options of "Doing Nothing" and "Sending in the Marines." That requires establishing a pattern of early and effective international response at the first signs of concern. The place to start is with concrete steps to build capacity—diplomatic, economic, legal, and military—in support of the principle of humanitarian protection. Universal adoption of the responsibility to protect has begun to remove the classical excuses for doing nothing in the face of mass atrocities. What is needed now is the capacity and political will to back it up.

Somalia's Terrorist Infestation

Eben Kaplan

EVER SINCE THE DEATHS of eighteen U.S. soldiers in a UN-backed intervention in 1993, Somalia has weighed on the minds of U.S. officials. Without a functioning government since 1991, the country has been home to a lawless society dominated by violence. Beyond the humanitarian concerns caused by such prolonged instability, there is evidence to suggest that international terrorist organizations are using the fractured state on the tip of Africa's Horn as a safe haven and base of operations. According to the U.S. State Department's most recent Country Reports on Terrorism, terrorist activities in Somalia are "threatening the security of the whole region."

WHAT IS SOMALIA'S RECENT HISTORY?

SOMALIA WAS CREATED in 1960 by the merger of British Somaliland Protectorate and the colony of Italian Somaliland. The United Republic of Somalia was ruled by a democratic government for nine years until it was toppled by a military coup and Major General Muhammad Siad Barre took power. Barre established a socialist state, which lasted until 1991 when opposition clans overthrew him. After Barre's expulsion, several northern clans declared independence as the Republic of Somaliland. Though unrecognized, the area has maintained a relatively stable existence under clan rule. In the south, however, violence between rival warlords vying for power killed thousands of civilians, prompting the UN Security Council to sponsor a U.S.-led intervention. The mission ended

---

This article was posted on CFR.org, June 6, 2006.

shortly after a disastrous firefight in the streets of Mogadishu led to unexpected U.S. losses.

WHAT EFFORTS ARE BEING MADE TO ESTABLISH A GOVERNMENT IN SOMALIA?

SINCE GENERAL BARRE's flight from power, thirteen different attempts to form a government have failed. A fourteenth effort, the product of two years of thorough international mediation, produced a transitional government known as the Somalia Transitional Federal Institutions (TFIs) in October 2004. This includes a 275-member parliamentary body that elected a president, the Ethiopian-backed warlord Abdullahi Yusuf Ahmed. Experts say warlords are members of the transitional parliament as well. Many of these warlords have an interest in preventing the establishment of a stable government, as the status quo enables them to maintain control over their fiefdoms.

Actually convening the government has been no easy task. Until June 2005, the TFIs existed in exile, and when they returned to Somalia several members of the government faced assassination attempts. When the transitional parliament finally convened on Somali soil in February 2006, they did so in the city of Baidoa, in large part because meeting in Mogadishu, the capital, was deemed too dangerous. Since then, renewed violence has caused experts to question whether the TFIs can introduce any semblance of stability.

International organizations have called for African Union peacekeepers to help establish a stable environment in which a government could flourish. Somali leaders have said they would welcome peacekeepers from Sudan and Uganda, but not from Djibouti, Ethiopia, or Kenya, as they are concerned their neighbors would be too eager to meddle in Somali affairs.

WHO HOLDS THE POWER IN SOMALIA?

AFTER FIFTEEN YEARS of recurring violence and absent leadership, Somalia is the very definition of a failed state. Providing a modicum of order in this power vacuum are sharia (Islamic law) courts, which have sprung up across much of southern Somalia over the past decade. More recently, these courts have obtained the support of Islamist militias, further projecting their influence. Just prior to this year's transitional parliament meeting, a group of Mogadishu-based warlords calling themselves the Alliance for the Restoration of Peace and Counter-Terrorism organized in opposition to the militias. Clashes between the alliance and the Islamist militias escalated in May 2006, resulting in some of the worst violence in Somalia in more than a decade, and on June 5, militia members announced they had seized complete control of Mogadishu. Members of the transitional parliament have accused the United States of supporting the allied warlords as part of the "war on terror."

WHAT IS THE EXTENT OF THE U.S. TIES TO THE WARLORDS OF THE ALLIANCE FOR THE RESTORATION OF PEACE AND COUNTER-TERRORISM?

U.S. POLICYMAKERS have not provided any information about their relationship with the aligned group of warlords, but the *Washington Post* reports that U.S. officials have anonymously confirmed contact with the alliance. Some Somalis say the group's "counterterrorism" name is just a gimmick to attract U.S. support. As Ted Dagne, an Africa analyst for the Congressional Research Service, explains, "The fact that these guys came up with that alliance name five years after the terrorist attacks in New York and Washington and considering their past and current brutal acts against their own people should tell you something."

The amount of U.S. support for the warlords, if any, is small. There are no U.S. troops in Somalia, and an arms embargo forbids providing weapons. Experts say the United States is likely communicating with the warlords and possibly providing them with some money. Even this level of involvement has caused some discontent within the TFIs. As Prime Minister Ali Mohamed Gedi told the *Washington Post*, "We would prefer that the U.S. work with the transitional government and not with criminals."

WHY IS SOMALIA AN ATTRACTIVE LOCATION FOR TERRORISTS?

MEMBERS OF SEVERAL terrorist groups, including al-Qaeda, have sought refuge in Somalia in recent years. The lack of a functioning central government means Somalia's borders can be crossed without visas, and once inside the country, there's no real law enforcement to speak of. Just a boat ride away from Yemen via well-traveled fishing and trade routes, Somalia has long served as a passageway from Africa to the Middle East.

The International Crisis Group (ICG) reports that despite repeated efforts, militant Islam has failed to take root in Somalia's seemingly "fertile ground." Nevertheless, Somalia is home to groups that are willing to offer protection and support to terrorists transiting through the country.

WHAT TERRORIST GROUPS ARE OPERATING IN SOMALIA?

AN ICG REPORT IDENTIFIES two active terrorist groups in Somalia. One is an al-Qaeda cell believed to be responsible for the 1998 bombing of the U.S. embassy in Kenya, and later for the simultaneous bombing of a Mombasa resort hotel and failed missile attack on an Israeli passenger jet in 2002. Despite the high profile of this cell's attacks, the ICG estimates the number of ranking al-Qaeda operatives in Somalia is less than half a dozen. The second terrorist group, composed largely of local jihadis, emerged in 2003 and has since carried out a number of massacres and assassinations, including the murder of an Italian nun. Led by Aden Hashi Ayro, who trained in Afghanistan, the group operates in decentralized units and has no clear ideological agenda. Some members of this new group, including Ayro, are former members of the now-defunct al-Itihaad al-Islaami, a Somali terrorist group from the 1990s whose militia once had more than 1,000 members, but was destroyed by Ethiopia after attacks on Ethiopian territory.

While terrorists have certainly taken advantage of Somalia's instability, experts say the country is of particular concern not as much for the terrorist haven it is today, but for the haven it has the potential to be. As yet, Dagne says, "There is no evidence that I know of linking Somali 'Islamist' groups to any international terrorist act, although Somalia may have been used as a transit for some terrorist individuals or a temporary resting place, as is the case more so for Kenya."

WHAT IS THE UNITED STATES DOING TO PREVENT TERRORISTS FROM OPERATING IN SOMALIA?

BEYOND THE SUPPORT THE United States may or may not be giving the Alliance for the Restoration of Peace and Counter-Terrorism, there are some 1,000 U.S. troops stationed in nearby Djibouti as part of the Combined Joint Task Force-Horn of Africa. This task force is charged with advancing the long-term stability of the region—building schools, hospitals, and wells—and preventing the spread of terrorism. Djibouti is home to France's largest military base, and French forces are also involved in development and counterterrorism operations.

Experts agree the most effective counterterrorism strategy for Somalia is one that seeks to establish a stable government, as well as an environment in which civil society organizations and moderate Muslim organizations can flourish.

Avoiding Conflict in the Horn of Africa: U.S. Policy Toward Ethiopia and Eritrea

Terrence Lyons

WHILE THE UNITED STATES has paid high-level attention to Sudan and to issues of counterterrorism in the Horn of Africa, policies toward the border stalemate and authoritarianism in Ethiopia and Eritrea have been reactive, episodic, and largely unsuccessful. Washington needs a new diplomatic strategy in the region that recognizes these growing risks and the links among the border stalemate, fragile and authoritarian regimes, and escalating proxy clashes in Somalia.

Washington has few good options to address the emergent threats in Somalia. There are, however, opportunities to push for full implementation of the peace agreement that ended the Ethiopia-Eritrea border conflict, which can help dampen the dynamic that contributes to escalation within Somalia. Ethiopia and Eritrea both need the involvement of the international community and the United States in particular to back away from the confrontation on the border. Washington should remain committed to the multilateral Witnesses to the Algiers Agreement and Eritrea Ethiopia Boundary Commission (EEBC) framework, pressing Ethiopia to demarcate the border and Eritrea to return

---

This piece is excerpted from the Council Special Report *Avoiding Conflict in the Horn of Africa: U.S. Policy Toward Ethiopia and Eritrea* (New York: Council on Foreign Relations Press, December 2006).

to talks and lift restrictions on the UN Mission in Ethiopia and Eritrea (UNMEE).

Washington must speak clearly and critically to both Ethiopia and Eritrea and lay out an unambiguous set of options and specify what types of relationships and assistance the regimes will lose if they persist in prolonging the border stalemate, suppressing internal dissent, and interfering in Somalia. Washington must also indicate what types of support the two countries can anticipate if they initiate real policies of regional cooperation and internal reform. Leaders on both sides will resist public pressures, and thus U.S. diplomacy will need to be subtle and discreet to be successful. Senior members of the U.S. administration must address these issues in direct, face-to-face meetings in the region. The U.S. government should also be prepared to offer substantial financial backing and use its influence within the international financial institutions to support demobilization, cross-border trade and communications, and normalization of regional relations.

Once the border issue is settled, the United States should pressure Asmara to permit basic political rights and Addis Ababa to release political prisoners, enter into a dialogue with the full range of opposition leaders, and return to the freedoms seen in early 2005. Development and military assistance programs should be tied to progress on these governance issues, and Washington should be prepared to reduce or slow nonhumanitarian programs if political conditions deteriorate further. Simultaneously, well-funded programs on democratization and rule of law should be offered to support positive political openings. Washington should also reach out to the wide spectrum of opposition groups both within Ethiopia and in the diaspora and encourage them to pursue strategies of peaceful electoral competition, rather than armed struggle.

Finally, the United States, international donors, and international organizations should support long-term regional peacebuilding initiatives. Building new relationships between communities split by the militarized border, groups displaced by the conflict, and families divided by loyalties to rival states will provide a context for new thinking and increased confidence about the formal peace process and for building healthier bilateral relations after the border dispute is settled.

THE ETHIOPIAN-ERITREAN BORDER CRISIS

BACKGROUND TO THE CONFLICT

The Ethiopian People's Revolutionary Democratic Front (EPRDF), led by Prime Minister Meles Zenawi, and the Eritrean People's Liberation Front (EPLF), led by President Isaias Afwerki, cooperated closely to overthrow the brutal Mengistu Haile Mariam regime in 1991. While the EPRDF joined with other parties to form the Transitional Government of Ethiopia, the EPLF assumed control of Eritrea and established a provisional government. The provisional government independently administered Eritrea until April 1993, when Eritreans voted overwhelmingly for independence in a UN-monitored referendum.

By 1998, however, relations between the two countries had degenerated. Disputes between Addis Ababa and Asmara arose over access to Eritrean ports, how the new Eritrean currency related to the Ethiopian currency, and the precise location of their poorly demarcated border. The classic imperatives of state- and nation-building drove both regimes to set forth unconditional goals and refuse compromise on those questions and the vital issues of territoriality, legitimacy, and identity. It is notable that Eritrea, Africa's newest state, has had border conflicts with each of its neighbors: Djibouti, Ethiopia, and Sudan.

In May 1998, Eritrean armed forces occupied the disputed, symbolically important border town of Badme, a use of military force that Ethiopia regarded as illegal territorial annexation. This skirmish quickly escalated into full-scale war. The historical links and rivalries between the two states, peoples, ruling parties, and leaders made the violence particularly painful. Deep personal animosity between leaders in both Ethiopia and Eritrea, along with the countries' shared political culture that values absolute victory and zero-sum calculations over compromise and joint gains, made deescalation difficult. The violence generated large casualties and huge costs on both sides. An estimated 70,000 to 100,000 people were killed, one million were displaced, and a generation of development opportunities was squandered.

After a period of military stalemate and unproductive negotiations, Ethiopia launched a major offensive in May 2000, broke through defenses, and forced Eritrea to pull its troops back to pre-May 1998 positions. In December 2000, the warring parties signed an internationally brokered agreement in Algiers. The United States played a particularly prominent role in these talks, thanks to the appointment of former National Security Adviser Anthony Lake as special envoy and the close relationships between several members of the William J. Clinton administration and the Ethiopian and Eritrean leaderships.

The Algiers Agreement created a 25-kilometer temporary security zone to be patrolled by UNMEE, as well as the EEBC to delimit the border, and a claims commission to assess liability for war damages. On the issue of the border, the agreement followed African practice and confirmed colonial borders. Under Article Four of the agreement, the EEBC was charged to "delimit and demarcate the colonial treaty border based on pertinent colonial treaties (1900, 1902, and 1908) and applicable international law," and this determination was final and binding. The commission explicitly was not empowered to make decisions *ex aequo et bono*, that is, on the basis of equity considerations.

Although the cease-fire has held, other provisions of the Algiers Agreement have been only partially implemented. In April 2002, the EEBC issued its determination and ruled that the town of Badme was on the Eritrean side of the border while other, less symbolically important areas claimed by Eritrea were on the Ethiopian side. Once the ruling was clear, shocked Ethiopian leaders strongly objected to it and did everything short of resumption of hostilities to delay compliance. Ethiopia appealed to the EEBC to take into account local situations and claimed that the decision divided towns and required adjustments. The EEBC, however, stated that the Algiers Agreement made the demarcation decision final and did not allow for decisions to be reopened.

Ethiopia resisted implementing the demarcation decision. In a September 2003 letter to UN Secretary-General Kofi A. Annan, President Meles dug in his heels and characterized the EEBC decision relating to Badme as "totally illegal, unjust, and irresponsible." Meles later issued a five-point peace initiative in November 2004 that declared acceptance of the border ruling in principle while simultaneously calling for peace-building dialogue. Although this initiative represented a move toward complying, it was insufficient to elicit a positive response from Asmara. Eritrea, reminding Addis Ababa that both had agreed in advance in the Algiers Agreement that the EEBC decision would be "binding and final," insisted that the border demarcation be implemented fully before other issues, including peace-building initiatives, are raised.

ESCALATION AND THE THREAT OF WAR, 2005–2006

Eritrea, frustrated both by Ethiopia and by what it considered international appeasement of Addis Ababa, took measures to force the issue of border demarcation in October 2005. Eritrea banned UNMEE helicopter flights, which led the UN to withdraw its forces from nearly half of its deployment sites. The helicopter ban prevented medical evacuations and was blamed for the death of an Indian peacekeeper as well as halted demining activities.

In November 2005, the UN Security Council passed Resolution 1640 demanding that Eritrea lift its restrictions, Ethiopia accept the EEBC's border demarcation decisions, and both states reverse recent troop mobilization. The resolution threatened to impose Article 41 (nonmilitary) sanctions against Eritrea if it did not remove the UNMEE restrictions. Eritrea reacted angrily to the pressure, protested that the international community was yet again unfairly accommodating Ethiopia's violations of the Algiers Agreement, expelled Western observers from UNMEE, and arrested UN volunteers and local Eritrean staff working with the UN.

In December 2005, the claims commission issued a series of rulings that held Eritrea had violated the UN Charter by resorting to armed force to attack and occupy Badme in May 1998. Eritrea was therefore determined to be liable to compensate Ethiopia for damages caused by this violation of international law even while the EEBC later determined that Badme is on Eritrea's side of the border.

In the context of new restrictions on UNMEE, many observers suggested that prospects for war were growing. A December 2005 International Crisis Group report, for example, argued there were "worrying signs that the countdown to renewed conflict may have begun."[1] In early 2006, UN observers characterized the border as "tense and potentially volatile," and UN Secretary-General Annan listed full withdrawal of UNMEE as an option. Although tensions were high in early 2006, the stalemate remained stable because neither Asmara nor Addis Ababa had compelling incentives to break the cease-fire. Eritrea continually threatened war unless Ethiopia implemented the EEBC agreement and constantly reiterated that its position was consistent with international law. But acting on these threats was unlikely due to the vastly larger Ethiopian military and because Eritrean leaders understood that they would lose the legal high ground if the country unilaterally reignited the war. Addis Ababa, which had security concerns on multiple fronts, knew that if it attacked Eritrea it would lose international support and face resistance for as long as its occupation lasts. The status quo was also acceptable to Ethiopia because it continued to occupy Badme and the UN-patrolled temporary security zone was on the Eritrean side of the border.

INTERNATIONAL RESPONSES

PERIODIC HUMANITARIAN EMERGENCIES in the Horn of Africa, the need to end the 1998–2000 border war between Eritrea and Ethiopia, the political crisis following the 2005 elections in Ethiopia, and the links between the Horn and terrorism in the Middle East have generated periodic interest in the United States and the international community. What has been lacking, however, is sustained attention and coherent diplomatic strategies that recognize the links among domestic, bilateral, and regional dynamics.

INITIATIVES TO MANAGE THE BORDER CRISIS

The international community in general, and the United States in particular, paid too little attention to the challenges of implementing the Algiers Agreement. UNMEE was deployed along the border, the cease-fire held, and the EEBC held its hearings and made its demarcation decision in 2002. Little was done to push Ethiopia to accept demarcation or to advance the larger tasks of addressing the underlying causes of the conflict and building a framework for normal regional relations. It was only after frustrations grew and Asmara imposed outrageous restrictions on UNMEE that the issue was forced back onto the international agenda.

By January 2006, UNMEE and the Algiers peace process were in crisis. Eritrea, unfazed by threatened sanctions, refused to lift restrictions as required in UN Security Council Resolution 1640 and some troop-contributing countries were advocating withdrawing the mission. The initial U.S. response to the crisis over UNMEE was an improvised unilateral initiative to break the impasse. U.S. Ambassador to the UN John R. Bolton asked the UN Security Council to delay action while Washington sent Assistant Secretary of State for African Affairs Jendayi E. Frazer to the region. She met top Ethiopian leaders in Addis Ababa and visited the disputed border from the Ethiopian side, but was denied a meeting with Eritrean leaders who were unwilling to discuss the border issues. Asmara insisted that the Algiers Agreement and the EEBC determination are legally binding and not open to any modifications. Nonetheless, this ad hoc initiative by Washington generated needed attention to the region—after years of neglect that contributed to Ethiopia's perception that it could avoid implementing the agreement and heightened Eritrea's frustrations—and activated a series of new or renewed initiatives.

Representatives of the Witnesses to the Algiers Agreement—the African Union (AU), European Union, UN, Algeria, and United States—convened in New York in February 2006 to discuss challenges to implementing the accord. In March and May 2006, the EEBC met in London with officials from both Ethiopia and Eritrea as well as representatives from the Algiers Witnesses. The U.S. government regarded as progress the fact that both parties attended the meetings, but they failed to generate substantial movement toward implementing the demarcation agreement or lifting the restrictions on UNMEE. Following the meetings, both sides restated their positions and blamed each other for the stalemate.

On May 31, 2006, the UN Security Council reacted to the lack of progress in the EEBC meetings and reduced the size of UNMEE's force from 3,300 to 2,300 while retaining the mission's peacekeeping mandate. Ambassador Bolton had proposed reducing the force to 1,800 and changing the mandate to a peace observation mission. Russia and Britain, among others, argued for less severe cuts. The U.S. position in New York linked the reduction in UNMEE's force to an increase in the troop levels for the UN mission in Côte d'Ivoire and seemed to focus on the politics and financing of UN peacekeeping rather than developments between Ethiopia and Eritrea.

In September, UN Secretary-General Annan warned of the potential for disaster if the "untenable" stalemate between the two sides was not resolved. The UN Security Council once again called on Eritrea to lift restrictions and Ethiopia to accept the final and binding border demarcation decision. UNMEE's mandate was extended until January 31, 2007, while the UN warned that it would consider ending the mission unless "demonstrated progress" took place. In October, a few weeks after the mission extension resolution was passed, Eritrea moved some 1,500 troops and fourteen tanks into the buffer zone in what the UN regarded as a "major breach" of the peace agreement. Eritrea claimed that the troops were in the demilitarized zone to "harvest crops."[2]

The EEBC and with it the Algiers peace process was in deep crisis in November 2006. After failing to bring Ethiopia and Eritrea together for talks in June, the EEBC concluded that, "The situation is one which is beyond the Commission's powers to remedy on the grounds of manifest implacability."[3] In November, the EEBC announced that it would unilaterally complete demarcation on paper and disengage from the thorny issues of joint demarcation on the ground. Both Addis Ababa and Asmara have rejected the plan as inconsistent with the Algiers Agreement. The EEBC's decision, driven by international frustration at both parties' intransigence, risks terminating the existing process before an alternative framework is in place. With fewer international constraints, the prospects that one or another party will attempt to achieve its objectives militarily increases.

With the multilateral efforts by the EEBC and the Algiers Witnesses group facing grave challenges, international policy toward the border stalemate continues to require a strong multilateral mechanism to pressure the parties to implement the peace agreement. If the EEBC talks collapse, the United States and others in the Algiers Witnesses group will need to construct a new mechanism for multilateral involvement in the protracted stalemate.

REACTIONS TO THE ETHIOPIAN POLITICAL CRISIS

The major donors responded to the 2005 crisis within Ethiopia with clear statements criticizing the government and with the suspension of significant levels of assistance. In November 2005, the United States and the European Union issued a joint statement calling for the release of all "political detainees," thereby challenging the government's contention that the leaders had been arrested on criminal grounds. The Development Assistance Group (DAG) for Ethiopia, which includes the United States and other major bilateral and multilateral donors, also adopted a tough posture and stated, "These disturbances weaken the environment for aid effectiveness and poverty reduction. . . . As a result of the situation, the DAG is collectively reviewing development cooperation modalities to Ethiopia."[4] In December 2005, international donors put $375 million in budget support on hold, sending another clear message that business as usual would not be possible in the context of this political crisis. In January 2006, a U.S. Department of State press release stated that, "Steps that appear to criminalize dissent impede progress on democratization."[5]

The Ethiopian government, however, remained unmoved. Addis Ababa repeatedly stated that the elections were free and fair, the response of security forces to demonstrations appropriate, and that charges against opposition politicians, journalists, and civil society leaders were based on solid evidence and long-standing Ethiopian law. When pressed to release the prisoners, Meles insisted that he could not interfere in the rule of law and had to allow the independent courts to follow their own procedures. The fact that Ethiopia dropped charges against five U.S. citizens who were Voice of America reporters suggests that pressures from Washington had some effect, even if the others under arrest remained in jail without bail.

The international donor community's tone also moderated in mid-2006. In April, the World Bank approved debt cancellation for Ethiopia along with other heavily indebted poor countries. In May, the World Bank approved the Protection of Basic Services Program that channeled $215 million to local governments providing basic health, education, agricultural, and water services. During a July visit, World Bank President Paul D. Wolfowitz noted that Ethiopia had been through a difficult period but that, "There is more reason to feel confident that people are learning the right lessons from the experiences of the last year."[6] Although the World Bank's plan emphasizes the need for improved governance and decentralization, because the EPRDF controls nearly all local government, the release of funds through regional authorities will bolster the government's structures of authority and administration.

U.S. POLICY RECOMMENDATIONS

THE ERITREA-ETHIOPIA BORDER stalemate, the potential for violent and chaotic political transitions in Ethiopia and Eritrea, and the ways these challenges are linked to Somalia, Sudan, and U.S. interests in counterterrorism, call for a new and more comprehensive U.S. policy. U.S. foreign policy toward the 2000 Ethiopia-Eritrea talks in Algiers and the north-south peace process in Sudan suggests that focused, high-level diplomatic attention, willingness to take risks and accept costs, and sustained work through broad, multilateral coalitions offer the best hope for success.

SETTLING THE BORDER STALEMATE

To break the border deadlock, the United States and other donor countries must impress upon Ethiopia that it is in its long-term interest to complete demarcation and withdraw from Badme, so that both parties can begin comprehensive peace negotiations.

Efforts to convince Ethiopia to demarcate the border should emphasize that accepting the EEBC's decision will not alter the overall domestic balance of forces. Some in Ethiopia argue that withdrawing from Badme would destabilize the EPRDF regime and thus should not be done. Those who oppose the regime will certainly use withdrawal as another point in their criticism of the EPRDF—but larger threats to the ruling party are likely to arise from Addis Ababa and other cities, from the Oromo region, or from instability in Somalia. Therefore, little is to be gained by further delay now that the 2005 elections are over and the new parliament is sitting. Furthermore, in the long run, ending the border stalemate will allow Ethiopia to shift its attention to other security threats and to delink the challenges of domestic political opposition from rivalries with neighboring states. If Ethiopia refuses to implement the EEBC decision, then donors should publicly and privately place the blame for the stalemate on Addis Ababa and reduce assistance.

At the same time, Washington and other major powers need to be unambiguous with Asmara: harassing UNMEE and refusing to lift restrictions on the UN is unacceptable. After a year without any progress and with harassment escalating, it is time for the international community to act on that threat and put multilateral sanctions in place. Given Eritrea's self-imposed isolation from international institutions and donors, such sanctions are likely to be largely symbolic.

Any efforts to apply sanctions against Eritrea for its failures to lift restrictions on UNMEE, against Ethiopia for failing to implement the Algiers Agreement, or against either one for violations of the arms embargo in Somalia should be multilateral. U.S. influence will be greatest if it is coordinated with broader, multilateral partnerships, such as the EEBC and the Algiers Witnesses group. The decision by the EEBC to unilaterally demarcate the border is dangerous and should be reconsidered because it threatens to remove the multilateral framework that plays a vital role in constraining Addis Ababa and Asmara.

Incentives for both sides for resolving the border conflict and normalizing relations—including projects to rebuild cross-border

infrastructure and trade, demine territory, demobilize and reinte-
grate populations, and support persons displaced by the conflict—
will require the support of the Europeans and international financial institutions. Such programs will cost hundreds of millions of
dollars, but will likely be less expensive than the UNMEE budget
of $200 million per year. A combination of tough multilateral
sanctions and generous incentives presented by a well-coordinated
group of donors holds the greatest promise for breaking the border impasse.

UNMEE continues to have an important role to play as a symbol
of international support for the peace process and as a mechanism to
reduce the chances of accidental war. The reduction of UNMEE's
forces in early 2006 does not prevent the mission from fulfilling
these goals. The United States and other major powers should not
seek to restrict the mission further or demand deeper reductions
in UNMEE's forces to balance increases elsewhere in Africa. Even
after demarcation, UNMEE will remain important to demining
and other cross-border peace-building initiatives.

The recommendations of this report include:

- The United States, UN, and other interested parties, within
  the multilateral Algiers Witnesses framework, should press
  Addis Ababa to unambiguously accept the EEBC decision
  and begin to demarcate the border. Only then will the broader
  talks on regional peace-building that Ethiopia wants be possible. If Ethiopia refuses, then Washington and other donors
  should reduce assistance and unambiguously condemn this
  violation of the peace agreement.
- The United States, UN, and other interested parties, within
  the multilateral Algiers Witnesses framework, should press
  the Eritrean government to be more accommodating to the
  diplomacy of working through the details of demarcation. By
  refusing to talk, Eritrea is obstructing the implementation of
  the Algiers Agreement. If Eritrea refuses to lift its restrictions
  on UNMEE, then sanctions should be applied as called for
  in Resolution 1640.
- The United States and other bilateral donors should work
  with international financial institutions to develop new

incentives, such as generous post-demarcation support packages, to encourage Addis Ababa to accept the EEBC decision and manage any domestic political fallout. Initiatives focused on regional development and cross-border trade will place the newly demarcated border in a less militarized context, thereby helping sustain a more normal cross-border relationship and sustainable peace.

- Washington should not push for further reductions in UNMEE's forces. Its continued presence increases confidence and serves as an important symbol of the international community's commitment to support implementation of the Algiers Agreement. In addition, UNMEE has important roles in facilitating and protecting demining and final demarcation and in coordinating regional peace-building initiatives after border demarcation.

- The United States and others in the Algiers Witnesses group should urge the EEBC to reconsider its decision to move forward with unilateral border demarcation. The multilateral framework represented by the EEBC, Algiers Witnesses, and UNMEE constrains Ethiopia and Eritrea and should not be weakened without a viable alternative framework in place.

CONCLUSION

HEIGHTENED BORDER TENSIONS, authoritarian governance, and growing regional dynamics of conflict in Somalia raise concerns of a potentially expanding crisis in the strategically important Horn of Africa. Washington needs a new, comprehensive diplomatic strategy with high-level support, adequate funding, and close coordination with allies and other donors to address these developments and protect U.S. interests in the region.

Policies backed with significant resources to push for implementation of the border settlement will open up opportunities to address the fragile governments in the region. Successful political reforms, in turn, will reinforce regional peace-building. Regional dialogue and peace-building efforts are desperately needed, as is evidenced by the rapidly and dangerously escalating crisis in Somalia and the potential for significant conflict between Ethiopia and Somalia. Given the stakes and the role the region plays with regard to the Arabian Peninsula and counterterrorism, the importance of democratization promotion globally, and the growing attention to the region on Capitol Hill and within diaspora communities, disengagement is not an option.

Blowing the Horn

John Prendergast and Colin Thomas-Jensen

WASHINGTON'S FAILINGS IN AFRICA

THE GREATER HORN OF AFRICA—a region half the size of the United States that includes Sudan, Eritrea, Ethiopia, Djibouti, Somalia, Kenya, and Uganda—is the hottest conflict zone in the world. Some of the most violent wars of the last half century have ripped the region apart. Today, two clusters of conflicts continue to destabilize it. The first centers on interlocking rebellions in Sudan, including those in Darfur and southern Sudan, and engulfs northern Uganda, eastern Chad, and northeastern Central African Republic. The main culprit is the Sudanese government, which is supporting rebels in these three neighboring countries—and those states, which are supporting Sudanese groups opposing Khartoum. The second cluster links the festering dispute between Ethiopia and Eritrea with the power struggle in Somalia, which involves the fledgling secular government, antigovernment clan militias, Islamist militants, and anti-Islamist warlords. Ethiopia's flash intervention in Somalia in December temporarily secured the ineffectual transitional government's position, but that intervention, which Washington backed and supplemented with its own air strikes, has sown the seeds for an Islamist and clan-based insurgency in the future.

Recent U.S. policy has only made matters worse. The region, which has both suffered attacks by al Qaeda and hosted its agents (including Osama bin Laden himself), is a legitimate concern of U.S. officials. But stemming the spread of terrorism and extremist ideologies has become such an overwhelming strategic objective

This article was published in *Foreign Affairs*, March/April 2007.

for Washington that it has overshadowed U.S. efforts to resolve conflicts and promote good governance; in everything but rhetoric, counterterrorism now consumes U.S. policy in the Greater Horn as totally as anticommunism did a generation ago. To support this critical but narrow aim, the Bush administration has too often nurtured relationships with autocratic leaders and favored covert and military action over diplomacy. Sometimes that has even included feting in Langley of Sudanese officials suspected of having a hand in the massacres in Darfur or handing suitcases full of cash to warlords on the streets of Mogadishu.

The results have been disastrous. Sudan's autocrats are reverting to the extremism of their roots. In Somalia, the core of the Islamist militant movement remains intact after Ethiopia's invasion, its members' passions inflamed by the intervention. The leaders of Ethiopia, Eritrea, and Uganda have used the specter of war and the imperative of counterterrorism as excuses to crack down on political opponents and restive populations at home. The humanitarian situation throughout the region, fragile even in times of peace, is now catastrophic: nearly nine million people have been displaced, and chronic insecurity severely constrains access to humanitarian aid for the more than 16 million people who need it.

The fundamental flaw in Washington's approach is its lack of a regional diplomatic strategy to tackle the underlying causes of the two clusters of conflicts. These crises can no longer be addressed in isolation, with discrete and uncoordinated ad hoc peace initiatives. Washington must work to stabilize the Greater Horn through effective partnerships with Africa's multilateral institutions, the European Union, and the new UN secretary-general. Until it does, long-term U.S. counterterrorism objectives will suffer—and the region will continue to burn.

DEATH ON THE NILE

SINCE GAINING ITS INDEPENDENCE in 1956, Sudan, the largest country in the region, has been engulfed in a series of civil wars pitting Arab-dominated governments in Khartoum against rebels from marginalized groups. In the face of continued unrest, the ruling National Congress Party (NCP), which took charge in a coup in 1989, has armed and trained ethnic-based militias in Sudan and throughout the region and granted them impunity for mass atrocities against civilians it suspects of supporting its opponents.

In the south, the 21-year civil war between Khartoum and the Sudan People's Liberation Army (SPLA) killed 2.2 million people—making it the second-deadliest conflict in the world since World War II, after the civil war in Congo, which killed 3.8 million people. The NCP enlisted the Lord's Resistance Army, a millenarian rebel group based in northern Uganda, to open a second front against the SPLA. Khartoum also backed it to punish the Ugandan government for supporting the SPLA. The result there has been 1.7 million people in displaced camps and, courtesy of the Lord's Resistance Army, the highest rate of child abductions in the world.

The war in southern Sudan officially ended in January 2005 with the signing of the Comprehensive Peace Agreement. The deal granted autonomy to the area and gave the SPLA majority control of the new Government of Southern Sudan, based in Juba, and a minority role in the Government of National Unity, in Khartoum. It also provided for a referendum in 2011, in which the people of southern Sudan will decide whether to secede from the rest of the country. But two years later, the situation is not encouraging. The implementation of critical components of the arrangement—notably the demobilization of the NCP's proxy militias in southern Sudan, the demarcation of borders in oil-producing areas, and the transparent disbursement of oil revenues—is lagging. War clouds have been forming again since John Garang, the SPLA's charismatic leader and a leading proponent of a unified Sudan, died in a helicopter crash in July 2005. Without him, the SPLA has failed to assert itself in the Government of National Unity.

Another problem is that the negotiations leading to the agreement did not involve opposition groups from Darfur and other northern areas. That left opponents of the government in Darfur feeling that they had no other recourse but to attack military outposts, police stations, and other government interests to win a place at the negotiating table. Since the rebellion broke out there in February 2003, the NCP has supported Arab militias, known as the Janjaweed, who routinely attack the non-Arab civilians backing the rebels. Some 200,000 to 450,000 Darfurians are estimated to have died since April 2003, 2.5 million have been driven from their homes, and two-thirds of all Darfurians—some 4.3 million people—now need humanitarian assistance of some kind. Partly thanks to U.S. efforts, the Darfur Peace Agreement was signed in May 2006, but the negotiators secured signatures from leaders of only one rebel faction, which alienated other groups and soon resulted in more fighting. The conflict has since spilled over into Chad and the Central African Republic—causing another two million people in those countries to require humanitarian assistance. Khartoum has been supporting an array of rebel groups and militias in both countries in the hope of overthrowing their governments and installing friendlier regimes.

In eastern Sudan, too, rebels took up arms against the regime, more than a decade ago. Although the Eritrean government mediated an agreement between the NCP and rebels there in October 2006, the deal has yet to face a serious test. In the meantime, the regime in Khartoum continues to respond ferociously to all uprisings—a sign that it is desperate to maintain power by any means and hold on to its growing oil wealth.

ALL TANGLED UP

THE SECOND CLUSTER of conflicts centers on Somalia and also involves Ethiopia, Eritrea, and northeastern Kenya. Somalia, the only country in the world without an operational government, has been headless since 1991, when the country's leader—and a U.S. ally—Muhammad Siad Barre, was overthrown. Warlords held sway in urban centers for over a decade after that, despite no fewer than 14 initiatives to create a central government. Finally, in 2004, under the impetus of the Intergovernmental Authority on Development, a regional organization, a fragile body known as the Transitional Federal Government was set up, headquartered first in Kenya and then, in mid-2005, in the Somali town of Baidoa. In the meantime, however, Somali Islamists had established in and around the capital, Mogadishu, 11 clan-based Islamic courts backed by militias, a few of which had close links to jihadists and terrorists suspected of being associated with al Qaeda.

The struggle for domination started coming to a head in mid-2006, when the Islamic courts defeated the warlords in Mogadishu and expanded their control over much of south-central Somalia. The courts managed to win over the population—which is Muslim but of a Sufi persuasion averse to the courts' radical Salafism—by providing security and basic services, which both the ineffectual transitional government and the predatory warlords had failed to assure. The Ethiopian government, having grown increasingly concerned about the Islamists' rising influence, sent troops across the border at the end of 2006. The fighting was over before it began. The Islamists melted into the civilian population, leaving a few militia groups to be pursued by Ethiopian forces.

The Ethiopian government had a number of reasons for taking out the Islamic courts. Ethiopia and Somalia have had a tense history, including three wars between 1960 and 1978. Somalia has hosted al-Itihaad al-Islamiya, a terrorist organization that planted several bombs in Ethiopia in the 1990s, prompting the Ethiopian government twice during that period to send troops into Somalia to destroy the group and dismantle its training camps. Last year, senior court officials made clear that they intended to incorporate Somali populations in the Somali region of southeastern Ethiopia into a greater Somalia. They were already backing Ethiopian opposition groups such as the Ogaden National Liberation Front and, in southern Oromia, the Oromo Liberation Front. This support was a direct challenge to Ethiopian Prime Minister Meles Zenawi, who, after a decade and a half of rule, faces internal political pressure from ethnic groups that feel underrepresented. Legislative elections in Ethiopia in 2005 were characterized by unprecedented openness, but after a strong showing by opposition parties, Meles' government cracked down.

These domestic troubles have also made it harder for Meles to budge on Ethiopia's border dispute with Eritrea—another threat to regional stability. In the early 1990s, when Eritrea won its independence from Ethiopia after three decades of fighting, Ethiopia became a landlocked state. The two states' leaders, Meles and Isaias Afwerki, had good relations at first, but they soon fell out over economic and political matters, particularly the countries' ill-defined border. The tensions spiraled into an especially savage war in the late 1990s. In 2000, Eritrea and Ethiopia signed a peace deal and agreed to submit their border dispute to "final and binding" resolution by an independent international commission. The ruling, issued in 2002, awarded the disputed town of Badme to Eritrea. Meles has steadfastly refused to implement it, however, arguing that the commission's methodology was flawed. He also objects because he is sensitive to the widespread sentiment among Ethiopians that he is responsible for losing the country's access to the Red Sea at Eritrea's independence; he is careful not to appear soft on Eritrea.

The Eritrean government, for its part, is increasingly frustrated by the international community's unwillingness to pressure Ethiopia to demarcate the border. In protest, President Isaias has restricted the UN peacekeeping force charged with observing the cease-fire and expelled international aid organizations. Continually invoking the prospect of imminent war, his government has clamped down on all opposition while needling Ethiopia by supporting the Ogaden National Liberation Front and the Oromo Liberation Front. Ethiopia, meanwhile, backs the Eritrean Democratic Alliance, an umbrella organization of groups opposed to the Eritrean government.

Even more worrisome for regional stability is the fact that Ethiopia and Eritrea are playing out their differences through their neighbors. While the Ethiopian government supports the Sudanese government, the Eritrean government—which accused Khartoum of wanting to expand its Islamist reach throughout the region and of backing a rebellion by the Eritrean Islamic Jihad Movement in the 1990s—maintains close relations with rebels in Darfur and eastern Sudan. At the same time, it has been providing weapons and forces to the Islamic courts in Somalia, principally in opposition to the Ethiopian government, which backs the transitional government there. The Sudanese government is also involved in Somalia's affairs. Using its temporary leadership of the Arab League, for example, it convened in Khartoum a meeting between representatives of the Somali transitional government and representatives of the Islamic courts in March 2006—a move that raised concerns among officials of the transitional government who are wary of ties between leaders of the Islamic courts, universities in Sudan, and Islamists in the NCP.

BACKDRAFT

THESE PROLIFERATING THREATS could have been mitigated by smart U.S. policy, but Washington's approach to the Greater Horn of Africa, which centers on counterterrorism, has been erratic and shortsighted. The United States' overweening focus on stemming terrorism began early in the Clinton presidency in response to Khartoum's aggressive promotion of its ties to international terrorist organizations. Al Qaeda operatives based in Somalia blew up the U.S. embassies in Kenya and Tanzania in 1998 and, Washington suspects, attacked a hotel and an El Al plane in Kenya in 2002. Following the attacks of 9/11, Washington expanded its counterterrorism efforts in the region. It has deployed over 1,500 troops in Djibouti to carry out civil-affairs programs and help gather intelligence on suspected terrorists and has earmarked $100 million a year to support counterterrorism efforts by local authorities. More than anything, however, the United States' counterterrorism policy in the Greater Horn of Africa now hinges on three strategies: almost unconditional support for the Ethiopian government, extremely close cooperation on counterterrorism with Khartoum, and occasional but spectacular forays into Somalia in the hope of killing or capturing al Qaeda suspects.

Ethiopia has been the United States' closest ally in the Greater Horn for the last decade, partly because the fight against Islamic extremism resonates powerfully with Ethiopian officials. Although the country is half Muslim and half Christian, its political and intellectual elites have historically been Christian. Ethiopia has also suffered firsthand from Islamist terrorism: radicals based in Sudan plotted an assassination attempt on Egyptian President

Hosni Mubarak in the capital, Addis Ababa, in 1995, and the Somalia-based al-Itihaad al-Islamiya has repeatedly staged attacks throughout the country. In 2001, the Bush administration declared Ethiopia the United States' principal counterterrorism ally in the region. Even the U.S. Agency for International Development—which gave Ethiopia over $460 million in food aid and assistance in fiscal year 2005—touts the country as being "of strategic importance to the United States because of its geographic position" and as "the linchpin to stability in the Horn of Africa and the Global War on Terrorism."

But Washington's narrow agenda has stifled U.S. efforts to press for more democracy and greater respect for human rights in Ethiopia. And it has undermined attempts to settle the border dispute between Ethiopia and Eritrea. In 1998, with full support from the State Department, the Defense Department, and the National Security Council, former National Security Adviser Anthony Lake led the multilateral efforts that eventually ended the Eritrean-Ethiopian war in 2000. But when Ethiopia started balking at implementing the 2002 border decision, rather than pursue diplomatic efforts to pressure it, the Bush White House did little, allowing its counterterrorism objectives to override peace-making. The two states have barely budged in the five years since, and the Eritrean government has grown deeply skeptical of the international community's intentions. From its point of view, the border issue has been settled and Ethiopia must be held to account before negotiations on other questions can begin. While the stale-mate lasts, U.S.-Eritrean relations sour: Washington now sees Isaias as unreliable and worries he is becoming friendlier to rogue states such as Iran, and Isaias continues to fume at what he considers to be favoritism toward Meles.

A second focus of the Bush administration's policy in the Greater Horn has been close cooperation on counterterrorism with Sudan. Khartoum's move away from its strong support for international terrorism started during the Clinton administration. From 1991 to 1996, bin Laden resided in Sudan, and the regime allowed numerous terrorists to travel on Sudanese passports and establish training camps on Sudanese soil. But then, in 1996, in response to U.S.-

led sanctions by the UN Security Council, Khartoum expelled bin Laden and dismantled al Qaeda's camps and commercial infrastructure. Relations deteriorated in the summer of 1998, when Washington retaliated for the embassy bombings in Kenya and Tanzania by blowing up a Sudanese factory that it alleged stored biological weapons. And they improved somewhat again after the attacks of 9/11, which reinforced Washington's emphasis on counterterrorism and prompted the Bush administration to engage more with Khartoum.

The Bush White House, which was eager to respond to conservative Christian constituents who were demanding an end to human rights abuses and religious persecution in southern Sudan, also intensified its support for a peace deal there. But as the SPLA and the NCP were closing in on an agreement in 2003, Darfur blew up, exposing the weakness of the narrow approach of Washington and its partners. At that point, the U.S. government had to decide whether to continue to press for peace in the south or broaden its effort to also respond aggressively to the escalating crisis in Darfur. It chose the first option for fear that choosing (and failing at) the second would jeopardize both peace between the NCP and the SPLA and Khartoum's cooperation on counterterrorism. By doing so, however, Washington unwittingly gave the Sudanese government the upper hand: Sudanese officials realized that they could delay a deal with the SPLA while underwriting brutalities in Darfur without facing serious consequences. In both October 2003 and April 2004, even as Sudanese armed forces and the Janjaweed were massacring civilians in Darfur, the White House reported to Congress that Khartoum was negotiating "in good faith" with the SPLA.

President George W. Bush and senior U.S. officials have spoken out against the crimes in Darfur (they have called them genocide), and a UN panel has blamed them in part on senior NCP officials, including the director of national intelligence, the minister of the interior, and the minister of defense. But thanks partly to increased cooperation with Washington on intelligence, Khartoum has managed to avoid punitive action, stifle diplomatic efforts to reach durable settlements with the rebels, and resist international efforts to send a robust peacekeeping force to Darfur. Last November, the Bush administration clearly stated that if Sudan did not agree by the end of the year to welcome a mixed force of UN and African Union (AU) troops to Darfur, Khartoum would face unspecified measures. But when the deadline came and went, the Bush administration issued no condemnation. Meanwhile, Khartoum has continued to cultivate its image as a counterterrorism partner—even as hard-liners in the NCP have been reconnecting with old terrorist allies. All along, the NCP's objective in cooperating on terrorism has been to make itself indispensable to Washington in order to lessen its exposure to international pressure over its human rights record. And it has succeeded: despite a vast grass-roots movement in the United States calling for a robust response to the atrocities in Darfur, no viable plan is forthcoming yet.

U.S. policy in Somalia has also been dangerously narrow. Washington intervened there as part of a UN humanitarian mission in 1992, but it quickly got bogged down and, following the killing of 18 U.S. troops in the streets of Mogadishu, withdrew all U.S. forces in 1994. Since then, its main goal has been to apprehend the foreign al Qaeda operatives it believes are being hidden and protected by Somali Islamists. (One suspected protector is Sheik Hassan Dahir Aweys, a one-time member of al-Itihaad al-Islamiya and now the chair of the Islamic courts.) To that end, Washington has funded Somali warlords to pursue terrorists on its behalf. By 2006, the enlisted warlords were calling themselves the Alliance for the Restoration of Peace and Counterterrorism—and getting, according to our interviews with some members, about $150,000 a month from Washington. In contrast, the United States contributed only $250,000 to the $10 million peace process that led to the formation of the Transitional Federal Government, and the United States gives far less humanitarian assistance to Somalia than to other countries in the region. The Bush administration has preferred to create a strategic partnership with warlords in the pursuit of a few terrorists rather than to address Somalia's chronic statelessness, which will continue to draw many more terrorists to the country.

Although Ethiopia's intervention this winter dislodged the potentially hostile Islamic courts—which can be considered a short-term counterterrorism success—it is too early for Washington to roll out the "Mission Accomplished" banners. Ethiopia's invasion has only displaced the most visible part of the Islamist movement; other elements have survived, including a network of mosques, madrasahs, and businesses, as well as a militant wing, known as the Shabaab, that has threatened to wage guerrilla war. Meanwhile, the courts' collapse has left a huge vacuum that the transitional government cannot fill. The courts had brought peace and stability, and their defeat has returned Mogadishu to the warlords who have preyed on Somalia for much of the past two decades. Two related insurgencies are likely to break out in the future, one led by the remnants of the courts, the other by disaffected clans.

This leaves the United States' interests in Somalia at risk. Having pursued the narrow objective of capturing or killing a few terrorist suspects, Washington has now become embroiled in Ethiopia's policies in Somalia, which may diverge significantly from its own in the long run. Focusing on hunting down suspects without also investing in state building is a strategy that could not have worked, and the decision to support Ethiopia's military invasion without devising a broader political strategy was a stunning mistake, especially considering the U.S. experience in Iraq. Predictably, resentment over foreign intervention has been building among Somalis. And U.S. air strikes against Islamist holdouts in the far south of the country have turned Somalia into a much more interesting target for al Qaeda than it once was; they could boost recruiting for the Islamists for a long time.

A THREE-PART PLAN

A NEW FRAMEWORK FOR engagement in the Greater Horn is urgently needed to reverse these trends. The United States' counterterrorism objectives would be best served by a new comprehensive diplomatic initiative focused on resolving conflict and promoting good governance throughout the region. Any new strategy must be wide-ranging and multilateral. It must focus all at once on resolving conflicts, keeping the peace, and punishing spoilers, and it will require working with the UN Security Council and the AU.

First, the United States should launch a Greater Horn peace initiative with the AU and the new UN secretary-general to devise a comprehensive approach to the two main clusters of conflicts surrounding Sudan and Somalia. This should entail coordinated efforts to resolve the related crises in Darfur, Chad, and the Central African Republic; secure a deal between the Lord's Resistance Army and the Ugandan government; broker a power-sharing arrangement in Somalia; and settle the ongoing disputes in southern Sudan and between Ethiopia and Eritrea, in order to see the two existing peace deals concerning them fully implemented. These efforts would require the creation of a conflict resolution cell in the region, staffed by senior diplomats reporting to the State Department and assigned for at least one year, who would coordinate peace talks and support their realization. This initiative could follow the models provided by the partnership between the United States, the United Kingdom, Norway, and the Intergovernmental Authority on Development that ended the war in southern Sudan and the partnership between the United States, the European Union, and the Organization of African Unity (the AU's predecessor) that ended the war between Ethiopia and Eritrea. Unfortunately, so far, in both Somalia and Darfur, the international community has put the cart before the horse, working furiously to send peacekeeping forces before having secured viable peace agreements.

Second, a concerted effort must be made to boost the peacekeeping capacity that would be needed to implement any peace deals. The United States and the European Union have spent hundreds of millions of dollars in the past decade to prepare African armies to participate more effectively in peacekeeping operations. But judging by the limitations of the AU operations in Darfur, peacekeeping objectives need to be refocused. Lacking an explicit mandate to protect civilians, the AU troops in Darfur have often been either irrelevant or counterproductive, serving as a lightning rod for local hostility and as an excuse for the inaction of the international community. The AU does not have enough forces to deploy in multiple theaters; it could barely scrape together the 7,500 troops it sent to Darfur. And with Western donors failing to fully fund the mission, the troops were ill equipped and remained unpaid for months. The inescapable conclusion from the AU's experience in Darfur is that the UN should lead peacekeeping operations in Africa (as it does elsewhere in the world), with substantial AU participation and a mandate to protect civilians.

Third, Washington must do a better job of garnering international support for using, or at least threatening to use, multilateral penalties of some type. In Sudan, Somalia, and Ethiopia, the U.S. government and some Western states have offered much and gained little in return, partly because they have failed to apply instruments of pressure; they are like barking dogs with no bite. Real leverage comes from the early use of multilateral punitive measures—such as prosecutions by the International Criminal Court, targeted sanctions against senior officials and rebels, and oil embargoes and other instruments of economic pressure—and from their suspension when compliance is achieved. How can the regime in Khartoum be expected to act any differently in Darfur if its activities bear no cost?

WALKING THE WALK

BOOSTING CONFLICT RESOLUTION, peacekeeping, and punitive measures will unquestionably be difficult, but it can be done if the United States builds multilateral partnerships to share the diplomatic and financial burdens. In Sudan, this will require preventing the NCP from continuing to channel U.S. policies into separate streams—one on southern Sudan, another on Darfur, another still on counterterrorism. Washington needs a cohesive Sudan policy that addresses all U.S. goals simultaneously and uses multilateral punitive actions to achieve them. Until the power-sharing agreement is fully implemented in the south and wealth and power devolve from the ruling elites in Khartoum to marginalized areas in Darfur and the east, the tensions that have fueled 50 years of civil war in Sudan will not subside.

Despite its flaws, the Comprehensive Peace Agreement in southern Sudan remains a key building block for altering the distribution of power and reestablishing democracy throughout the country—

but only if it is fully implemented. Enforcement means overcoming several major obstacles: the NCP's failure to demobilize its proxy militia forces in southern Sudan, its refusal to accept a border commission's ruling regarding the oil-producing region of Abyei, and the lack of transparency in the division of oil revenues between the Government of National Unity in Khartoum and the Government of Southern Sudan in Juba. NCP hard-liners simply will not implement key elements of the agreement—or abandon their militaristic policies in Darfur—unless Western governments subject them to the coordinated pressure of UN sanctions, asset freezes, and criminal indictments.

At the same time, the United States and other donors must live up to their commitment to help build the capacity of the nascent Government of Southern Sudan. International donors pledged $4.5 billion for Sudan at a conference following the Comprehensive Peace Agreement in Oslo in May 2005, but they did not fulfill their obligations fully because of mounting concern over Khartoum's role in the atrocities in Darfur. They must now refocus on the south to prevent a return to conflict. And they must prepare for the increasing likelihood that the region will vote to secede in the 2011 referendum. Southern Sudanese participating in focus groups convened by the National Democratic Institute in April 2006 expressed near-total support for independence. With little progress in their relations with Khartoum, it is unlikely that southerners will change their minds in the next four years. But Khartoum will probably return to war rather than allow the referendum to occur and risk losing access to 80 percent of its oil resources. More focused international support for the Government of Southern Sudan, especially for helping the SPLA become a regular army, would not only decrease insecurity in the south in the run-up to the referendum but also help deter the NCP from resuming the conflict (or at least give southerners the means to defend themselves if it did).

With Sudan's oil revenues up to $4 billion a year, Khartoum is now driven more by greed than by Islamist ideology. This presents an opportunity for the United States to increase economic pressure on Khartoum. But Washington cannot make the most of this without engaging more deeply with China and Arab League countries, which have strong economic interests in Sudan and regularly run interference for the regime. In response to U.S. economic sanctions in the 1990s, the Sudanese oil sector established close ties with China and, to a lesser extent, with Malaysia and India; as a result, Beijing is now reluctant to lean on Khartoum. But the growing perception that Beijing is turning a blind eye to continuing atrocities in Darfur could mar its international image as it prepares to host the 2008 Olympics. Recent efforts to build consensus among China, Russia, and the Arab League for enhancing peacekeeping forces in Darfur are a good start. But it is also necessary to build multilateral support for a comprehensive peace strategy that would force Khartoum to stop supporting rebel groups in Chad and the Central African Republic, negotiate amendments to the flawed Darfur Peace Agreement, and accept a properly mandated international peacekeeping force—with UN troops under UN command and control—to protect civilians and dismantle the Janjaweed. The United States should work through the UN Security Council to freeze the assets of senior NCP officials and their businesses and impose travel bans on them, as well as facilitate the flow of information about suspected war criminals to the International Criminal Court. In case the situation deteriorates and Khartoum continues to obstruct peace efforts, the international community should urgently plan for deploying ground and air forces to protect civilians without Khartoum's consent.

In Somalia, too, a multilateral approach to peace building is necessary to prevent protracted insurgencies from engulfing the region. There has been little history of sectarian violence in Ethiopia, but many Ethiopians now worry that an extended war with Somali Islamists could create religious divisions at home, pitting, in particular, Muslims against the government. Rather than relying primarily on military force, regular intelligence from and occasional intervention by Ethiopia, anti-Islamist warlords, and a weak transitional government, as it has done, Washington must adopt a more nuanced approach to Somalia. It should work with the European Union, the AU, the Arab League, and the Intergovernmental Authority on Development to pressure all parties into negotiating a power-sharing deal between the transitional government, clan leaders in Mogadishu, and the Islamic courts. The Somali transitional government will negotiate only if pressed by Ethiopia, and the United States has more clout with Ethiopia than does any other external actor. By contrast, Washington lacks direct leverage with the Islamic courts and excluded clan elders, and so U.S. diplomacy on that front should focus on getting governments in the region and in the Arab League to persuade them to accept a government of national unity.

None of this will be easy. Washington must appoint full-time envoys to press for a power-sharing deal in Somalia and to nudge Ethiopia and Eritrea toward accommodation. Letting these disputes fester would ensure the advent of Islamist and clan-based insurgencies in Somalia and increase the possibility of another war between Ethiopia and Eritrea. Both developments would be disastrous for the people of the Greater Horn and for long-term U.S. counterterrorism objectives.

The essential lesson of U.S. counterterrorism policy over the last five years—apparently unheeded by the Bush administration— is that in order for local Muslim populations to take the United States' counterterrorism agenda seriously, the United States must take their state-building and power-sharing agendas seriously, too. Ironically, the strategy is already there on paper. In its 2002 National Security Strategy and elsewhere, the Bush administration has argued that failing states foster terrorism and has laid out a comprehensive approach to counterterrorism that involves promoting peace building, state reconstruction, and good governance. When it comes to the Greater Horn, however, the Bush administration has simply not implemented its own policies. By relying on sporadic military strikes and continued support for autocrats without broader political planning, it has combined the worst elements of its current strategy in Iraq with the Cold War–era policy of cronyism. Conflict resolution and good governance are, in fact, the keys to countering terrorism in the Greater Horn over the long term. Failing to recognize this will likely result in hundreds of thousands more deaths, billions of dollars more spent on emergency humanitarian aid—and the increased prospect of another terrorist attack against U.S. interests in the region. With a few more dollars spent on preventive diplomacy, these outcomes could be avoided altogether.

III

Next Steps:
Ideas for the Present and Future of Africa

Africa is not easily generalized. There are fifty-three countries in Africa of different races, religions, cultures, and stages of development. Yet it is also true that sub-Saharan Africa is by and large poor, victim to some of the world's deadliest diseases, and plagued by a history of poor governance and many devastating conflicts. A number of African countries are moving out of this morass. Ghana is stably democratic, enjoying solid economic growth, has instituted a national health insurance system, and is moving to reduce the economic disparities within the country. South Africa has maintained one of the strongest constitutional democracies in Africa or for that matter most anywhere in the developing world. Mozambique, Botswana, Mali, Benin, and other African states are moving ahead on both better governance and sound economic management. But issues of governance and deeply entrenched aspects of poverty remain for most of the continent.

While much of the literature on African development focuses on economic issues, in this section two authors address more fundamental issues of governance and leadership. Stephen Ellis takes a hard look at the problems of weak or failing states and criticizes the international community for its responses to date. Ellis believes a longer-term focus on building strong institutions and stronger state capacities, along with better accountability, will be the determining factor in whether weak African states fall back into conflict or, almost as bad, stagnation. Robert I. Rotberg focuses on the failure of African leadership since independence and how to build a new generation of more responsible and capable leaders. Rotberg's analysis corresponds with the view of many African analysts of the fundamental problem in Africa to date.

Laurie Garrett calls attention to another more subtle challenge to African success. Some years ago, Jeffrey Sachs pointed out why improvements in health, vital to productivity, needed to be addressed as an investment in growth, not the by-product of economic development. Garrett indicates how health in Africa not only impedes African development but endangers global health. In this age of globalized commerce, heavy international travel, and the emergence of new health threats such as avian flu or drug-resistant tuberculosis, health crises can spread rapidly from Africa to the United States and other countries. She points out how international health protection relies on monitoring systems, quick reaction capabilities, and institutional strengths that often do not exist in much of Africa. Once the interdependence of the world's health systems is understood, the challenge of addressing Africa's health needs becomes more than a humanitarian undertaking, but one essential to the health of all.

How to Rebuild Africa

Stephen Ellis

THE LORDS OF MISRULE

THIS PAST MARCH, a UN panel revealed that Liberian officials had signed a secret contract with an obscure European company, giving it a virtual monopoly on mining diamonds in the troubled country—even though Liberia has been banned by the UN from selling its diamonds since 2001. The arrangement, it was disclosed, had involved members of the new transitional government operating under the (supposed) scrutiny of a large UN mission.

The discovery should not have come as a surprise. Liberia's new government, supposedly a model of national reconciliation, is largely made up of former militia members. During 15 years of war, armed gangs ravaged Liberia, turning it into a classic example of a failed state. Since the fighting stopped in August 2003, the erstwhile warlords have been quick to set aside their differences—at least when doing so helps them acquire more loot. The mining deal was just one in a long series of similar scandals perpetrated by senior members of the transitional government, who are rapidly signing away their country's future in return for personal financial gain.

It did not have to be this way. The new regime was established in October 2003 as part of a peace agreement brokered by West African states and supported by Washington—and backed up by a powerful UN peacekeeping mission. The UN force, originally led by Jacques Klein (a former U.S. diplomat with strong military credentials), has worked to disarm local fighters, build a working bureaucracy, organize democratic elections, and establish a basis

---

This article was published in *Foreign Affairs*, September/October 2005.

for lasting peace. Preparations for presidential and parliamentary elections are proceeding on schedule, with voting expected to take place in October.

Unfortunately, the interim government has used the time to make things worse. Liberian warlords and politicians have found it easy to outmaneuver the UN and the international community in the conduct of what locals, with their habitual grim humor, call "business more than usual." Despite claims that they are struggling for peace, democracy, and reconciliation, the warlords and their henchmen continue to use the country's institutions for personal profit. Even if one of the few respectable candidates wins the presidential election in October, there is little chance that he or she will be able to rectify matters. And if the UN starts to wind down its mission after the elections, as it currently plans to do, the most likely outcome will be a resumption of politics-as-plunder and war. Nothing worthwhile will have come of the hundreds of millions of dollars poured into Liberia by international donors or of the hundreds of lives lost by foreign peacekeepers.

Liberia is just one example on a long list of African states that have spent years on the brink of collapse (or have long since succumbed) despite international efforts to help them. Together, these countries (the list also includes Sierra Leone, the Democratic Republic of the Congo, and Somalia) point to a stark truth: the conventional approach for helping Africa's failed and failing states does not work.

Part of the problem involves the way that the international community understands failed states in the first place. The conventional view relies on a misleading mechanical metaphor, which leads policymakers to suppose that, like broken machines, failed African countries can be repaired by good mechanics. In fact, dysfunctional governments are more like sick people. Like humans, states fall ill in a variety of ways, can continue to function (after a fashion) even when sick, and do not all respond to treatment the same way. Some illnesses can be treated quickly, whereas others require long-term care. Most important, serious illnesses often leave their victims—whether people or governments—permanently changed, unable to return to their former condition.

Keeping this in mind, a better approach to dysfunctional states in Africa would begin with a diagnosis that takes full account of their individual characters and does not assume that the same therapy will work on all of them. The international community cannot get heavily involved in all of Africa's problem countries anytime soon. However, there are a few places, such as Liberia, where the outside world is already deeply entangled. New efforts should be focused in these states.

Achieving real gains will take time, however, and the international community must start thinking about how to help African states in more than just three- to five-year increments (the current life span of most UN mandates). International actors should be prepared to spend ten years or longer on Africa's hardest cases. A new approach will also require new institutional frameworks that draw in all interested parties, including some of Africa's more capable states and regional institutions. International financial bodies, especially the World Bank and the International Monetary Fund (IMF), must also be brought onboard.

In some cases, a form of international trusteeship will be required. This idea, anathema since the end of colonialism, deserves rehabilitation. Done properly, it need not involve the wholesale dismantling of national sovereignty, a precedent that would rightly worry many parties. Instead, trusteeship should entail a new, enhanced form of international responsibility.

Not all African states will need such radical intervention. The continent's countries lie along a spectrum of effective statehood. At one end are South Africa, Botswana, and Mauritius—the few sub-Saharan success stories in terms of both governance and economics. At the other end lie the abject failures, including Liberia, Sierra Leone, and Somalia. And in between fall the majority. Notwithstanding the optimistic talk of international development officials, the vast bulk of Africa's countries are doing just about enough to get by. A few, such as Uganda, have pulled themselves back from the brink of ruin. Several others—including Benin, Ghana, Kenya, Mali, Mozambique, Senegal, and perhaps Malawi and Zambia—are functioning democracies that may be on the road to recovery. Still, of the African Union's 53 members, eight or nine could currently be described as war zones, and there are plenty more—such as Chad, Togo, and Guinea—that could go that way at any moment. It is past time that the world's leading states found a better way to help them.

DEFINING DEVIANCY DOWN

ALTHOUGH THEY VARY in their details, dysfunctional states share two key characteristics: they cannot guarantee law and order throughout their territory, and they cannot fulfill certain critical international obligations. Of these two problems, the former tends to matter most to the state's own citizens, since they are the primary victims. But the latter creates the most widespread concern.

The attacks of September 11, 2001, made it very clear just how dangerous failed states can be for the rest of the world. The U.S. government has discovered that even the most obscure country can become a base for America's enemies—a notion underscored in late 2001 when it was disclosed that Charles Taylor, Liberia's then president, had sold diamonds to al Qaeda. This discovery—made not by a U.S. intelligence agent but by a reporter from *The Washington Post*—highlighted the way that even nonideological leaders may cooperate with dangerous anti-Western forces. Even when they want to, moreover, dysfunctional states are often unable to comply with Washington's counterterrorism efforts (or with any other policy, for that matter). In such cases, providing military assistance (as the United States is doing in some parts of Africa) only makes matters worse.

Aside from these basic failures, no two problem states are exactly the same, and it helps to break them down into categories more nuanced than simply "working" or "failing." Nine years ago, the political scientist Jean-Germain Gros proposed a useful typology that the international community should adopt. He identified five types of dysfunctional states: "anarchic" states, such as Somalia, which lack a central government; "phantom," or "mirage," states, such as Congo (formerly Zaire), which exercise only a semblance of central authority and can manage just a few core tasks (such as protecting the president and his circle); "anemic" states, which are enervated by an insurgency or where, as in Haiti, "the engines of modernity were never put in place"; "captured" states, such as Rwanda, where a strong centralized authority has been taken over by an insecure elite that is primarily concerned with defending itself against rival elites; and "aborted" states, such as Angola, which failed before they were ever consolidated.

This framework underscores the fact that not all problem countries are amenable to the same treatment. Somalia, for example, may work better without a real state than it did with one, since the lack of a central government there has prevented any one warlord from capturing all the resources and aid money for himself. Rwanda, meanwhile, remains a problem not because its government is feeble, but because the paranoid Tutsi political elite regards any moderation as weakness. Crafting a strategy for dealing with these enormously varied situations might seem impossible, but it should not cause officials to despair. There are a number of African states that are now good candidates for international attention, and they should be made the focus of outside help.

THREE STRIKES

BEFORE EXPLAINING HOW best to provide aid, it helps to understand why past efforts have not worked. Large international state-fixing missions are currently under way in Burundi, Côte d'Ivoire, Congo, Liberia, Sierra Leone, and Sudan. These ventures share three major inadequacies.

The first problem is with their time frames: healing a seriously troubled state requires a comprehensive medium-term strategy, not a quick fix. "Medium term" here means longer than the four-year policy cycle typical in Washington; fixing dysfunctional African states can take ten years or more. Thinking in long time frames is not easy for Western governments, but they can do it when they have to, as they have shown with energy policy. And where Africa is concerned, there is little alternative; too many outside interventions have been undermined by the expectation of instant results.

The second flaw in the current approach is its historical imprecision. Foreign officials tend to talk as though they can restore

African states to a degree of efficiency that existed at some vague time in the past. But much of Africa never enjoyed anything like what is now considered good governance. Before 1980, for example, Liberia was run by a few families who claimed U.S. ancestry, under a system analogous to apartheid. It would be a terrible mistake to resurrect such a system today, and Liberians would never accept it. What period, then, should Liberia aspire to reproduce? Even in its heyday, Monrovia never functioned well.

Although Liberia, which was never formally a colony, has an unusual history, its story is similar in important respects to those of many other problem states in Africa. In the majority, colonial administrations ruled for decades, relying on village chiefs and other rural notables to keep the masses quiet. Only from the 1940s onward did most colonial governments begin to try to develop their territories economically and to endow local administrations with some democratic credentials. When most African countries gained independence in the 1960s, they had very little experience with management or governance.

Still, independence came during the height of the Cold War and at the midpoint of the longest and widest economic boom in the modern history of the world (lasting roughly from 1945 to 1973). Prices for agricultural commodities were high, outside aid was easy to attain, and the development community felt very optimistic—and very generous. Conditions have obviously changed since then.

This is not to say that African countries can never regain the sense of optimism and progress they enjoyed in the mid-twentieth century, or that their public administrations can never gain a reasonable degree of efficiency and honesty. But in order for them to do so, they must first face up to modern realities. Prices for many agricultural commodities have declined and may never return to their 1960s or 1970s high point. Most African states have shown themselves unable to industrialize and incapable of absorbing capital; instead, outside money has been used to enrich tiny political elites and their partners abroad. Today, many African governments are further than ever from being able to finance themselves through their own resources, and they rely on permanent subsidies from donor countries for their very existence. Population growth has changed the relationship of people to the land, in both economic and cultural terms. Many of the most dynamic and best-educated Africans have emigrated to Europe or North America. Young people express little hope for a better future. And HIV/AIDS is cutting a cruel swath through the continent, with long-term implications that are hard to predict.

Outsiders also tend to ignore the historical roots of today's conflicts. Virtually since independence, much of Africa has been consumed with warfare—in the Great Lakes region and Sudan since the 1950s, for example, and in Liberia since the 1980s. Today's strife is not just the product of the end of the Cold War or the withdrawal of military funding by the superpowers. Many of Africa's current conflicts are just the latest twists in a long and bloody history that goes back to the circumstances of decolonization. Understanding this history is essential for rebuilding today.

The third and final weakness of current attempts to rebuild Africa is that most are too narrowly oriented toward individual states. This was one of the mistakes made by the World Bank and the IMF in the 1980s, when prescriptions for economic reform were given to neighboring countries with little thought of their cumulative consequences. In a similar fashion, Africa's wars are today often erroneously understood as internal, rather than interstate, conflicts. The truth is that most combatants receive support from neighboring governments, making Africa's wars regional in fact if not in name. Indeed, Congo's "civil" war—a conflagration that has persisted, in one form or another, since 1997 and has claimed more than three million lives—has involved forces from at least eight countries. And the ongoing chaos in Liberia has helped to destabilize neighboring Sierra Leone, Côte d'Ivoire, and Guinea.

To have a chance at success, peacemaking efforts and rebuilding strategies must take these regional dynamics into account. Regionwide cooperation is also necessary on economic issues, such as facilitating cross-border trade and ensuring that people can travel, work, and own property outside their home countries. Achieving such cooperation may require the creation of international customs administrations, for example, and pooled revenue arrangements.

TEST CASES

No AFRICAN STATE HAS been undergoing major repairs for longer than Sierra Leone. As a result, it has become something of a laboratory experiment in state sickness and remedy. And it serves as a good test case for just what is wrong and what is right about the international approach to Africa.

Sierra Leone started out as colony under British auspices in 1787, serving as a refuge for homeless black people from the streets of London (many of them veterans of the wrong side of the American War of Independence). After the British departed in 1961, the new country quickly succumbed to corruption and misrule under the long reign of Siaka Stevens (1968–85). War broke out in 1991 and began to taper off only after British troops arrived in May 2000.

Since then, the international effort to reconstruct Sierra Leone has been intense. Under UN and British auspices, its army and police force have been reorganized and retrained, law courts and police stations have been rebuilt, and a government has been democratically elected. Many officials in the new government, however, have murky pasts—including ties to a militia that committed atrocities during the war. They and their colleagues have shown little interest in making more than a rhetorical commitment to good governance. Many officials are also highly corrupt and have paid scant attention to the deep social problems (such as bad education and unemployment) that led to war in the first place. Government ministers and senior officials seldom venture outside the capital city, Freetown, where they drive around in luxury SUVs paid for with international aid money. Meanwhile, nothing has changed for the impoverished veterans of Sierra Leone's vicious wars—or for their victims. Some former fighters say they would pick up arms again at the first opportunity; at least the militias provided them with jobs. If the UN and the British leave Sierra Leone in the near future, there is every reason to believe the state will once again collapse.

The same goes for neighboring Liberia, which is now a wreck—despite having boasted the world's second-fastest-growing economy during the 1950s and having been home, more recently, to the largest UN mission in the world and a recovery process to which the United States is estimated to have contributed some $750 million.

In both countries, as in many other parts of Africa, ruling cliques have developed a vested interest in disorder and show little interest in seeing an efficient state emerge. This is not a problem of education: Africa's elites include people with degrees from leading universities around the world. Many of Liberia's warlords studied in the United States, for example, and the president of Sierra Leone, Ahmad Tejan Kabbah, is a former UN official.

And the problem goes deeper than crooked officials. Countries such as Sierra Leone, Liberia, and Somalia, which have suffered through fighting for almost a generation now, lack not just honest, competent leaders but also clerks and bureaucrats. Not enough people have been educated or trained for effective government work. An entire range of social and economic institutions also needs fixing. Reconstruction will take a minimum of ten years and could require as many as 50.

None of these problems can be solved by simply throwing more cash at Africa. Many on the continent have come to see foreign aid as nothing more than a cow to be milked. Unfortunately, much of the international community has yet to recognize this. Consider *Our Common Interest*, the report published earlier this year by the Commission for Africa (convened by the British government). While it cites the need for reform, the report also recommends a major injection of new aid—as if Africa's main problem was a lack of capital. The commission did not adequately consider why that formula has failed so badly, and so often, in the past.

Now the G-8 (the coalition of the world's leading industrialized powers) has made a similar mistake. At the recent summit at the Gleneagles resort in Scotland, leaders promised to increase by 2010 official development assistance to Africa by $25 billion a year, doubling current totals. But Africa's real problem is not a lack of money. In fact, new aid from the West will only make matters worse unless it is integrated into a strategy that also involves much more incisive political input from donor countries.

TOUGH LOVE

INSTEAD OF MORE MONEY, what Africa really needs is governments that are responsible to their own voters, that are largely self-financing, that are internationally respectable, and that can attract home some of the hundreds of thousands of talented Africans who currently live in the West. New infusions of aid would likely just perpetuate the kleptocratic regimes that have slowly strangled the continent since independence.

Healthier states will need to reflect the actual politics of their societies, including some unconventional arrangements. In Somaliland (a region in the north of Somalia), for example, a relatively competent though still-unrecognized independent government has sprung up, funded by local business leaders and remittances from abroad—which turn out to have a much more salutary effect on government than does foreign aid. Premature recognition of Somaliland could kill it by turning it into another aid junkie. But the territory deserves some form of legal status to recognize its impressive development and to take it out of its present limbo.

Of course, providing basic security remains an essential first step in any rebuilding effort. Africa's lack of security—physical, political, and economic—has wreaked such psychological havoc that it will be hard to redress through conventional government techniques. Few Africans can muster the confidence to invest in their countries, whether financially, professionally, or personally. Persuading them to reengage will require providing military and economic security; only then will the climate improve enough to permit the training and retention of professional and administrative personnel.

But traditional peacekeeping is not enough. Even well-meaning international efforts can do more harm than good. As the academics Denis Tull and Andreas Mehler have pointed out, often the worst violence in Africa has occurred after the outside world intervened to create power-sharing deals between rival elites; think of the slaughter in Angola in 1992, in Burundi in 1993, and in Rwanda in 1994. What was missing, in each of these cases, was enough international pressure and outside resources to keep fragile and sometimes misconceived peace treaties in place.

To craft a better approach to Africa, one other problem must be confronted head-on: effective intervention is going to occasionally require overriding traditional national sovereignty. Certain African governments have never managed to create durable working administrations. In these countries, sovereignty has become a mere legal fiction, one that provides cover for all sorts of internal abuses. For too long, legitimate worries about infringing on Africa's independence have stymied international efforts to address this problem.

Fortunately, there is now a growing body of international jurisprudence defining the circumstances in which the international community is justified, or even required, to bypass such nominal sovereignty in order to protect people who have been abandoned or abused by their governments. And several African governments, most notably Nigeria's and South Africa's, have started to signal a new flexibility on this question, as have the leaders of the new African Union (AU). All seem to agree that in some cases, when states are unable or unwilling to prevent massive human rights abuses, intervention is appropriate—whether local powers like it or not. Intrusive outside meddling often smacks of colonialism and is thus a bitter pill for African nationalists to swallow. But sometimes there is simply no alternative.

This understanding should allow for a new form of international engagement in Africa: namely, trusteeships for certain failed states. No one is advocating a return to the UN's old trusteeship system. Under the new paradigm, locals would remain full partners in any arrangement. What is called for now are multilateral joint ventures in which certain countries and institutions share control over key operations. In such missions, the UN should still play a fundamental role (although not an administrative one), since it alone can confer the kind of legitimacy critical to such projects. In this regard, it would help enormously if the UN Security Council were expanded to include a representative from sub-Saharan Africa, since this would give Africans a sense that they were full partners in the body.

The most obvious current candidate for such a trusteeship is Liberia. Congo and Sudan might equally need help, but they are too large in political, economic, and population terms, and have too many self-interested outside actors involved to allow a novel international arrangement to succeed. Liberia, by contrast, has far less to lose and fewer outside influences and allies. Liberians are also so deeply attached to the United States that many locals would likely support a U.S.-led effort.

Any trusteeship established to oversee the country should include representatives of the U.S. government, as well as of the other parties to the international "contact group" on Liberia, which was formed in September 2002 to track the country's progress (the group also includes representatives from the UN, the EU, the AU, the Economic Community of West African States [ECOWAS], France, Morocco, Nigeria, Senegal, and the United Kingdom). The IMF and the World Bank should also be included, as well as whoever is elected as Liberia's president in October.

One of the main priorities of the trusteeship of Liberia should be to encourage some of the many Liberians living abroad to return home. These returnees and other exiles could be organized into a continent-wide international corps of administrators who could be deployed wherever in Africa they are needed. The international community, however, must avoid simply giving control of all aspects of the country's public administration to the new trusteeship. To ensure that Liberia starts to govern itself effectively, foreign administrators should concentrate on securing the boundaries of the political field while allowing new local arrangements to emerge. This can best be accomplished by taking control of the main sources of revenue and ensuring that money is then passed on to the Liberian Treasury on agreed terms. A comparable system has been pioneered for oil revenues in Chad, an example that should be studied for future cases. Another option is the arrangement some analysts have proposed for Congo: requiring both local and international businesses to pay taxes not to the central government but into a series of provincial trust funds jointly run by locals and foreigners. Such innovations could be very useful for these countries and many others throughout the continent.

Although the trusteeship idea might sound complicated and costly, the sums of money involved in restoring African states to health will be small—far less than what is now pouring into Iraq or is given as aid to a range of other countries. In many cases, the new paradigm would involve no new allocations, but would simply spread out over longer periods what has already been budgeted. Expensive, large-scale peacekeeping forces would not generally be required, certainly not for the long term. Where peacekeepers are needed, the best approach would be to copy the Sierra Leone model: use a small number of Western soldiers (800 British troops were deployed in Sierra Leone) to spearhead a larger force of regional peacekeepers (such as the West African troops deployed in Côte d'Ivoire or the AU forces sent to Burundi and, more recently, to Darfur). The AU has expressed interest in creating an African standby force, but this may take years to assemble and organize.

Such forces should not occupy whole territories, but simply guarantee effective military intervention in defined circumstances—such as if a legitimately elected government is threatened by a coup or if a troubled country is threatened by invasion. As the British armed forces have shown in Sierra Leone, the credible threat of a deployment by an "over the horizon" force serves as an effective deterrent when part of a wider political strategy.

A NEW AFRICA

ONE OF THE FEW HOPEFUL developments to come out of Africa's many dysfunctional states is the way power vacuums have been spontaneously filled by new structures with deep roots in Africa's history. These institutions, such as Somalia's subclans or West Africa's initiation societies, do not figure in textbooks on government and sometimes play a negative role. In other cases, however—as in the self-governing Somaliland—they have made a positive contribution. At present, UN administrators tend to ignore such networks and often spend an entire tour of duty patiently rebuilding formal new governments without noticing the alternate structures already in existence right under their noses.

Administrators should learn to take advantage of such indigenous political institutions. Over the next few decades, governance in many parts of Africa must be substantially reinvented, and the more solidly it is grounded, the better. Not all local institutions that have a historical pedigree should be preserved. But because certain deep-rooted local structures are not going to disappear, it makes sense to think about how they can play a role. Some self-defense and vigilante groups, for example, could be incorporated into local police forces or national guard units.

With every month that goes by, it becomes clearer that the chapter of African history that opened in 1945 has now closed. The golden age of decolonization and nationalism in Africa did not lead, in most cases, to successful sovereign states. This fact may be hard for Africans to admit, but it is even harder for them to live with.

Too often, Westerners ask only whether Africa's problems affect their security and, learning that they do not, decide to ignore them. Such short-term thinking must now change, especially given the new, global threats that have emerged since September 11. The West should adopt a new, enlightened form of self-interest and be open to engaging in new sorts of involvement in Africa. Sick states there cannot be restored with the medicines and surgical techniques of a bygone era. What is required instead are international joint ventures as discussed above. These arrangements would avoid the evils of colonialism and the errors of more recent peace-keeping and state-building efforts. The outcome—a healthier, more stable, and more secure Africa—would benefit everyone, on the continent and around the world.

Strengthening African Leadership

There Is Another Way

Robert I. Rotberg

AFRICA HAS LONG BEEN SADDLED with poor, even malevolent, leadership: predatory kleptocrats, military-installed autocrats, economic illiterates, and puffed-up posturers. By far the most egregious examples come from Nigeria, the Democratic Republic of the Congo, and Zimbabwe—countries that have been run into the ground despite their abundant natural resources. But these cases are by no means unrepresentative: By some measures, 90 percent of sub-Saharan African nations have experienced despotic rule in the last three decades. Such leaders use power as an end in itself, rather than for the public good; they are indifferent to the progress of their citizens (although anxious to receive their adulation); they are unswayed by reason and employ poisonous social or racial ideologies; and they are hypocrites, always shifting blame for their countries' distress.

Under the stewardship of these leaders, infrastructure in many African countries has fallen into disrepair, currencies have depreciated, and real prices have inflated dramatically, while job availability, health care, education standards, and life expectancy have declined. Ordinary life has become beleaguered: General security has deteriorated, crime and corruption have increased, much-needed public funds have flowed into hidden bank accounts, and

This article was published in *Foreign Affairs*, July/August 2004.

officially sanctioned ethnic discrimination—sometimes resulting in civil war—has become prevalent. This depressing picture is brought into even sharper relief by the few but striking examples of effective African leadership in recent decades. These leaders stand out because of their strength of character, their adherence to the principles of participatory democracy, and their ability to overcome deep-rooted challenges. The government of Mozambique, for example, brought about economic growth rates of more than 10 percent between 1996 and 2003, following the economic catastrophe wrought by that country's civil war (which ended in 1992). And in Kenya, President Mwai Kibaki has strengthened civil society, invested in education, and removed barriers to economic entrepreneurship instated during the repressive rule of Daniel arap Moi.

The best example of good leadership in Africa is Botswana. Long before diamonds were discovered there, this former desert protectorate, which was neglected by the British under colonialism, demonstrated a knack for participatory democracy, integrity, tolerance, entrepreneurship, and the rule of law. The country has remained democratic in spirit as well as form continuously since its independence in 1966—an unmatched record in Africa. It has also defended human rights, encouraged civil liberties, and actively promoted its citizens' social and economic development.

GOOD APPLES

WHAT HAS ENABLED Botswana to succeed where so many other African nations have failed? Some observers point to the relative linguistic homogeneity of the country. But Somalia, which remains unstable despite a similar uniformity, shows that this factor is far from sufficient. Others point to the century-old teachings of the congregational London Missionary Society—the peaceful, pragmatic outlook that is inextricably bound up in the country's political culture. But this explanation also fails to explain why the same positive effects have not been witnessed in other countries with a history of Christian teaching, such as in neighboring Zambia. Nor are Botswana's plentiful diamond reserves responsible: Angola, Gabon, and Nigeria all have abundant natural resources, but none has seen comparable returns for its people.

It is Botswana's history of visionary leadership, especially in the years following independence, that best explains its success. Sir Seretse Khama, Botswana's founding president, came from a family of Bamangwato chiefs well regarded for their benevolence and integrity. When Khama founded the Botswana Democratic Party in 1961 and led his country to independence, he was already dedicated to the principles of deliberative democracy and market economy that would allow his young country to flourish. Modest, unostentatious as a leader, and a genuine believer in popular rule, Khama forged a participatory and law-respecting political culture that has endured under his successors, Sir Ketumile Masire and Festus Mogae.

Although operating in very different circumstances, Mauritius' first leader, Sir Seewoosagur Ramgoolam, held to the same leadership codes as Khama. Ramgoolam gave Mauritius a robust democratic beginning, which has been sustained by a series of wise successors from different backgrounds and parties. Both Khama and Ramgoolam could have emulated many of their contemporaries by establishing strong, single-man, kleptocratic regimes. But they refused to do so.

Effective leadership has proved the decisive factor in South Africa, too: without Nelson Mandela's inclusive and visionary leadership, his adherence to the rule of law, his insistence on broadening the delivery of essential services, and his emphasis on moving from a command economy toward a market-driven one, South Africa would probably have emerged from apartheid as a far more fractured and autocratic state than it did.

Too few African leaders have followed the examples of Mandela, Khama, and Ramgoolam. Ghana, Lesotho, Mali, and Senegal are all showing promise. But in many other African countries, leaders have begun their presidential careers as democrats only to end up, a term or two later, as corrupt autocrats: Bakili Muluzi of Malawi, Moi of Kenya, and, most dramatically of all, Robert Mugabe of

Zimbabwe. Other leaders, such as Sam Nujoma of Namibia and Yoweri Museveni of Uganda, may be heading in the same direction.

A BOLD INITIATIVE

To BUILD ON the positive leadership examples, a select group of prominent past and present African leaders who met over the last year decided to confront the continent's pathology of poor leadership with deeds as well as words. At the conclusion of a series of private meetings (the final one of which was held in Mombasa, Kenya), they established the African Leadership Council, promulgated a Code of African Leadership with 23 commandments, issued a Mombasa Declaration promoting better leadership, and proposed a series of courses to train their political successors in the art of good government.

Members of the council believe that absolute standards of leadership are both appropriate and attainable. Good leaders deliver security of the state and of the person, the rule of law, good education and health services, and a framework conducive to economic growth. They ensure effective arteries of commerce and enshrine personal and human freedoms. They empower civil society and protect the environmental commons. Crucially, good leaders also provide their citizens with a sense of belonging to a national enterprise.

Conscious that Africa's poor are getting poorer and that good governance is essential for successful economic development, the council sees itself at the vanguard of fundamental reform in the continent. Its approach certainly goes far beyond the New Partnership for Africa's Development (NEPAD) and proposals for the African Union. The Code of African Leadership, for example, says in its first commandment that leaders should "offer a coherent vision of individual growth and national advancement with justice and dignity for all," implying that most leaders today do not. Other commandments demand that African leaders encourage "broad participation," adhere to the letter and spirit of their national constitutions (especially term limits), encourage dissent and disagreement, respect human rights and civil liberties, strengthen the rule of law, promote policies that eradicate poverty and improve the well-being of their citizens, ensure a strong code of ethics, refuse to use their offices for personal gain, oppose corruption, and bolster essential personal freedoms.

This uncommonly bold agenda seeks to avoid renewed patrimonial leadership debacles, such as those presided over by Mobutu Sese Seko in Zaire, Moi in Kenya, Idi Amin in Uganda, and Jean-Bedel Bokassa in the Central African Republic. The council is highly conscious, too, of the hijacking of Zimbabwe's government by Mugabe, which has resulted in starvation and drastically reduced living standards.

The council is chaired by former President Sir Ketumile Masire of Botswana and includes former Nigerian head of state General Yakubu Gowon, Vice President Moody Awori of Kenya, former Prime Minister Hage Geingob of Namibia, and a dozen other present and former prime ministers and cabinet ministers from Sierra Leone to Kenya, Malawi, and Uganda. All are regarded throughout Africa as men of unusual personal probity and esteem and as accomplished proponents of good governance. The council intends to recruit additional members from the ranks of Africa's outstanding democratic leaders, Francophone and Anglophone, female and male. Together they will serve the continent by advising international organizations, individual countries, and donor agencies on how to improve leadership.

The group stands ready to assist civil societies in countries undergoing serious leadership crises. It will also urge greedy national leaders to attack corrupt practices and adhere to term limits (the current presidents of Gabon, Malawi, Namibia, Uganda, and Zambia, for example, have all had pangs of desire for illegal third terms). Next year, it expects to begin holding special seminars for cabinet ministers and others. The council's curriculum emphasizes constitutionalism, the rule of law, ethics, accountability, diversity, good fiscal management, coalition building, and the fundamentals of modern micro- and macroeconomics. Training courses will soon be launched.

Whether the efforts of the African Leadership Council will reduce bloodshed, diminish corruption, and encourage more prosperity for citizens across Africa is by no means certain. But as a unique African response to the continent's immense needs, this innovative endeavor is a promising, dramatic step forward.

The Challenge of Global Health

Laurie Garrett

BEWARE WHAT YOU WISH FOR

LESS THAN A DECADE AGO, the biggest problem in global health seemed to be the lack of resources available to combat the multiple scourges ravaging the world's poor and sick. Today, thanks to a recent extraordinary and unprecedented rise in public and private giving, more money is being directed toward pressing heath challenges than ever before. But because the efforts this money is paying for are largely uncoordinated and directed mostly at specific high-profile diseases—rather than at public health in general—there is a grave danger that the current age of generosity could not only fall short of expectations but actually make things worse on the ground.

This danger exists despite the fact that today, for the first time in history, the world is poised to spend enormous resources to conquer the diseases of the poor. Tackling the developing world's diseases has become a key feature of many nations' foreign policies over the last five years, for a variety of reasons. Some see stopping the spread of HIV, tuberculosis (TB), malaria, avian influenza, and other major killers as a moral duty. Some see it as a form of public diplomacy. And some see it as an investment in self-protection, given that microbes know no borders. Governments have been joined by a long list of private donors, topped by Bill and Melinda Gates and Warren Buffett, whose contributions to today's war on disease are mind-boggling.

This article was published in *Foreign Affairs*, January/February 2007.

Thanks to their efforts, there are now billions of dollars being made available for health spending—and thousands of nongovernmental organizations (NGOs) and humanitarian groups vying to spend it. But much more than money is required. It takes states, health-care systems, and at least passable local infrastructure to improve public health in the developing world. And because decades of neglect there have rendered local hospitals, clinics, laboratories, medical schools, and health talent dangerously deficient, much of the cash now flooding the field is leaking away without result.

Moreover, in all too many cases, aid is tied to short-term numerical targets such as increasing the number of people receiving specific drugs, decreasing the number of pregnant women diagnosed with HIV (the virus that causes AIDS), or increasing the quantity of bed nets handed out to children to block disease-carrying mosquitoes. Few donors seem to understand that it will take at least a full generation (if not two or three) to substantially improve public health—and that efforts should focus less on particular diseases than on broad measures that affect populations' general well-being.

The fact that the world is now short well over four million health-care workers, moreover, is all too often ignored. As the populations of the developed countries are aging and coming to require ever more medical attention, they are sucking away local health talent from developing countries. Already, one out of five practicing physicians in the United States is foreign-trained, and a study recently published in *JAMA: The Journal of the American Medical Association* estimated that if current trends continue, by 2020 the United States could face a shortage of up to 800,000 nurses and 200,000 doctors. Unless it and other wealthy nations radically increase salaries and domestic training programs for physicians and nurses, it is likely that within 15 years the majority of workers staffing their hospitals will have been born and trained in poor and middle-income countries. As such workers flood to the West, the developing world will grow even more desperate.

Yet the visionary leadership required to tackle such problems is sadly lacking. Over the last year, every major leadership position on the global health landscape has turned over, creating an unprecedented moment of strategic uncertainty. The untimely death last May of Dr. Lee Jong-wook, director general of the World Health Organization (WHO), forced a novel election process for his successor, prompting health advocates worldwide to ask critical, long-ignored questions, such as, Who should lead the fight against disease? Who should pay for it? And what are the best strategies and tactics to adopt?

The answers have not been easy to come by. In November, China's Dr. Margaret Chan was elected as Lee's successor. As Hong Kong's health director, Chan had led her territory's responses to SARS and bird flu; later she took the helm of the WHO's communicable diseases division. But in statements following her election, Chan acknowledged that her organization now faces serious competition and novel challenges. And as of this writing, the Global Fund to Fight AIDS, Tuberculosis, and Malaria remained without a new leader following a months-long selection process that saw more than 300 candidates vie for the post and the organization's board get mired in squabbles over the fund's mission and future direction.

Few of the newly funded global health projects, meanwhile, have built-in methods of assessing their efficacy or sustainability. Fewer still have ever scaled up beyond initial pilot stages. And nearly all have been designed, managed, and executed by residents of the wealthy world (albeit in cooperation with local personnel and agencies). Many of the most successful programs are executed by foreign NGOs and academic groups, operating with almost no government interference inside weak or failed states. Virtually no provisions exist to allow the world's poor to say what they want, decide which projects serve their needs, or adopt local innovations. And nearly all programs lack exit strategies or safeguards against the dependency of local governments.

As a result, the health world is fast approaching a fork in the road. The years ahead could witness spectacular improvements in the health of billions of people, driven by a grand public and private effort comparable to the Marshall Plan—or they could see poor societies pushed into even deeper trouble, in yet another tale of well-intended foreign meddling gone awry. Which outcome will emerge depends on whether it is possible to expand the developing world's local talent pool of health workers, restore and improve crumbling national and global health infrastructures, and devise effective local and international systems for disease prevention and treatment.

SHOW ME THE MONEY

THE RECENT SURGE IN FUNDING started as a direct consequence of the HIV/AIDS pandemic. For decades, public health experts had been confronted with the profound disparities in care that separated the developed world from the developing one. Health workers hated that inequity but tended to accept it as a fact of life, given that health concerns were nested in larger issues of poverty and development. Western AIDS activists, doctors, and scientists, however, tended to have little experience with the developing world and were thus shocked when they discovered these inequities. And they reacted with vocal outrage.

The revolution started at an international AIDS meeting in Vancouver, Canada, in 1996. Scientists presented exhilarating evidence that a combination of anti-HIV drugs (known as antiretrovirals, or ARVs) could dramatically reduce the spread of the virus inside the bodies of infected people and make it possible for them to live long lives. Practically overnight, tens of thousands of infected men and women in wealthy countries started the new treatments, and by mid-1997, the visible horrors of AIDS had almost disappeared from the United States and Europe.

But the drugs, then priced at about $14,000 per year and requiring an additional $5,000 a year for tests and medical visits, were unaffordable for most of the world's HIV-positive population. So between 1997 and 2000, a worldwide activist movement slowly developed to address this problem by putting pressure on drug companies to lower their prices or allow the generic manufacture of the new medicines. The activists demanded that the Clinton administration and its counterparts in the G-8, the group of advanced industrial nations, pony up money to buy ARVs and donate them to poor countries. And by 1999, total donations for health-related programs (including HIV/AIDS treatment) in sub-Saharan Africa hit $865 million—up more than tenfold in just three years.

In 2000, some 20,000 activists, scientists, doctors, and patients gathered in Durban, South Africa, for another international AIDS conference. There, South Africa's former president, Nelson Mandela, defined the issue of ARV access in moral terms, making it clear that the world should not permit the poor of Harare, Lagos, or Hanoi to die for lack of treatments that were keeping the rich of London, New York, and Paris alive. The World Bank economist Mead Over told the gathering that donations to developing countries for dealing with HIV/AIDS had reached $300 million in 1999—0.5 percent of all development assistance. But he characterized that sum as "pathetic," claiming that the HIV/AIDS pandemic was costing African countries roughly $5 billion annually in direct medical care and indirect losses in labor and productivity.

In 2001, a group of 128 Harvard University faculty members led by the economist Jeffrey Sachs estimated that fewer than 40,000 sub-Saharan Africans were receiving ARVs, even though some 25 million in the region were infected with HIV and perhaps 600,000 of them needed the drugs immediately. Andrew Natsios, then director of the U.S. Agency for International Development (USAID), dismissed the idea of distributing such drugs, telling the House International Relations Committee that Africans could not take the proper combinations of drugs in the proper sequences because they did not have clocks or watches and lacked a proper concept of time. The Harvard faculty group labeled Natsios' comments racist and insisted that, as Sachs put it, all the alleged obstacles to widespread HIV/AIDS treatment in poor countries "either don't exist or can be overcome," and that three million people in Africa could be put on ARVs by the end of 2005 at "a cost of $1.1 billion per year for the first two to three years, then $3.3 billion to $5.5 billion per year by Year Five."

Sachs added that the appropriate annual foreign-aid budget for malaria, TB, and pediatric respiratory and diarrheal diseases was about $11 billion; support for AIDS orphans ought to top $1 billion per year; and HIV/AIDS prevention could be tackled for $3 billion per year. In other words, for well under $20 billion a year, most of it targeting sub-Saharan Africa, the world could mount a serious global health drive.

What seemed a brazen request then has now, just five years later, actually been eclipsed. HIV/AIDS assistance has effectively spearheaded a larger global public health agenda. The Harvard group's claim that three million Africans could easily be put on ARVs by the end of 2005 proved overoptimistic: the WHO's "3 by 5 Initiative" failed to meet half of the three million target, even combining all poor and middle-income nations and not just those in Africa. Nevertheless, driven by the HIV/AIDS pandemic, a marvelous momentum for health assistance has been built and shows no signs of abating.

MORE, MORE, MORE

IN RECENT YEARS, the generosity of individuals, corporations, and foundations in the United States has grown by staggering proportions. As of August 2006, in its six years of existence, the Bill and Melinda Gates Foundation had given away $6.6 billion for global health programs. Of that total, nearly $2 billion had been spent on programs aimed at TB and HIV/AIDS and other sexually transmitted diseases. Between 1995 and 2005, total giving by all U.S. charitable foundations tripled, and the portion of money dedicated to international projects soared 80 percent, with global health representing more than a third of that sum. Independent of their government, Americans donated $7.4 billion for disaster relief in 2005 and $22.4 billion for domestic and foreign health programs and research.

Meanwhile, the Bush administration increased its overseas development assistance from $11.4 billion in 2001 to $27.5 billion in 2005, with support for HIV/AIDS and other health programs representing the lion's share of support unrelated to Iraq or Afghanistan. And in his 2003 State of the Union address, President George W. Bush called for the creation of a $15 billion, five-year program to tackle HIV/AIDS, TB, and malaria. Approved by Congress that May, the President's Emergency Plan for AIDS Relief (PEPFAR) involves assistance from the United States to 16 nations, aimed primarily at providing ARVs for people infected with HIV. Roughly $8.5 billion has been spent to date. PEPFAR's goals are ambitious and include placing two million people on ARVs and ten million more in some form of care by early 2008. As of March 2006, an estimated 561,000 people were receiving ARVs through PEPFAR-funded programs.

The surge in giving has not just come from the United States, however. Overseas development assistance from every one of the nations in the Organization for Economic Cooperation and Development (OECD) skyrocketed between 2001 and 2005, with health making up the largest portion of the increase. And in 2002, a unique funding-dispersal mechanism was created, independent of both the UN system and any government: the Global Fund to Fight AIDS, Tuberculosis, and Malaria. The fund receives support from governments, philanthropies, and a variety of corporate-donation schemes. Since its birth, it has approved $6.6 billion in proposals and dispersed $2.9 billion toward them. More than a fifth of those funds have gone to four nations: China, Ethiopia, Tanzania, and Zambia. The fund estimates that it now provides 20 percent of all global support for HIV/AIDS programs and 66 percent of the funding for efforts to combat TB and malaria.

The World Bank, for its part, took little interest in health issues in its early decades, thinking that health would improve in tandem with general economic development, which it was the bank's mission to promote. Under the leadership of Robert McNamara (which ran from 1968 to 1981), however, the bank slowly increased direct investment in targeted health projects, such as the attempted elimination of river blindness in West Africa. By the end of the 1980s, many economists were beginning to recognize that disease in tropical and desperately poor countries was itself a critical impediment to development and prosperity, and in 1993 the bank formally announced its change of heart in its annual *World Development Report*. The bank steadily increased its health spending in the following decade, reaching $3.4 billion in 2003 before falling back to $2.1 billion in 2006, with $87 million of that spent on HIV/ AIDS, TB, and malaria programs and $250 million on child and maternal health. The bank, along with the International Monetary Fund (IMF), the OECD, and the G-8, has also recently forgiven the debts of many poor nations hard-hit by AIDS and other diseases, with the proviso that the governments in question spend what would otherwise have gone for debt payments on key public services, including health, instead.

When the Asian tsunami struck in December 2004, the world witnessed a profound level of globalized generosity, with an estimated $7 billion being donated to NGOs, churches, and governments, largely by individuals. Although health programs garnered only a small percentage of that largess, many of the organizations that are key global health players were significantly bolstered by the funds.

In January 2006, as the threat of avian influenza spread, thirty-five nations pledged $1.9 billion toward research and control efforts in hopes of staving off a global pandemic. Since then, several G-8 nations, particularly the United States, have made additional funding available to bolster epidemiological surveillance and disease-control activities in Southeast Asia and elsewhere.

And poor nations themselves, finally, have stepped up their own health spending, partly in response to criticism that they were underallocating public funds for social services. In the 1990s, for example, sub-Saharan African countries typically spent less than 3 percent of their budgets on health. By 2003, in contrast, Tanzania spent nearly 13 percent of its national budget on health-related goods and services; the Central African Republic, Namibia, and Zambia each spent around 12 percent of their budgets on health; and in Mozambique, Swaziland, and Uganda, the figure was around 11 percent.

For most humanitarian and health-related NGOs, in turn, the surge in global health spending has been a huge boon, driving expansion in both the number of organizations and the scope and depth of their operations. By one reliable estimate, there are now more than sixty thousand AIDS-related NGOs alone, and there are even more for global health more generally. In fact, ministers of health in poor countries now express frustration over their inability to track the operations of foreign organizations operating on their soil, ensure those organizations are delivering services in sync with government policies and priorities, and avoid duplication in resource-scarce areas.

ONE MIGHT THINK THAT with all this money on the table, the solutions to many global health problems would at least now be in sight. But one would be wrong. Most funds come with strings attached and must be spent according to donors' priorities, politics, and values. And the largest levels of donations are propelled by mass emotional responses, such as to the Asian tsunami. Still more money is needed, on a regular basis and without restrictions on the uses to which it is put. But even if such resources were to materialize, major obstacles would still stand in the way of their doing much lasting good.

One problem is that not all the funds appropriated end up being spent effectively. In an analysis prepared for the second annual meeting of the Clinton Global Initiative, in September 2006, Dalberg Global Development Advisors concluded that much current aid spending is trapped in bureaucracies and multilateral banks. Simply stripping layers of financing bureaucracy and improving health-delivery systems, the firm argued, could effectively release an additional 15–30 percent of the capital provided for HIV/AIDS, TB, and malaria programs.

A 2006 World Bank report, meanwhile, estimated that about half of all funds donated for health efforts in sub-Saharan Africa never reach the clinics and hospitals at the end of the line. According to the bank, money leaks out in the form of payments to ghost employees, padded prices for transport and warehousing, the siphoning off of drugs to the black market, and the sale of counterfeit—often dangerous—medications. In Ghana, for example, where such corruption is particularly rampant, an amazing 80 percent of donor funds get diverted from their intended purposes.

Another problem is the lack of coordination of donor activities. Improving global health will take more funds than any single donor can provide, and oversight and guidance require the skills of the many, not the talents of a few compartmentalized in the offices of various groups and agencies. In practice, moreover, donors often function as competitors, and the only organization with the political credibility to compel cooperative thinking is the WHO. Yet, as Harvard University's Christopher Murray points out, the WHO itself is dependent on donors, who give it much more for disease-specific programs than they do for its core budget. If the WHO stopped chasing such funds, Murray argues, it could go back to concentrating on its true mission of providing objective expert advice and strategic guidance.

This points to yet another problem, which is that aid is almost always "stovepiped" down narrow channels relating to a particular program or disease. From an operational perspective, this means that a government may receive considerable funds to support, for example, an ARV-distribution program for mothers and children living in the nation's capital. But the same government may have no financial capacity to support basic maternal and infant health programs, either in the same capital or in the country as a whole. So HIV-positive mothers are given drugs to hold their infection at bay and prevent passage of the virus to their babies but still cannot obtain even the most rudimentary of obstetric and gyneco-logical care or infant immunizations.

Stovepiping tends to reflect the interests and concerns of the donors, not the recipients. Diseases and health conditions that enjoy a temporary spotlight in rich countries garner the most attention and money. This means that advocacy, the whims of foundations, and the particular concerns of wealthy individuals and governments drive practically the entire global public health effort. Today the top three killers in most poor countries are maternal death around childbirth and pediatric respiratory and intestinal infections leading to death from pulmonary failure or uncontrolled diarrhea. But few women's rights groups put safe pregnancy near the top of their list of priorities, and there is no dysentery lobby or celebrity attention given to coughing babies.

The HIV/AIDS pandemic, meanwhile, continues to be the primary driver of global concern and action about health. At the 2006 International AIDS Conference, former U.S. President Bill

Clinton suggested that HIV/AIDS programs would end up helping all other health initiatives. "If you first develop the health infrastructure throughout the whole country, particularly in Africa, to deal with AIDS," Clinton argued, "you will increase the infrastructure of dealing with maternal and child health, malaria, and TB. Then I think you have to look at nutrition, water, and sanitation. All these things, when you build it up, you'll be helping to promote economic development and alleviate poverty."

But the experience of bringing ARV treatment to Haiti argues against Clinton's analysis. The past several years have witnessed the successful provision of antiretroviral treatment to more than 5,000 needy Haitians, and between 2002 and 2006, the prevalence of HIV in the country plummeted from six percent to three percent. But during the same period, Haiti actually went backward on every other health indicator.

Part of the problem is that most of global HIV/AIDS-related funding goes to stand-alone programs: HIV testing sites, hospices and orphanages for people affected by AIDS, ARV-dispersal stations, HIV/AIDS education projects, and the like. Because of discrimination against people infected with HIV, public health systems have been reluctant to incorporate HIV/AIDS-related programs into general care. The resulting segregation has reinforced the anti-HIV stigma and helped create cadres of health-care workers who function largely independently from countries' other health-related systems. Far from lifting all boats, as Clinton claims, efforts to combat HIV/AIDS have so far managed to bring more money to the field but have not always had much beneficial impact on public health outside their own niche.

DIAMONDS IN THE ROUGH

ARGUABLY THE BEST EXAMPLE of what is possible when forces align properly can be found in the tiny African nation of Botswana. In August 2000, the Gates Foundation, the pharmaceutical companies Merck and Bristol-Myers Squibb, and the Harvard AIDS Initiative announced the launching of an HIV/AIDS treatment program in collaboration with the government of Botswana. At the time, Botswana had the highest HIV infection rate in the world, estimated to exceed 37 percent of the population between the ages of 15 and 40. The goal of the new program was to put every single one of Botswana's infected citizens in treatment and to give ARVs to all who were at an advanced stage of the disease. Merck donated its anti-HIV drugs, Bristol-Myers Squibb discounted its, Merck and the Gates Foundation subsidized the effort to the tune of $100 million, and Harvard helped the Botswanan government design its program.

When the collaboration was announced, the target looked easily attainable, thanks to its top-level political support in Botswana, the plentiful money that would come from both the donors and the country's diamond wealth, the free medicine, and the sage guidance of Merck and Harvard. Unlike most of its neighbors, Botswana had an excellent highway system, sound general infrastructure, and a growing middle class. Furthermore, Botswana's population of 1.5 million was concentrated in the capital city of Gaborone. The national unemployment rate was 24 percent—high by Western standards but the lowest in sub-Saharan Africa. The conditions looked so propitious, in fact, that some activists charged that the parties involved had picked an overly easy target and that the entire scheme was little more than a publicity stunt, concocted by the drug companies in the hopes of deflecting criticism over their global pricing policies for AIDS drugs.

But it soon became apparent that even comparatively wealthy Botswana lacked sufficient health-care workers or a sound enough medical infrastructure to implement the program. The country had no medical school: all its physicians were foreign trained or immigrants. And although Botswana did have a nursing school, it still suffered an acute nursing shortage because South Africa and the United Kingdom were actively recruiting its English-speaking graduates. By 2005, the country was losing 60 percent of its newly trained health-care workers annually to emigration. (In the most egregious case, in 2004 a British-based company set up shop in a fancy Gaborone hotel and, in a single day, recruited 50 nurses to work in the United Kingdom.)

By 2002, the once-starry-eyed foreigners and their counterparts in Botswana's government had realized that before they could start handing out ARVs, they would have to build laboratories and clinics, recruit doctors from abroad, and train other health-care personnel. President Festus Mogae asked the U.S. Peace Corps to send doctors and nurses. Late in the game, in 2004, the PEPFAR program got involved and started working to keep HIV out of local hospitals' blood supplies and to build a network of HIV testing sites.

After five years of preparation, in 2005 the rollout of HIV treatment commenced. By early 2006, the program had reached its goal of treating 55,000 people (out of an estimated HIV-positive population of 280,000) with ARVs. The program is now the largest such chronic-care operation—at least per capita—in the world. And if it works, Botswana's government will be saddled with the care of these patients for decades to come—something that might be sustainable if the soil there continues to yield diamonds and the number of people newly infected with HIV drops dramatically.

But Kwame Ampomah, a Ghana-born official for the Joint UN Programme on HIV/AIDS, based in Gaborone, now frets that prevention efforts are not having much success. As of 2005, the incidence of new cases was rising eight percent annually. Many patients on ARVs may develop liver problems and fall prey to drug-resistant HIV strains. Ndwapi Ndwapi, a U.S.-trained doctor who works at Princess Marina Hospital, in Gaborone, and handles more of the government's HIV/AIDS patients than anyone else, also frets about the lack of effective prevention efforts. In slums such as Naledi, he points out, there are more bars than churches and schools combined. The community shares latrines, water pumps, alcohol—and HIV. Ndawpi says Botswana's future rests on its ability to fully integrate HIV/AIDS care into the general health-care system, so that it no longer draws away scarce doctors and nurses for HIV/AIDS-only care. If this cannot be accomplished, he warns, the country's entire health-care system could collapse.

Botswana is still clearly somewhat of a success story, but it is also a precariously balanced one and an effort that will be difficult to replicate elsewhere. Ampomah says that other countries might be able to achieve good results by following a similar model, but "it requires transparency, and a strong sense of nationalism by leaders, not tribalism. You need leaders who don't build palaces on the Riviera. You need a clear health system with equity that is not donor-driven. Everything is unique to Botswana: there is a sane leadership system in Gaborone. So in Kenya today maybe the elite can get ARVs with their illicit funds, but not the rest of the country. You need a complete package. If the government is corrupt, if everyone is stealing money, then it will not work. So there is a very limited number of African countries that could replicate the Botswana experience." And despite the country's HIV/AIDS achievements and the nation's diamond wealth, life expectancy for children born in Botswana today is still less than 34 years, according to CIA estimates.

BRAIN DRAIN

As in Haiti, even as money has poured into Ghana for HIV/AIDS and malaria programs, the country has moved backward on other health markers. Prenatal care, maternal health programs, the treatment of guinea worm, measles vaccination efforts—all have declined as the country has shifted its health-care workers to the better-funded projects and lost physicians to jobs in the wealthy world. A survey of Ghana's health-care facilities in 2002 found that 72 percent of all clinics and hospitals were unable to provide the full range of expected services due to a lack of sufficient personnel. Forty-three percent were unable to provide full child immunizations; 77 percent were unable to provide 24-hour emergency services and round-the-clock safe deliveries for women in childbirth. According to Dr. Ken Sagoe, of the Ghana Health Service, these statistics represent a severe deterioration in Ghana's health capacity. Sagoe also points out that 604 out of 871 medical officers trained in the country between 1993 and 2002 now practice overseas.

Zimbabwe, similarly, trained 1,200 doctors during the 1990s, but only 360 remain in the country today. In Kadoma, eight years ago there was one nurse for every 700 residents; today there is one for every 7,500. In 1980, the country was able to fill 90 percent of its nursing positions nationwide; today only 30 percent are filled. Guinea-Bissau has plenty of donated ARV supplies for its people, but the drugs are cooking in a hot dockside warehouse because the country lacks doctors to distribute them. In Zambia, only 50 of the 600 doctors trained over the last 40 years remain today. Mozambique's health minister says that AIDS is killing the country's health-care workers faster than they can be recruited and trained: by 2010, the country will have lost 6,000 lab technicians to the pandemic. A study by the International Labor Organization estimates that 18–41 percent of the health-care labor force in Africa is infected with HIV. If they do not receive ARV therapy, these doctors, nurses, and technicians will die, ushering in a rapid collapse of the very health systems on which HIV/AIDS programs depend.

Erik Schouten, HIV coordinator for the Malawi Ministry of Health, notes that of the country's 12 million people, 90,000 have already died from AIDS and 930,000 people are now infected with HIV. Over the last five years, the government has lost 53 percent of its health administrators, 64 percent of its nurses, and 85 percent of its physicians—mostly to foreign NGOs, largely funded by the U.S. or the British government or the Gates Foundation, which can easily outbid the ministry for the services of local health talent. Schouten is now steering a $270 million plan, supported by PEPFAR, to use financial incentives and training to bring back half of the lost health-care workers within five years; nearly all of these professionals will be put to use distributing ARVs. But nothing is being done to replace the health-care workers who once dealt with malaria, dysentery, vaccination programs, maternal health, and other issues that lack activist constituencies.

Ibrahim Mohammed, who heads an effort similar to Schouten's in Kenya, says his nation lost 15 percent of its health work force in the years between 1994 and 2001 but has only found donor support to rebuild personnel for HIV/AIDS efforts; all other disease programs in the country continue to deteriorate. Kenya's minister of health, Charity Kaluki Ngilu, says that life expectancy has dropped in her country, from a 1963 level of 63 years to a mere 47 years today for men and 43 years for women. In most of the world, male life expectancy is lower than female, but in Kenya women suffer a terrible risk of dying in childbirth, giving men an edge in survival. Although AIDS has certainly taken a toll in Kenya, Ngilu primarily blames plummeting life expectancy on former President Daniel arap Moi, who kept Kenyan spending on health down to a mere $6.50 per capita annually. Today, Kenya spends $14.20 per capita on health annually—still an appallingly low number. The country's public health and medical systems are a shambles. Over the last ten years, the country has lost 1,670 physicians and 3,900 nurses to emigration, and thousands more nurses have retired from their profession.

Data from international migration-tracking organizations show that health professionals from poor countries worldwide are increasingly abandoning their homes and their professions to take menial jobs in wealthy countries. Morale is low all over the developing world, where doctors and nurses have the knowledge to save lives but lack the tools. Where AIDS and drug-resistant TB now burn through populations like forest fires, health-care workers say that the absence of medicines and other supplies leaves them feeling more like hospice and mortuary workers than healers.

Compounding the problem are the recruitment activities of Western NGOs and OECD-supported programs inside poor countries, which poach local talent. To help comply with financial and reporting requirements imposed by the IMF, the World Bank, and other donors, these programs are also soaking up the pool of local economists, accountants, and translators. The U.S. Congress imposed a number of limitations on PEPFAR spending, including a ceiling for health-care-worker training of $1 million per country. PEPFAR is prohibited from directly topping off salaries to match government pay levels. But PEPFAR-funded programs, UN agencies, other rich-country government agencies, and NGOs routinely augment the base salaries of local staff with benefits such as housing and education subsidies, frequently bringing their employees' effective wages to a hundred times what they could earn at government-run clinics.

USAID's Kent Hill says that this trend is "a horrendous dilemma" that causes "immense pain" in poor countries. But without tough guidelines or some sort of moral consensus among UN agencies, NGOs, and donors, it is hard to see what will slow the drain of talent from already-stressed ministries of health.

GOING DUTCH?

THE MOST COMMONLY SUGGESTED solution to the problematic pay differential between the wages offered by local governments and those offered by international programs is to bolster the salaries of local officials. But this move would be enormously expensive (perhaps totaling $2 billion over the next five years, according to one estimate) and might not work, because of the problems that stem from injecting too much outside capital into local economies.

In a recent macroeconomic analysis, the UN Development Program (UNDP) noted that international spending on HIV/AIDS programs in poor countries doubled between 2002 and 2004. Soon it will have doubled again. For poor countries, this escalation means that by the end of 2007, HIV/AIDS spending could command up to ten percent of their GDPs. And that is before donors even begin to address the health-care-worker crisis or provide subsidies to offset NGO salaries.

There are three concerns regarding such dramatic escalations in external funding: the so-called Dutch disease, inflation and other economic problems, and the deterioration of national control. The UNDP is at great pains to dismiss the potential of Dutch disease, a term used by economists to describe situations in which the spending of externally derived funds so exceeds domestic private-sector and manufacturing investment that a country's economy is destabilized. UNDP officials argue that these risks can be controlled through careful monetary management, but not all observers are as sanguine.

Some analysts, meanwhile, insist that massive infusions of foreign cash into the public sector undermine local manufacturing and economic development. Thus, Arvind Subramanian, of the IMF, points out that all the best talent in Mozambique and Uganda is tied up in what he calls "the aid industry," and Steven Radelet, of the Center for Global Development, says that foreign-aid efforts suck all the air out of local innovation and entrepreneurship. A more immediate concern is that raising salaries for health-care workers and managers directly involved in HIV/AIDS and other health programs will lead to salary boosts in other public sectors and spawn inflation in the countries in question. This would widen the gap between the rich and the poor, pushing the costs of staples beyond the reach of many citizens. If not carefully managed, the influx of cash could exacerbate such conditions as malnutrition and homelessness while undermining any possibility that local industries could eventually grow and support themselves through competitive exports.

Regardless of whether these problems proliferate, it is curious that even the most ardent capitalist nations funnel few if any resources toward local industries and profit centers related to health. Ministries of health in poor countries face increasing competition from NGOs and relief agencies but almost none from their local private sectors. This should be troubling, because if no locals can profit legitimately from any aspect of health care, it is unlikely that poor countries will ever be able to escape dependency on foreign aid.

Finally, major influxes of foreign funding can raise important questions about national control and the skewing of health-care policies toward foreign rather than domestic priorities. Many governments and activists complain that the U.S. government, in particular, already exerts too much control over the design and emphasis of local HIV/AIDS programs. This objection is especially strong regarding HIV-prevention programs, with claims that the Bush administration has pushed abstinence, fidelity, and faith-based programs at the expense of locally generated condom- and needle-distribution efforts.

Donor states need to find ways not only to solve the human resource crisis inside poor countries but also to decrease their own dependency on foreign health-care workers. In 2002, stinging from the harsh criticism leveled against the recruitment practices of the NHS (the United Kingdom's National Health Service) in Africa, the United Kingdom passed the Commonwealth Code of Practice for the International Recruitment of Health Workers, designed to encourage increased domestic health-care training and eliminate recruitment in poor countries without the full approval of host governments. British officials argue that although the code has limited efficacy, it makes a contribution by setting out guidelines for best practices regarding the recruitment and migration of health-care personnel. No such code exists in the United States, in the EU more generally, or in Asia—but it should.

Unfortunately, the U.S. Congress has gone in the opposite direction, acceding to pressure from the private health-care sector and inserting immigration-control exemptions for health-care personnel into recent legislation. In 2005, Congress set aside 50,000 special immigration visas for nurses willing to work in U.S. hospitals. The set-aside was used up by early 2006, and Senator Sam Brownback (R-Kans.) then sponsored legislation eliminating all caps on the immigration of nurses. The legislation offers no compensation to the countries from which the nurses would come—countries such as China, India, Kenya, Nigeria, the Philippines, and the English-speaking Caribbean nations.

American nursing schools reject more than 150,000 applicants every year, due less to the applicants' poor qualifications than to a lack of openings. If it fixed this problem, the United States could be entirely self-sufficient in nursing. So why is it failing to do so? Because too few people want to be nursing professors, given that the salaries for full-time nurses are higher. Yet every year Congress has refused to pass bills that would provide federal support to underfunded public nursing schools, which would augment professors' salaries and allow the colleges to accept more applicants. Similar (although more complex) forms of federal support could lead to dramatic increases in the domestic training of doctors and other health-care personnel.

Jim Leach, an outgoing Republican member of the House of Representatives from Iowa, has proposed something called the Global Health Services Corps, which would allocate roughly $250 million per year to support 500 American physicians working abroad in poor countries. And outgoing Senator Bill Frist (R-Tenn.), who volunteers his services as a cardiologist to poor countries for two weeks each year, has proposed federal support for sending American doctors to poor countries for short trips, during which they might serve as surgeons or medical consultants.

Although it is laudable that some American medical professionals are willing to volunteer their time abroad, the personnel crisis in the developing world will not be dealt with until the United States and other wealthy nations clean up their own houses. OECD nations should offer enough support for their domestic health-care training programs to ensure that their countries' future medical needs can be filled with indigenous personnel. And all donor programs in the developing world, whether from OECD governments or NGOs and foundations, should have built into their funding parameters ample money to cover the training and salaries of enough new local health-care personnel to carry out the projects in question, so that they do not drain talent from other local needs in both the public and the private sectors.

WOMEN AND CHILDREN FIRST

INSTEAD OF SETTING A HODGEPODGE of targets aimed at fighting single diseases, the world health community should focus on achieving two basic goals: increased maternal survival and increased overall life expectancy. Why? Because if these two markers rise, it means a population's other health problems are also improving. And if these two markers do not rise, improvements in disease-specific areas will ultimately mean little for a population's general health and well-being.

Dr. Francis Omaswa, leader of the Global Health Workforce Alliance—a WHO-affiliated coalition—argues that in his home country of Zambia, which has lost half of its physicians to emigration over recent years, "maternal mortality is just unspeakable." When doctors and nurses leave a health system, he notes, the first death marker to skyrocket is the number of women who die in childbirth. "Maternal death is the biggest challenge in strengthening health systems," Omaswa says. "If we can get maternal health services to perform, then we are very nearly perfecting the entire health system."

Maternal mortality data is a very sensitive surrogate for the overall status of health-care systems since pregnant women survive where safe, clean, round-the-clock surgical facilities are staffed with well-trained personnel and supplied with ample sterile equipment and antibiotics. If new mothers thrive, it means that the health-care system is working, and the opposite is also true.

Life expectancy, meanwhile, is a good surrogate for child survival and essential public health services. Where the water is safe to drink, mosquito populations are under control, immunization is routinely available and delivered with sterile syringes, and food is nutritional and affordable, children thrive. If any one of those factors is absent, large percentages of children perish before their fifth birthdays. Although adult deaths from AIDS and TB are pushing life expectancies down in some African countries, the major driver of life expectancy is child survival. And global gaps in life expectancy have widened over the last ten years. In the longest-lived society, Japan, a girl who was born in 2004 has a life expectancy of 86 years, a boy 79 years. But in Zimbabwe, that girl would have a life expectancy of 34 years, the boy 37.

The OECD and the G-8 should thus shift their targets, recognizing that vanquishing AIDS, TB, and malaria are best understood not simply as tasks in themselves but also as essential components of these two larger goals. No health program should be funded without considering whether it could, as managed, end up worsening the targeted life expectancy and maternal health goals, no matter what its impacts on the incidence or mortality rate of particular diseases.

Focusing on maternal health and life expectancy would also broaden the potential impact of foreign aid on public diplomacy. For example, seven Islamic nations (Afghanistan, Egypt, Iraq, Pakistan, Somalia, Sudan, and Yemen) lose a combined 1.4 million children under the age of five every year to entirely preventable diseases. These countries also have some of the highest maternal mortality rates in the world. The global focus on HIV/AIDS offers little to these nations, where the disease is not prevalent. By setting more encompassing goals, government agencies such as USAID and its British counterpart could both save lives in these nations and give them a legitimate reason to believe that they are welcome members of the global health movement.

Legislatures in the major donor nations should consider how the current targeting requirements they place on their funding may have adverse outcomes. For example, the U.S. Congress and its counterparts in Europe and Canada have mandated HIV/AIDS programs that set specific targets for the number of people who should receive ARVs, be placed in orphan-care centers, obtain condoms, and the like. If these targets are achievable only by robbing local health-care workers from pediatric and general health programs, they may well do more harm than good, and should be changed or eliminated.

In the philanthropic world, targeting is often even narrower, and the demand for immediate empirical evidence of success is now the norm. From the Gates Foundation on down to small family foundations and individual donors, there is an urgent need to rethink the concept of accountability. Funders have a duty to establish the efficacy of the programs they support, and that may require use of very specific data to monitor success or failure. But it is essential that philanthropic donors review the relationship between the pressure they place on recipients to achieve their narrow targets and the possible deleterious outcomes for life expectancy and maternal health due to the diversion of local health-care personnel and research talent.

SYSTEMS AND SUSTAINABILITY

PERCHED ALONG THE VERDANT HILLSIDES of South Africa's Kwa-Zulu-Natal Province are tin-roofed mud-and-wood houses, so minimal that they almost seem to shiver in the winter winds. An observant eye will spot bits of carved stone laying flat among the weeds a few steps from the round houses, under which lay the deceased. The stones are visible evidence of a terrifying death toll, as this Zulu region may well have the highest HIV prevalence rate in the world.

At the top of one hill in the Vulindlela area resides Chief Inkosi Zondi. A quiet man in his early 40s, Zondi shakes his head over the AIDS horror. "We can say there are 40,000 people in my 18 subdistricts," he says. "Ten thousand have died. So about 25 percent of the population has died." In this rugged area, only about ten percent of the adults have formal employment, and few young people have much hope of a reasonable future. Funerals are the most commonplace form of social gathering. Law and order are unraveling, despite Chief Zondi's best efforts, because the police and the soldiers are also dying of AIDS.

In such a setting, it seems obvious that pouring funds into local clinics and hospitals to prevent and treat HIV/AIDS should be the top priority. For what could be more important than stopping the carnage?

But HIV does not spread in a vacuum. In the very South African communities in which it flourishes, another deadly scourge has emerged: XDR-TB, a strain of TB so horribly mutated as to be resistant to all available antibiotics. Spreading most rapidly among people whose bodies are weakened by HIV, this form of TB, which is currently almost always lethal, endangers communities all over the world. In August 2006, researchers first announced the discovery of XDR-TB in KwaZulu-Natal, and since then outbreaks have been identified in nine other South African provinces and across the southern part of the continent more generally. The emergence of XDR-TB in KwaZulu-Natal was no doubt linked to the sorry state of the region's general health system, where TB treatment was so poorly handled that only a third of those treated for regular TB completed the antibiotic therapy. Failed therapy often promotes the emergence of drug-resistant strains.

There is also an intimate relationship between HIV and malaria, particularly for pregnant women: being infected with one exacerbates cases of the other. Physicians administering ARVs in West Africa have noticed a resurgence of clinical leprosy and hepatitis C, as latent infections paradoxically surge in patients whose HIV is controlled by medicine. HIV-positive children face a greater risk of dying from vaccine-preventable diseases, such as measles, polio, and typhoid fever, if they have not been immunized than do those nonimmunized children without HIV. But if financial constraints force health-care workers to reuse syringes for a mass vaccination campaign in a community with a Vulindlela-like HIV prevalence, they will almost certainly spread HIV among the patients they vaccinate. And if the surgical instruments in clinics and hospitals are inadequately sterilized or the blood-bank system lacks proper testing, HIV can easily spread to the general population (as has happened in Canada, France, Japan, Kazakhstan, Libya, Romania, and elsewhere).

As concern regarding the threat of pandemic influenza has risen worldwide over the last two years, so has spending to bolster the capacities of poor countries to control infected animal populations, spot and rapidly identify human flu cases, and isolate and treat the people infected. It has become increasingly obvious to the donor nations that these tasks are nearly impossible to perform reliably in countries that lack adequate numbers of veterinarians, public health experts, laboratory scientists, and health-care workers. Moreover, countries need the capacity to coordinate the efforts of all these players, which requires the existence of a public health infrastructure.

At a minimum, therefore, donors and UN agencies should strive to integrate their infectious-disease programs into general public health systems. Some smaller NGOs have had success with community-based models, but this needs to become the norm. Stovepiping should yield to a far more generalized effort to raise the ability of the entire world to prevent, recognize, control, and treat infectious diseases—and then move on to do the same for chronic killers such as diabetes and heart disease in the long term. Tactically, all aspects of prevention and treatment should be part of an integrated effort, drawing from countries' finite pools of health talent to tackle all monsters at once, rather than dueling separately with individual dragons.

David de Ferranti, of the Brookings Institution, reckons that meeting serious health goals—such as getting eight million more people on ARVs while bringing life expectancies in poor countries up to at least the level of middle-income nations and reducing maternal mortality by 15–20 percent—will cost about $70 billion a year, or more than triple the current spending.

Even if such funds could be raised and deployed, however, for the increased spending to be effective, the structures of global public health provision would have to undergo a transformation.

As Tore Godal, who used to run the neglected-diseases program at the WHO, recently wrote in *Nature*, "There is currently no systemic approach that is designed to match essential needs with the resources that are actually available." He called for a strategic framework that could guide both donations and actions, with donors thinking from the start about how to build up the capabilities in poor countries in order to eventually transfer operations to local control—to develop exit strategies, in other words, so as to avoid either abrupt abandonment of worthwhile programs or perpetual hemorrhaging of foreign aid.

In the current framework, such as it is, improving global health means putting nations on the dole—a $20 billion annual charity program. But that must change. Donors and those working on the ground must figure out how to build not only effective local health infrastructures but also local industries, franchises, and other profit centers that can sustain and thrive from increased health-related spending. For the day will come in every country when the charity eases off and programs collapse, and unless workable local institutions have already been established, little will remain to show for all of the current frenzied activity.

DOC-IN-A-BOX
As a thought experiment, the Council on Foreign Relations' Global Health Program has conceived of Doc-in-a-Box, a prototype of a delivery system for the prevention and treatment of infectious diseases. The idea is to convert abandoned shipping containers into compact transportable clinics suitable for use throughout the developing world.

Shipping containers are durable structures manufactured according to universal standardized specifications and are able to be transported practically anywhere via ships, railroads, and trucks. Because of trade imbalances, moreover, used containers are piling up at ports worldwide, abandoned for scrap. Engineers at Rensselaer Polytechnic Institute converted a sample used container into a prototype Doc-in-a-Box for about $5,000, including shipping. It was wired for electricity and fully lit and featured a water filtration system, a corrugated tin roofing system

(continued next page)

DOC-IN-A-BOX *(cont'd.)*

equipped with louvers for protection during inclement weather, a newly tiled floor, and conventional doors and windows. Given economies of scale and with the conversions performed in the developing world rather than New York, it is estimated that large numbers of Doc-in-a-Boxes could be produced and delivered for about $1,500 each.

Staffed by paramedics, the boxes would be designed for the prevention, diagnosis, and treatment of all major infectious diseases. Each would be linked to a central hub via wireless communications, with its performance and inventory needs monitored by nurses and doctors.

Governments, donors, and NGOs could choose from a variety of models with customizable options, ordering paramedic training modules, supplies, and systems-management equipment as needed. Doc-in-a-Boxes could operate under a franchise model, with the paramedics involved realizing profits based on the volume and quality of their operations. Franchises could be located in areas now grossly underserved by health clinics and hospitals, thus extending health-care opportunities without generating competitive pressure for existing facilities.

On a global scale, with tens of thousands of Doc-in-a-Boxes in place, the system would be able to track and respond to changing needs on the ground. It would generate incentives to pull rapid diagnostics, easy-to-take medicines, new types of vaccines, and novel prevention tools out of the pipelines of biotechnology and pharmaceutical companies. Supplies could be purchased in bulk, guaranteeing low per-unit costs. And the sorts of Fortune 500 companies that now belong to the Global Business Coalition on HIV/AIDS, TB, and Malaria would be able to provide services and advice.

Over time, Doc-in-a-Boxes could emerge as sustainable local businesses, providing desperately needed health-care services to poor communities while generating investment and employment, like branches of Starbucks or McDonald's.

IV

Our Role:
What the United States Can Do

If Africa is of growing importance to the United States, then treating Africa as a focus of foreign policy concern is essential. The tendency in the past to treat Africa primarily as a region of "humanitarian" concern masks the other significant American interests in Africa, throwing them into the shadows or addressing them only fitfully without overall policy direction. Taking Africa seriously as a region of strategic importance will also in fact improve the ways in which the United States addresses the issues of poverty, disease, and conflict that make up much of the humanitarian concern. All too often the humanitarian issues are addressed through emergency aid, or with widely swinging areas of focus—agriculture for a period, primary education the next—lacking the long-term commitment to fundamental problems that these issues demand.

In 2005, the world had the opportunity to focus more attention on Africa than it had for many years. There were studies, commissions, public campaigns, and in the end—at the G8 Summit at Gleneagles, Scotland—major commitments made for increased aid, debt relief, and trade reform. But whether these efforts will translate into a consistent and effective partnership between the industrialized countries and Africa, and lead to a more stable and productive continent—something very much in the interests of the United States—remains to be seen. The opportunities, and the challenges, were set forth in the Council's Independent Task Force Report, *More Than Humanitarianism: A Strategic U.S. Approach Toward Africa*.

It was the Year for Africa, But We Missed the Point

In June 2005, two billion people around the world viewed the "Live 8" concerts, headed by famous rock musicians Bono and Bob Geldof, which passionately appealed for an end to poverty in Africa. A week later the leaders of eight leading industrial nations pledged to double aid to Africa, forgive the debts of fourteen of Africa's poorest countries, and bring life-saving drugs to all individuals suffering from AIDS by 2010. President George W. Bush joined in this dramatic moment, outlining how the United States would, along with others, double its aid to Africa. These were noble commitments that reflected deep humanitarian impulses. They responded to real needs in one of the world's poorest regions.

But the point that was missing—amid the music, the communiqués, and the commitments—is that Africa is becoming steadily more central to the United States and to the rest of the world in ways that transcend humanitarian interests. Africa now plays an increasingly significant role in supplying energy, preventing the spread of terrorism, and halting the devastation of HIV/AIDS. Africa's growing importance is reflected in the intensifying competition with China and other countries for both access to African resources and influence in this region. No less important, these events did not speak to how Africa continues to test the resolve of the international community and the United States to prevent

This article is excerpted from the Independent Task Force report *More Than Humanitarianism: A Strategic U.S. Approach Toward Africa.* Anthony Lake and Christine Todd Whitman, chairs; Princeton N. Lyman and J. Stephen Morrison, project directors (New York: Council on Foreign Relations Press, 2006).

mass killings and genocide, as the continuing atrocities in the Darfur region of Sudan most clearly demonstrate.

These public events also reinforced an outdated view of Africa. Not a single African leader, teacher, doctor, or nurse was featured on the Live 8 stages. Africa's leaders in all walks of life are not passive objects but active players with influence over the dynamics in their region. A core of democratically elected presidents is leading the continent in the direction of greater democracy, improved governance, and sound economic policies. Civil society workers, officials, and businesspeople are working to improve their countries at all levels of African life. This rising level of African leadership—some 40 percent of African states are electoral democracies—offers an opportunity to build strong partnerships in areas of mutual interest.

The Task Force finds that Africa is of growing strategic importance to the United States in addition to being an important humanitarian concern. In a world where economic opportunity, security threats, disease, and even support for democracy transcend borders, a policy based on humanitarian concerns alone serves neither U.S. interests nor those of Africa. Furthermore, the Task Force report finds that critical humanitarian interests would be better served by a more comprehensive U.S. approach toward Africa. In sum, it is not valid to treat Africa more as an object of charity than as a diverse continent with partners the United States can work with to advance shared objectives.

CURRENT U.S. POLICY

THERE HAS BEEN A STEADY increase in attention to Africa in both the Clinton and Bush administrations. Each president made at least one high-profile visit to the continent, each has frequently spoken publicly about Africa, and each harnessed bipartisan congressional support since the mid-1990s for steady increases in assistance and support of U.S. programs to mitigate violent conflicts.

The Bush administration launched two new assistance programs, the Millennium Challenge Account (MCA) and the President's

Emergency Plan for AIDS Relief (PEPFAR), which direct significant amounts of new resources to Africa. These two programs figure prominently in President Bush's pledge to double U.S. aid to Africa by 2010. The African Growth and Opportunity Act (AGOA) opened up more of the U.S. market to African countries as the result of a bipartisan initiative within the Congress in 2000. AGOA was welcomed and enhanced by the Clinton administration, and since that time has been supported and elaborated by the Bush administration. President Bush has made a strong commitment to eliminating subsidies and other barriers to Africa's agricultural exports, if other countries, most importantly members of the European Union (EU), do the same. Several antiterrorism programs have been initiated since 9/11, including stationing 1,200–1,800 U.S. and allied troops in Djibouti, patrolling Africa's east coast, assisting countries in tracking terrorists in the Sahel region of West Africa, and helping several countries in East Africa to enhance their intelligence capacities. The wealthy G8 member countries have agreed to a U.S. proposal to train up to 40,000 African peacekeepers to help implement negotiated peace settlements. Secretary of State Condoleezza Rice has specifically included Africa in the U.S. priority focus on enhancing democracy around the world and has singled out Zimbabwe for special attention. The Bush administration has given sustained high-level attention to resolving the civil war in Sudan, helping to establish a more legitimate broad-based government there, and addressing the vast humanitarian toll and continued threat of mass atrocities, including genocide, in Sudan's Darfur region.

At the same time, the public rhetoric surrounding Africa policy has continued to emphasize humanitarian concerns more than other multiple and rising U.S. stakes. Recent increases in U.S. aid to Africa have been primarily in emergency assistance, with long-term investments in growth essentially flat. Congress, moreover, has not followed through on earlier pledges of assistance, most recently cutting back on the president's request for the MCA. While democracy has been stated as a major objective, there are very limited funds for Africa within worldwide democracy programs, and no articulated strategy to address the major challenges to democracy that loom in the influential states of Ethiopia, Nigeria, and Uganda, or the tyranny in Zimbabwe that was singled out by Secretary Rice. Antiterrorism programs have been primarily military in nature without adequate political oversight or complementary political, public diplomacy, or economic programs. Nothing similar to the high-level attention given to Sudan has been devoted to other major conflicts that threaten the stability and economic development of major subregions, such as the civil war in the Democratic Republic of Congo (DRC), and the threat of renewed war between Ethiopia and Eritrea, where the United States had played a significant role in resolving the earlier fighting. And Darfur begs for still greater U.S. action to mobilize international support in order to secure the ground and compel a negotiated settlement.

The United States has yet to make a geopolitical shift to pay sufficient attention to West Africa's energy-rich Gulf of Guinea, where billions of dollars are changing hands with impact that is both positive and negative. U.S. policy has not responded to the implications of intensifying activity in Africa by China along with other Asian countries. This activity may have consequences not only for access to resources but perhaps more importantly for the pursuit of important U.S. objectives of good governance, protection of human rights, and sound economic policies.

CONSEQUENCES OF CONTINUING DOWN THE SAME PATH

A BROADER BASIS FOR U.S. policy toward Africa is a more sustainable one for engagement with Africa. Recent assistance and humanitarian initiatives will likely suffer without a more comprehensive elaboration of U.S. interests in Africa, both to Congress and the public. A better understanding of the challenges in Africa, as well as the positive changes taking place in African leadership, good governance, sound economic policies, and cooperation with the United States on terrorism, democracy, and trade, will bolster confidence in a deeper U.S.-Africa relationship. The consequences of not doing so are becoming apparent. Growing domestic concern over deficits and the growing cost of natural disasters, as well as the war in Iraq, is already beginning to put pressure on foreign assistance funds. Congress has reduced the president's fiscal year (FY) 2006 request for the MCA by more than half, putting into jeopardy the president's pledge to double aid to Africa by 2010. The United States has begun to pressure the United Nations to cut back on its peacekeeping operations in West Africa, largely as a cost-saving measure, even though the peace processes in that subregion are still quite fragile. Aside from assistance, eliminating U.S. subsidies and trade protection for American agricultural producers is vital to integrating Africa more fully into the global economy. Such a move will be politically difficult and must be justified on both national security as well as humanitarian grounds to overcome strong domestic opposition.

The United States must thus recognize and act on its rising national interests on the continent through a far higher mobilization of leadership and focused resources that target Africa's new realities. A business-as-usual approach will squander historic opportunities to change the course of Africa's development and advance U.S. interests. Africa's poverty will persist. Conflicts and instability will likely continue to trouble many countries. The ability of Africa to resist terrorist infiltration and extremist appeals will be weak; stability and corruption in the energy-producing states will be a cause for public concern as well as a threat to predictable production; and U.S. influence will decline. Quite remarkably, U.S.-Africa policy still retains a strong bipartisan base of support in Congress and enjoys a widening and deepening support within American society. A more robust and comprehensive policy is therefore within reach.

We will know that the response to this opportunity has failed, however, if in another ten years, U.S. policymakers link hands once again with other world leaders around Africa's problems and the world witnesses another global concert to end Africa's poverty.

The United States cannot afford to let another decade go by without effective solutions, and Africa deserves far better.

WHAT IS NEW?

AFRICA IS BECOMING MORE STRATEGICALLY IMPORTANT

Energy

AFRICA IS BECOMING MORE important because of its growing role in supplying the world with oil, gas, and nonfuel minerals. Now supplying the United States with 15 percent of oil imports, Africa's production may double in the next decade, and its capacity for natural gas exports will grow even more. In the next decade, Africa could be supplying the United States with as much energy as the Middle East.

The United States is facing intense competition for energy and other natural resources in Africa. China, India, Malaysia, North Korea, and South Korea are all becoming active in the search for these resources and for both economic and political influence on the continent. European countries and Brazil are stepping up their aid and investments as well.

China presents a particularly important challenge to U.S. interests and values. China does not share U.S. concern for issues of governance, human rights, or economic policy. For example, China combines its large stake in Sudan's oil industry with protection of the government of Sudan from UN sanctions for the ongoing attacks in Darfur.

Terrorism

Africa is becoming more important in the war on terrorism. Terrorist cells struck U.S. embassies in Kenya and Tanzania in 1998. Terrorist organizations more recently have sought refuge in West Africa's Sahel region. Africans are being recruited for terrorism in Iraq and have been implicated in the subway bombings in London.

Disease

Africa is more important today because it is the epicenter of the HIV/AIDS pandemic, which is rapidly reaching the stage where it will not only take a steadily rising death toll but will also undermine social and political stability as well as the prospects for economic progress on the continent. What the United States learns in Africa, and what it is able to achieve, will be critical to whether it is possible to stem this pandemic as it spreads across Asia and into Russia.

Global Cooperation

African states are beginning to cooperate on the global stage. For example, African nations, with nearly a third of the votes in the World Trade Organization (WTO), are in a position to provide critical support to the United States in the current world trade negotiations. At the same time, African countries, together with other developing nations, are challenging the United States and Europe to make major changes in agricultural trade practices that would enable Africa to build its export capacity and become better integrated into the world economy.

Stopping and Preventing Genocide

In Darfur, the world is once again being tested as to its readiness and willingness to halt acts of genocide and crimes against humanity. Two years into the Darfur crisis, the situation remains unresolved despite strong U.S. and other denunciations of these acts and the introduction of African peacekeepers. Over two million displaced persons continue to suffer from periodic attacks and the breakdown of humanitarian operations.

AFRICAN GOVERNANCE AND CAPACITIES ARE IMPROVING

Many African leaders have strengthened their commitment to constitutional rule, improved economic policy, good governance, and conflict resolution. While there is a long way to go before these commitments are fulfilled across the continent, several concrete steps have been taken to achieve them.

[205]

Africa has dispatched its own peacekeepers to almost all of the countries in conflict. Africans need outside assistance to maintain these deployments and to bring about an end to the most serious conflicts. However, they are prepared to act with external support and additional capacity.

Africa's most influential and capable countries (e.g., South Africa, Nigeria, Kenya, Ghana, and Senegal) are providing important leadership. Burundi is a good example, where genocide on the scale of Rwanda could have taken place. Determined South African leadership in mediating a new political consensus and the readiness of the AU to deploy peacekeepers quickly, ahead of UN forces, combine to enable the United States, Europe, and the UN to play important supportive roles, but without anywhere near as much high-level involvement and investment of resources as needed in Sudan.

BIPARTISAN SUPPORT FOR AFRICA IS GROWING IN THE UNITED STATES

Aid levels to Africa have been rising steadily since the mid-1990s, through Democratic and Republican administrations, and with bipartisan support in Congress. President Bush pledged to double aid to Africa again by 2010. AGOA, a major opening of the U.S. market to African exporters, was fashioned with bipartisan congressional support during the Clinton administration, and has been steadily expanded during the Bush administration.

The United States brought the HIV/AIDS issue to the UN Security Council in January 2000—the first time a health issue was recognized as a threat to international peace and security. In 2003, President Bush galvanized international support for addressing this pandemic with a dramatic pledge of $15 billion over five years.

Since the late 1990s, the United States has supported a steadily increased UN peacekeeping presence to contain conflicts in Africa. President Bush and the other members of the G8 have pledged under the Global Peace Operations Initiative (GPOI) to support the training of 40,000 African peacekeepers over the next five years.

In addition, the public constituency for Africa is broadening. Joining a long tradition of support for Africa from the African-American community, humanitarian organizations, and select members of Congress, an increasing number of religious groups have become engaged in African issues. Evangelical Christian groups played a leading role in galvanizing U.S. leadership in resolving Sudan's decades-long civil war. They have been active in raising public awareness of the atrocities in Darfur. Evangelical and other religious groups have become principal advocates for debt relief for poor African countries and in the fight against HIV/AIDS.

Student groups are taking up African issues. A coalition of college students created the "Save Darfur" campaign, advocating stronger U.S. action on the Darfur situation, and lobbying for divestment in the China National Petroleum Corporation (CNPC).

U.S. military commands in Europe and the Middle East have recognized the strategic role of Africa, with an emphasis on the terrorist threat in Africa and the security of energy installations. This sharply contrasts with the traditional Pentagon view that Africa has little strategic importance.

The rapidly increasing programs to combat HIV/AIDS have enlisted interest and involvement from public health schools and professional organizations, along with rising numbers of nongovernmental organizations (NGOs).

POSITIVE MOVEMENT BUT SIGNIFICANT CHALLENGES

U.S. policy has begun to respond to new realities and opportunities, but the policy is fragmented and geared more toward short-term emergencies than to long-term investments.

As noted above, the United States launched several valuable foreign assistance initiatives that are international in scope but focus particularly on Africa, such as the MCA that was scheduled to increase U.S. foreign aid worldwide by 50 percent by 2007; PEPFAR; the major trade initiative, AGOA; and a $1.2 billion malaria initiative. New programs for counterterrorism, such as the

Combined Joint Task Force in Djibouti and the Trans-Sahara Counterterrorism Initiative (TSCTI), were launched after 9/11.

Nevertheless, the slow start of the MCA and Congress's decision to cut the president's request for 2006 in half call into question the prospect for doubling aid to Africa by 2010. Almost all of the fivefold increase in U.S. aid to Africa over the past ten years has been in emergency aid, rather than in the long-term investments that could lift Africa out of poverty. Investment in Africa's agricultural development declined sharply during the 1990s, higher education programs were largely terminated in the same period, and infrastructure projects continue to be rare. Even with new initiatives aimed at humanitarian need (e.g., educational exchanges and safe drinking water), Africa often loses out to regions considered to be of greater strategic importance. President Bush's clean water initiative in FY 2000 earmarked only $1.4 million for Africa out of an $80 million program, with the balance going to Afghanistan and the Middle East.

Support for HIV/AIDS programs, which grew substantially after President Bush's $15 billion initiative, has begun to slip. At the last meeting of the Global Fund to Fight AIDS, Tuberculosis, and Malaria (hereafter the Global Fund), only half the required funds for the coming year were pledged.

U.S. diplomatic presence in several of the energy-producing and other critically important countries is minimal. There is no ambassadorial presence in Khartoum; no American diplomatic presence in northern Nigeria, home to Africa's largest Muslim population, which exceeds 60 million persons; and none along the Mombasa coast in Kenya, where terrorist cells persist. Political oversight of the counterterrorist programs is insufficient. The Pan Sahel Initiative (PSI) worked with two regimes, Mauritania and Chad, without sufficient U.S. attention to either country's poor human rights and governance records.

The direction of U.S.-Africa policy and programs is fragmented. There are three separately administered major foreign assistance programs operating in Africa. Antiterrorist programs are being directed by three separate military commands. The National Security Council (NSC) has not taken sufficient lead on global energy issues in a way that would focus attention on Africa's growing role and the attendant challenges it creates. Peacekeeping programs are underbudgeted and divided between separate bureaus and departments.

SHAPING A MORE COMPREHENSIVE AFRICA POLICY

THE GUIDING PREMISE OF THIS report is that Africa is of strategic as well as humanitarian importance to the United States. The long-standing emphasis on humanitarian interest outside this broader context serves neither African nor U.S. interests today. Failure to broaden the basis for U.S. policy will make it exceedingly difficult, in the face of growing budget pressures in the United States, to maintain and deepen promising commitments for development, HIV/AIDS, and security initiated in the past several years. The recent congressional cutback of MCA funding and shortfalls in support of UN peacekeeping are harbingers of this danger.

The Task Force believes it is critical to develop a new, comprehensive U.S. policy toward Africa that maintains the historic and principled concern for humanitarian issues, while broadening the basis for U.S. engagement. Such a comprehensive policy should place Africa squarely in the mainstream of U.S. global policy objectives. The Task Force recommends that the United States advance a policy to help integrate Africa more fully into the global economy. The new policy would also mean making Africa an active partner in U.S. programs to assure safe and reliable supplies of energy for the world market, combat terrorism, reduce conflict, control pandemic diseases, and enlarge the worldwide community of democracies.

This is a big agenda. Africa policy is made even more challenging by the fact there are forty-eight countries in sub-Saharan Africa with quite different circumstances, influence, and potential. At the same time, many of the most challenging problems, such as disease, conflict, and terrorist activity, extend across borders, demanding both bilateral and regional responses. Sometimes the most disturbing crises occur in countries not thought of as strategically important. Rwanda in 1994 was such a case, where the crisis and the ensuing genocide touched the most basic values of the American people.

But the growing African capacity and willingness to lead on many of these issues, the bipartisan support that can be mobilized for a more comprehensive policy, and the partners with whom the United States can share responsibility make this challenge manageable. Several of these policy objectives are also mutually reinforcing. Integrating Africa more fully into the global economy, and helping various states to overcome conflict, will strengthen African states and their societies' resistance to extremism and terrorism. Better use of oil and gas proceeds will enhance stability and increase the ability of influential states like Nigeria and Angola to contribute to peace, growth, and stability throughout the continent. Moreover, the alternative to a comprehensive policy is to go along, as in the past, with admirable but insufficient programs, with the high probability that Africa will remain outside the mainstream of the world economy, still poor and heavily dependent upon aid, and still vulnerable to instability and future crises with possible genocidal dimensions. All the new and vital U.S. interests in Africa would suffer. The United States can do much better, and must, for its own sake. The Task Force has identified the following priorities and goals as integral to a comprehensive Africa policy.

Integrate Africa into the Global Economy

Trade reform is one of the most critical priorities if Africa is to grow and become more fully integrated into the global economy. The G8 leaders' pledge to double aid is welcome and can be used to bolster Africa's economic and social condition. But this commitment alone will not fully integrate Africa into the global economy or reduce aid dependency by the end of the next decade. It will not address the fundamental problems of poverty or conflict that wrack the continent today.

Together with adequate technical assistance and trade reform within Africa, the elimination of U.S. and European barriers to Africa's agricultural exports could add hundreds of millions of dollars annually to African earnings, reduce substantially rural poverty, and place many countries on the path to self-sufficiency. The United States should follow through on the president's commitment at the UN to eliminate all tariff and subsidy barriers in agricultural trade if other nations do so, by urging all the members of the WTO to set firm timetables for going down this path. The current Doha trade round is the crucial period for doing this, and the opportunity should not be lost.

Reform and Prioritize U.S. Assistance

In doubling aid, consistent long-term commitments of non-emergency assistance are needed. The United States should fulfill the president's pledge at the 2005 G8 Summit to double U.S. aid to Africa by 2010, but with an emphasis on aid for long-term investments in growth and development, not counting emergency aid that may be necessary during that time period.

Increases in aid should give consistent attention, not just for five but for ten to twenty years, to development areas where the United States has special strength and that address some of Africa's most important needs: agricultural development; private sector facilitation; science and technology; HIV/AIDS, malaria, and children's health needs; education; population; a sustainable environment; and—in support of all of these—democratization.

These programs should all emphasize building and supporting African leadership, institutions, and expertise, involving African governments, civil society, the New Partnership for Africa's Development (NEPAD), and the AU. Democracy is making progress across Africa, but the United States needs to focus especially on influential states where the democratic process is under stress. Special attention should thus be paid over the next two years to supporting constitutionally based political transitions and electoral processes in Nigeria, Sudan, Uganda, and Ethiopia. Success in those countries will reinforce the AU's ability to promote democracy more broadly. The United States should also help build AU institutions for enforcing human rights. To combat deeply ingrained patterns of corruption, which are major obstacles to development and democracy, the United States and European countries should provide strong support to African anticorruption efforts through assistance to civil society, advocacy organizations, and through help in both criminal investigations and recovery of illegally obtained assets.

Population programs must be restored to their earlier priority. Ideological issues and shifting of attention to HIV/AIDS have led to a diminution of U.S. leadership in this area. Yet the demographic projections in Africa should give the United States serious concern. Famine-prone countries like Ethiopia and Niger have doubled their population in the past two decades and the projections suggest further sharp increases in the future. In particular, the social and political impact of the growing youth bulge should garner more attention to population policy, as this bulge presages more conflict, unemployment, and potential recruitment for extremist activity.

The United States needs to urge the World Bank to develop a more coordinated strategy for overall donor assistance to Africa that will reduce overlap, assure consistent attention to all key sectors, and relieve some of the administrative problems burdening developing countries. Presidential and congressional leadership is required to reduce the heavy U.S. reliance on its own procedures, the many "earmarks" in the aid legislation that limit U.S. flexibility, and the resistance to allowing other donors to lead and coordinate policies in various sectors. The United States should support greatly expanding the UN emergency reserve fund of both food and funding so that recurring natural calamities such as drought do not turn into full-blown famines, which then demand the highest level of U.S. policy attention and massive emergency responses.

Confront the True Scale and Complexity of the HIV/AIDS Pandemic

Strong presidential leadership, well beyond this administration, will be needed to fulfill not only the $15 billion commitment under PEPFAR but the even greater amount of resources needed in the decades ahead. The commitment by the G8 in 2005 to see that all those in need worldwide have access to treatment represents an enormous commitment to future funding that has yet to be calculated. The United Nations Programme on HIV/AIDS

(UNAIDS), however, projects a 50 percent increase in requirements in just the next four years.

The United States must mobilize other donors to commit to a rising level of support for HIV/AIDS programs as the pandemic reaches major proportions across the continent. In particular, the United States must press other countries to meet two-thirds of the required budget for the Global Fund. Congress has limited the U.S. contribution to one-third of what is pledged.

Other donors should also be urged to fund the broader health infrastructure needed in Africa to complement the U.S. focus on emergency programs and HIV/AIDS-specific delivery systems. Donors, host governments, and the private sector need to come together to develop new, more appropriate models for delivery of health services in the poorer and most affected countries. The shortage of skilled health workers and infrastructure, aggravated by the recruitment of African doctors and nurses by developed countries, is one of the major limiting factors in delivering HIV/AIDS programs as well as addressing Africa's other critical health needs.

Along with other donors and African countries, the United States must give greater attention to prevention, or else the pandemic will constantly run ahead of the international community's ability to bring it under control. Ideological differences must be set aside and support given to all those prevention programs that work, including Abstinence, Be faithful, use Condoms (ABC). Much more research is needed on how to change social behavior, including gender dynamics, and more African leadership needs to be mobilized behind that objective. New approaches must be developed to increase testing, as the vast majority of those believed to be infected do not know they have the virus and are thus not accessible for counseling or treatment.

Promote a Reliable Supply of Energy from Africa

A geopolitical shift is needed in U.S. energy policy. The United States should establish a U.S.-Africa energy forum, at the cabinet or subcabinet level, to promote regional cooperation and to discuss shared problems of security, transparency, and marketing. The

United States should upgrade its diplomatic presence in energy-producing countries, especially in the Niger Delta region, Equatorial Guinea, and São Tomé and Príncipe. Cabinet-level visits to energy-producing states should be undertaken more often.

Nigeria, Angola, Chad, Equatorial Guinea, São Tomé and Príncipe, Gabon, and Cameroon will soon be joined by Mauritania, and perhaps Namibia and South Africa, as well as states along Africa's east coast, as energy producers. Oil and gas can provide much-needed earnings for these countries to address the needs of their people. But oil has too often been a curse, leading to corruption, waste, environmental degradation, decline of the nonenergy sectors of the economy, and unrest. A reliable and responsible policy for assuring the supply of energy from these states therefore requires not only investment in production facilities, which the private sector will do, but encouraging responsible use of oil and gas proceeds by the producing states. Few of these states will qualify for the MCA or traditional forms of aid. The United States should therefore utilize other sources of aid (e.g., the Economic Support Fund) to provide training, education, democratization programs, and security assistance, and to develop public-private partnerships to build infrastructure. Strong support should be given to civil society groups to advocate for greater transparency by the government in the use of energy proceeds and for better investment in development, environmental protection, and job creation for people in oil-producing areas.

Military assistance should be provided to help states in the Gulf of Guinea improve security of coastal environments and develop regional maritime security programs. Security assistance and intelligence sharing should be provided to combat the large-scale theft of oil, arms trafficking, and money laundering that fuel violent instability in the Niger Delta region. A recently announced program between the United States and Nigeria for this purpose is a positive development.

Build Security Against Failed States and Other Sources of Terrorism

The president has already indicated that failing states are potential breeding grounds for terrorism. Africa, however, does not receive sufficient political attention on the threat or sufficient funding to combat it.

The Department of State should exert more political oversight of counterterrorism programs to avoid collusion or unintended support of repressive regimes, as happened in Mauritania. Special attention must be paid to human rights concerns, the misuse of the terrorist label to punish legitimate opposition, and the use of the military for oppression of ethnic or religious groups.

The United States needs to rebuild its intelligence capabilities in Africa to understand better the dimensions of the threat, the sources of unrest, the warning signs of collapse, and the most appropriate forms of U.S. response, whether economic, cultural, political, or military. Nigeria and Somalia are examples of where such intelligence is badly needed.

More funding for Africa should be added to the president's Transitional Initiative for fragile and post-conflict states. Currently, $275 million out of a total of $325 million is designated for four countries: Afghanistan, Ethiopia, Haiti, and Sudan. This leaves insufficient funding for fragile countries in Africa such as the DRC, Liberia, Sierra Leone, Angola, Burundi, Rwanda, and the Central African Republic. The Transitional Initiative can fund democratization, civil society, civil security, and conflict resolution programs, all of which are essential in these states.

The administration has proposed for FY 2006 an expanded program of education and exchanges for countries with significant Muslim populations. But only the trans-Sahel region of Africa is mentioned, though this program would be valuable in many other African countries as well.

The U.S. Agency for International Development (USAID) should reverse the 1995 decision to close its missions in Niger, Chad, and other African states that are now important to the war on terrorism. These are the very states where U.S. European Command (EUCOM) is providing military assistance, but where broader development programs would be equally, if not more, important.

Roaming bands of former militia and child soldiers pose a specific threat to stability and are a ripe source of recruitment for rebels and terrorist groups. Peacekeeping budgets need to be expanded to cover the costs of Disarmament, Demobilization, and Reintegration (DDR) programs for ex-combatants in post-conflict countries. Currently these programs are inadequately funded through sundry bilateral and multilateral sources and, when funded, the financing often arrives too late to achieve the successful integration of ex-combatants. Liberia, Sierra Leone, and the DRC are prime examples of where more funding is urgently needed.

Dedicate High-Level Leadership to Reducing Conflict

High-level attention from the White House and senior officials in the Department of State must be given to resolving major conflicts in Africa, especially those that threaten whole subregions or involve large-scale atrocities. Africans have taken a strong leadership position in bringing conflicts to an end, but they often lack the political influence, the resources, and the peacekeeping capacity to do it alone. The success of U.S. interventions can be seen from their use in bringing an end to the Ethiopia-Eritrea war in 2000 and, most recently, the civil war in Sudan.

Such attention should be now devoted to the DRC, where some four million people have died, civil strife continues, and the peace process is extremely precarious. Two other targets for such attention are the continuing tension between Ethiopia and Eritrea, where U.S. counterterrorism interests are affected; and the still-fragile peace processes in Liberia and Sierra Leone. A return to conflict in either country could engulf the whole West Africa subregion. Budgeting and funding of UN peacekeeping need reform. The administration's budget requests to Congress do not take into account even known new peacekeeping operations, let alone allow for rapid support in fast-breaking crises. For example, full U.S. funding is not yet available for the anticipated UN mission to Sudan, which may be one of the largest ever, and which may have to be expanded further to address the crisis in Darfur. Recently, the United States opposed the UN secretary-general's request for an expansion of the UN peacekeeping force in the DRC in advance of elections there, as well as the extension of the full UN peacekeeping mission in Liberia past March 2006, largely for budgetary reasons.

In both the DRC and Liberia, the U.S. position risks weakening the peace process. Such reasoning also undermines effective peacekeeping and efforts to meet UN mandates with adequate capacities.

The budgets and policy direction for U.S. bilateral support for African peacekeeping also need reform. They are divided among several programs, departments, and bureaus to a degree that makes both long-term planning and the assessment of the total resources being devoted to this objective difficult. Policy direction should be consolidated at a sufficiently high level in the Department of State, and plans made for both short- and long-term programs. For example, the president's commitment under the GPOI to train up to 40,000 African peacekeepers over five years is a major positive step. But funding requests beyond FY 2005, when funding was obtained from the Department of Defense, do not provide sufficient funds to keep this program on track. It is also not clear how the needed increases in funding for the crisis in Darfur will affect GPOI's funding or from what source such funding will be found at all.

Prevent Future Atrocities

Failure to prevent the genocide in Rwanda was a major moral failure for the international community. The loss of life was horrific. It was also a political failure, lowering the credibility of the international community's readiness to live up to its commitments under the Convention on the Prevention and Punishment of the Crime of Genocide and the promises of "Never Again." The genocide also touched off the instability and warfare that has engulfed Central Africa ever since.

Nevertheless, the ongoing fighting in Darfur represents another deeply disturbing instance of genocidal acts and crimes against humanity. President Bush wrote "Not on my watch," when he read of the earlier Rwanda debacle. As a result, the United States condemned the killings in Darfur as genocide, urging strong UN actions against the government of Sudan and, along with the EU, assisting the deployment of an African peacekeeping force. Currently, Deputy Secretary of State Robert Zoellick is devoting his personal attention to the issue and has assigned Roger Winter, special envoy for Darfur, to help resolve this crisis and work on the other aspects of peace in Sudan. Yet, two years and as many as 100,000 deaths later, the international response remains woeful. More than two million people remain displaced from their homes, subject to periodic attack, and without sufficient protection by either AU or other peacekeepers. Meanwhile, the government of Sudan, the sponsor of the acts that the United States and the UN have condemned, remains free of serious sanctions.

The United States must press for urgent international action. First, the AU must be convinced that, despite its efforts to do so, it is not capable of mobilizing and deploying the full 13,000 peacekeepers it has promised. The AU is concerned about losing credibility if it seeks outside help in deployment and command. But it risks an even worse loss of credibility if the situation continues to deteriorate. The AU should request that the UN authorize a coalition of willing countries to provide a protective force, including some from Africa, for the internally displaced persons within Sudan. This coalition could serve as a bridging force to UN "blue helmets" (i.e., UN soldiers). The need is urgent and only a non-UN coalition could deploy rapidly enough to meet the current need. The force should have a mandate to defend the population against further attacks and to take military action, as necessary, to counter the threat. This includes enforcing the no-fly zone against the government of Sudan. An AU request would moreover serve to override previous Sudanese objections to a non-African force.

The UN Security Council remains blocked by the Chinese and Russians from imposing strong sanctions against the government of Sudan. The United States and its European partners should begin to impose further sanctions of their own on companies doing business in Sudan and on arms shipments to Sudan, and should even consider ways to inhibit Sudanese oil exports. China should be put on notice that continued blocking of UN sanctions is a serious issue for the United States, and that U.S. and European sanctions are in the works. China should be made aware that this issue could well provoke a serious confrontation between China and the United States.

The rebel forces continue to be part of the problem. Now splintered and without a clearly defined political agenda, they are poorly equipped to participate in the negotiations to end the conflict hosted by the AU. Rebel forces are increasingly guilty of attacking aid workers and stealing humanitarian supplies. The United States, together with interested European countries, must continue to engage the rebels on these matters, as Deputy Secretary Zoellick began doing in Nairobi, and provide technical assistance to them for political negotiations. The United States must also take a strong position against further attacks on humanitarian missions. The United States should make great efforts with Eritrea, Chad, and factions in southern Sudan to cease material support to the rebels and to help guide the rebels to a more constructive negotiating position.

The United States should press southern Sudanese leaders, now members of the central government, to take a much more active role in stopping government attacks in Darfur. Southern attention to Darfur has declined with the death of former Sudan People's Liberation Movement (SPLM) leader John Garang. The United States should condition the delivery of the large amounts of aid pledged to southern Sudan on active southern involvement in achieving a negotiated settlement in Darfur.

The Darfur crisis is part of a larger situation in Sudan in which the Khartoum government has failed to share power and resources with outlying regions. Both northern and southern members of the government of Sudan should be put on notice that, without broadening representation in the government and sharing resources with marginalized areas of the country like Darfur and eastern Sudan, the United States will not provide the full political or economic support promised under the Comprehensive Peace Agreement, signed in January 2005, which ended the north-south civil war.

Beyond Darfur

Neither the United States nor the UN has developed an adequate system for preventing or even containing such calamities in the future. Article 8 of the Genocide Convention, an injunction to prevent genocide, is the most important responsibility in the convention, much more so than acting after genocide has happened.

The United States should actively seek agreement that the UN secretary-general be charged with bringing to the attention of the Security Council evidence of impending large-scale atrocities, whether or not to be formally labeled as genocide, as clear threats to international peace and security. The new UN special adviser on the prevention of genocide, now a part-time post with a limited mandate, should be charged with, at the early stage of such crises, assembling reports of mass killings or impending disasters from official and nonofficial sources; convening as necessary those with field knowledge; evaluating the evidence; and reporting to the secretary-general on the need for bringing the matter urgently to the Security Council.

As with Darfur, the United States and its allies must be ready to take appropriate action, including sanctions and, if necessary, military intervention, if the Security Council is blocked from doing so.

Answer China's Challenge

The United States has to recognize that there is a new playing field in Africa that requires new resources and more active diplomacy. To compete more effectively with China, the United States must provide more encouragement and support to well-performing African states, develop innovative means for U.S. companies to compete, give high-level attention to Africa, and engage China on those practices that conflict with U.S. interests. Specifically:

- The MCA should begin to provide dramatically higher levels of assistance to African states performing well in governance, human rights, and development policies, in contrast to China's assistance packages that ignore these criteria. Congress must be persuaded to fully fund the projected increases for the MCA, with half of MCA's funding going to Africa.
- Presidential and other high-level visits are important and should include a presidential visit to the AU, where emphasis

can be placed on its support for good governance and sound development policies.

- The United States should develop public-private partnerships, utilizing the Export-Import Bank (EX-IM Bank), the Overseas Private Investment Corporation (OPIC), and USAID, in combinations that would enable the United States and U.S. companies to participate and compete more effectively for infrastructure and other projects needed in Africa.

- The United States should engage China on "rules of the road" in Africa, to end support for egregious violators of human rights, reduce incentives for corruption, protect the environment, improve the long-term prospects for stability, and reduce unfair business practices. Deputy Secretary Zoellick's broaching with China its protection of "rogue states," in September 2005, and Assistant Secretary of State for African Affairs Jendayi E. Frazer's discussions in China later in the year, are good steps in this direction.

- The United States should also look to cooperate with China in Africa on programs where both countries are active, especially health and peacekeeping.

Improve Policy Direction and Coordination

Implementing a complex and multifaceted policy requires high-level attention along with the necessary multiplicity of program instruments. At present, the programmatic instruments are not sufficiently led and coordinated to achieve maximum impact, nor do they constitute a balanced application of political, economic, and security assets.

There are various ways in which the government might be strengthened to provide more coordinated policy direction and to assure that there is sustained support for multiyear funding for development and security programs, and trade reform. This could be done through one or more of the following: a stronger NSC role in chairing an Africa policy committee, the creation of new high-level positions to coordinate critical parts of the policy (e.g., energy, postconflict stabilization and reconstruction, and joint military command structures), or by elevating the responsibilities and staff resources of the Department of State specifically charged with Africa policy. The Task Force does not recommend any one of these over another, but urges the U.S. government to give high priority to improving coordination through these or other means.

The United States should appoint a fully accredited ambassador to the AU. The United States has taken this step with nearly every other regional organization (e.g., the North Atlantic Treaty Organization [NATO], the Organization of American States [OAS], the Association of South East Asian Nations [ASEAN], and the EU) to the considerable benefit of U.S. foreign policy interests. Such an appointment, if given adequate authority and staff support, will help ensure consistency in the U.S. approach, signal the seriousness of U.S. purpose, and allow a single focal point for U.S. engagement on both immediate priorities and long-term challenges facing the AU. Also, it will provide additional valuable oversight of the multiple streams of U.S. assistance to the AU.

The several congressional committees that address African issues must be partners in the development and oversight of a new Africa policy. These committees will need to provide consistent, long-term support to both the development and security programs discussed in this report. The plethora of earmarks and restrictive conditions that are present in most aid legislation should be reduced, or at least consolidated, in ways that are consistent with the broad and comprehensive approach to Africa that this report recommends. Congress should also provide the executive branch with a peacekeeping emergency reserve that would allow the administration, with appropriate consultation with Congress, to respond rapidly to new or expanding demands in conflict situations.

Trade reform will demand exceptional and farsighted leadership in Congress. Hearings on Africa, including those on security interests and on the role Africa plays in the overall trade negotiations important to the United States, should help in garnering support for ways to reduce U.S. agricultural support programs and tariffs with appropriate adjustment assistance to affected farm communities.

A UNIQUE OPPORTUNITY

THIS "YEAR OF AFRICA" provides an exceptional opportunity to turn all the attention, and the added resources that may flow from it, into a far more comprehensive and effective policy toward Africa. It could lead to a deeper understanding of U.S. interests in Africa and to a more comprehensive and productive long-term policy. Or it could be but a superficial, passing phase for U.S. policy, a feel-good era of promises, in which the United States fails to grasp the deeper shifts that are occurring and fails to graduate to a more coherent, strategic approach to Africa, backed by adequate human and financial resources.

The newer, broader approach this report advocates requires high-level leadership—the voices of the president, the secretary of state, and others—articulating a new integrated vision of how to advance U.S. interests in Africa. The vision must encompass Africa's growing importance to the United States—in energy, security, global health, and trade. It must impart to the American people a sense of commitment to addressing U.S. interests more effectively, including embarking upon a long-term commitment to helping achieve a fundamental improvement in Africa's place in the world. The vision must recognize the changing playing field in which the West's interests are being challenged, especially by a strongly competitive China and other fast-growing economies in Asia. This vision must make clear the diversity of Africa and the positive changes taking place that make wisely planned, increased investment there much more likely to be successful.

With this vision, the year of Africa can be a turning point; not a passing phase, but rather the beginning of a serious long-term commitment to achieving the United States' and Africa's best interests.

Endnotes

Nigeria: Elections and Continuing Challenges

1. About 54 percent of Nigerian oil exports go to the United States, 10 percent to Brazil.

2. Peter M. Lewis, "Getting the Politics Right: Governance and Economic Failure in Nigeria," in Robert I. Rotberg (ed.), *Crafting the New Nigeria: Confronting the Challenges* (Boulder, 2004), p. 121.

3. HDI measures life expectancy, educational attainment and literacy, adjusted real income, and standards of living.

4. Daniel J. Smith, "HIV/AIDS in Nigeria: the Challenges of a National Epidemic," in Rotberg, p. 200.

5. World Health Organization, WHO Report 2006: Global Tuberculosis Control: Surveillance, Planning, Financing, WHO/HTM/TB/2006.362 (Geneva, 2006).

South Africa in Retrospect

1. Study Commission on U.S. Policy Toward South Africa, *South Africa: Time Running Out*, Berkeley, University of California Press, 1986.

2. Marq de Villiers, *White Tribe Dreaming* (New York: Penguin Books, 1987), p. 361.

3. Trevor Huddleston, *Return to South Africa* (London: Fount Paperbacks), p. 138.

4. Stephen John Stedman, ed., *South Africa: The Political Economy of Transformation* (Boulder, CO: Lynne Rienner, 1994), pp. 12–13, 24, 187–88.

5. R.W. Johnson, "When That Great Day Comes," *London Review of Books*, July 22, 1993, p. 9.

6. Stedman, p. 38.

7. Princeton N. Lyman, *Partner to History: The U.S. Role in South Africa's Transition to Democracy* (Washington, DC: United States Institute of Peace, 2002), p. 257.

8. Quoted on O'Malley, p. 133.

9. *IMF Executive Board Concludes Article IV Consultations with South Africa*, Public Information Notice No. 06/102, September 7, 2006.

10. Trevor Manuel, Minister of Finance, *Budget Speech 2006*, pp. 4–5.

11. Ibid, p. 4.

12. Stedman, pp. 37–38.

13. Padraig O'Malley, ed., *Southern Africa: The People's Voices* (Cape Town: National Democratic Institute of International Affairs, 1999), p. 117.

14. Ibid, p. 130.

15. Ibid, p.151.

16. Ibid, p. 162.

17. Quoted in Ibid, p. 174. For polls on jobs and other issues, see pp. 188, 190.

18. Ibid, p. a58.

19. *Department of Trade and Industry Deputy Minister Thabethe Addresses in South Africa*, September 20, 2005.

20. *AIDS Analysis Africa*, Southern Africa Edition, Rivonia, South Africa, Aug./Sept. 1994, p. 2.

21. Amnesty International, *Summary of South Africa, 2004.* http://web.amnesty.org/web.nsf/print/2004-zaf.summary-eng.

22. Stedman, p. 148.

23. O'Malley, Ibid, p. 194.

Zimbabwe: The Limits of Influence

1. Actually Zimbabwe quit the Commonwealth after having been suspended.

2. Richard Joseph, ed., *State, Conflict, and Democracy in Africa* (Boulder, Co.: Lynne Rienner, 1999), pp. 244–45, 259–61. See also "Zimbabwe: Fast Track Land Reform in Zimbabwe," Human Rights Watch, March 2002.

3. For analyses of Zimbabwe's recent elections see the reports of the International Crisis Group, especially *Post-Election Zimbabwe: What Next?*, Africa Report No. 93, June 7, 2005. The ICG concludes that in the election of March 2005, through a range of legal and extralegal means, the election was decided well before the first voter reached the polls.

4. Michael Clemens and Todd Moss, *Costs and Causes of Zimbabwe's Crisis*, Center for Global Development CGD Notes, July 2005, pp. 1, 4.

5. These include references to "the gay government of the gay United Kingdom." Ibid, p. 2.

6. Ibid.

7. Ibid, p. 4.

8. Stephen Collinson, "Bush hardens line on Zimbabwe," slamming Mugabe's "Bad Governance." *Agence France Press*, July 23, 2003, http://www/nexis/com/research/search/documentDiplay?_m = 7ee3a. The article notes that while Bush made some harsh statements about Zimbabwe in his stop in Botswana, he did not repeat them in South Africa.

Endnotes

9. Anna Kajumulo Tibaijuka, "Report of the Fact-Finding Mission to Zimbabwe to Assess the Scope and Impact of Operation Murambatsvina by the UN Special Envoy on Human Settlements Issues in Zimbabwe," United Nations, July 2005.

10. Richard Williamson, "African Leaders' Condemnation," *Chicago Sun-Times,* January 23, 2006, p. 39.

11. "IMF insincere, Says Zimbabwe state media," *Business Day,* February 10, 2006, www.businessday.co.za/PrintFriendly.aspx?ID = BD4A145921.

12. Todd Moss and Stewart Patrick, *The Day After Comrade Bob: Applying Post-Conflict Recovery Lessons to Zimbabwe.*

Darfur and Beyond: What Is Needed to Prevent Mass Atrocities

1. A recent Zogby survey found that 70 percent of the public supports the U.S. implementation of a no-fly zone over Darfur to prevent aerial attacks on civilians. Additionally, 62 percent of Americans agree that the United States "has a responsibility to help stop the killing in the Darfur region," and 58 percent believe more can be done diplomatically in order to help end the crisis in Sudan. The broad support among Americans for action in Sudan is consistent with findings observed in previous polls by the Program on International Policy Attitudes (PIPA). In 2005, a PIPA survey revealed that a majority of the public (71 percent) supported NATO and U.S. involvement in Sudan by providing assistance to the African Union peacekeeping force in Darfur. See, http://www.globalsolutions.org/programs/glob_engage/news/Zogby_poll_march06.html, http://www.worldpublicopinion.org/pipa/articles/brafricara/71.php?nid = &id = &pnt = 71&lb = bthr, and http://www.worldpublicopinion.org/pipa/articles/btjusticehuman_rightsra/110.php?nid = &id = &pnt = 110&lb = bthr.

2. International Crisis Group (ICG), "Getting the UN into Darfur," *Africa Briefing* No. 43. Nairobi/Brussels, October 12, 2006; Joseph Loconte, "The Failure to Protect: Lessons from Darfur," *The American Interest,* Vol. 2, No. 3, January/February 2007.

3. Gérard Prunier, *Darfur: The Ambiguous Genocide* (Ithaca: Cornell University Press, 2005), p. 100.

4. Ibid, p. 91.

5. Jan Egeland, "Briefing to the Security Council," UN Department of Public Information, November 22, 2006.

6. Kofi A. Annan, "Report of the Secretary-General on Darfur," S/2006/591, July 28, 2006, p. 16.

7. Alex de Waal, "I Will Not Sign," *London Review of Books,* Vol. 28, No. 23, November 30, 2006.

8. France, Italy, and Germany dispatched troops quickly, speeding the initial deployment of troops to an expanded UNIFIL operation.

9. Morton Abramowitz, "A New Tact on Darfur," *The Washington Post,* October 23, 2006.

10. The ICG report, "Getting the UN into Darfur," identifies a series of economic sanctions and other penalties to pursue.

11. Sudan lacks the capability to fly into Darfur from bases in the south, so it is possible to limit the most likely sources of attacks.

12. See Loconte, "The Failure to Protect: Lessons from Darfur."

13. Newt Gingrich and George Mitchell, *American Interests and UN Reform: A Report of the Congressional Task Force on the United Nations* (Washington, DC: United States Institute of Peace, 2005), p. 4.

Avoiding Conflict in the Horn of Africa: U.S. Policy Toward Ethiopia and Eritrea

1. International Crisis Group, *Ethiopia and Eritrea: Preventing War*, Africa Report No. 101, December 22, 2005, p. i.

2. "Eritrea Says Troops in Buffer Zone to Harvest Crops," Agence France-Press, October 17, 2006.

3. Martin Plaut, "Crisis Talks over Horn Border Row," BBC News, June 15, 2006.

4. Statement by the Development Assistance Group, Addis Ababa, November 11, 2005.

5. U.S. Department of State, press statement, "Political Dissent and Due Process in Ethiopia," January 6, 2006.

6. "World Bank Resumes Aid to Ethiopia," Reuters, July 12, 2006.

Additional Resources

The Council's website—CFR.org—is the premier online resource on international affairs and U.S. foreign policy. The site is a valuable tool for staying abreast of current events, even when "under the radar." In addition to a wide range of Council material—including work from the Council's Studies Program, interviews with experts, meeting transcripts, and articles—users will find analysis and documents from other sources that have been carefully selected by the website's editorial staff for their relevance and quality. These editorial franchises include the popular Backgrounder Q&As, Expert Interviews, Daily Analysis, News Briefings, and Online Debates. In addition, the site includes Podcast audio interviews on selected topics, the *Daily Brief* email newsletter offering a roundup of world news every morning, and Crisis Guides, information-rich multimedia interactives offering a unique perspective on some of the most pressing international issues.

To explore some of these specific resources and to learn more about Africa, visit the following sites on CFR.org:

- Africa Regional Page: http://www.cfr.org/region/143/africa.html—this webpage offers all the latest and most relevant Council material on Africa.
- Darfur Multimedia Crisis Guide: an interactive look at the crisis in Darfur using graphics and other multimedia.

The full texts of all Council publications are also available on CFR.org for downloading. The publications posted on the site and excerpted in this volume include:

- Independent Task Force reports: consensus documents on U.S. foreign policy developed through private and nonpartisan deliberations. Two articles excerpted in this book come from the Task Force report *More Than Humanitarianism*.

- Council Special Reports: concise policy briefs that provide timely responses to developing crises or contributions to current policy dilemmas. Because a Special Report can be prepared quickly, it can have an impact when changing events create a space for useful involvement. Previous Council Special Reports about Africa have addressed elections in Nigeria, mass atrocities in Darfur, and conflict in the Horn of Africa. For a complete list of all Council publications go to www.cfr.org/publications.

Since 1922, the Council has published *Foreign Affairs*, America's most influential publication on international affairs and foreign policy. It is more than a magazine—it is the international forum of choice for the most important new ideas, analysis, and debate on the most significant issues in the world. Inevitably, articles published in *Foreign Affairs* shape the political dialogue for years to come. The website for *Foreign Affairs* (www.foreignaffairs.org) offers a collection of old and new articles. For those on Africa, please visit the Africa Regional Page: http://www.foreignaffairs.org/gs/africa.html.

For more information about the Caravan project, please visit its website: www.caravanbooks.org.

About the Contributors

PATRICIA DORFF is director of publishing at the Council on Foreign Relations, a position she has held since 1995. Previously she was associate editor for *Foreign Affairs* magazine and editor of the *Foreign Affairs Chronology*.

STEPHEN ELLIS is a senior researcher at the African Studies Centre in Leiden, the Netherlands, and the former director of the Africa program at the International Crisis Group. He is the coauthor (with Gerrie ter Haar) of *Worlds of Power: Religious Thought and Political Practice in Africa* (2006).

LEE FEINSTEIN is senior fellow for U.S. foreign policy and international law at the Council on Foreign Relations. He was senior adviser for peacekeeping and peace enforcement policy in the office of the secretary of defense from 1994–95, and principal deputy director of the policy planning staff under Secretary of State Madeline K. Albright. His articles on national security and foreign policy have appeared in *Foreign Affairs*, the *National Interest*, the *Financial Times*, the *Los Angeles Times*, the *Washington Post*, and many other publications.

ADAM P. FRANKEL was a Rosenthal Fellow in the Office of the Coordinator for Counterterrorism at the U.S. Department of State and has worked in the Office of Presidential Speechwriting at the White House.

MICHELLE D. GAVIN is an international affairs fellow at the Council on Foreign Relations. Prior to joining the Council, Ms. Gavin served as legislative director to U.S. Senator Ken Salazar (D-CO). She previously spent six years as Senator Russ Feingold's (D-WI) primary foreign policy adviser, where she worked on a broad range of initiatives, including the creation of U.S. policy reforms related to HIV/AIDS treatment abroad. She also served as the staff director of the Senate Foreign Relations Committee's subcommittee on African affairs.

LAURIE GARRETT is a senior fellow for global health at the Council on Foreign Relations. Ms. Garrett was the president of the National Association of Science Writers during the mid-1990s. Ms. Garrett is the only writer ever to have been awarded all three of the Big "Ps" of journalism: the Peabody, the Polk, and the Pulitzer, and has been honored with two doctorates in humane letters honoris causa, from Weslayan Illinois University and the University of Massachusetts, Lowell. Her expertise includes global health systems, chronic and infectious diseases, and bioterrorism. Ms. Garrett is the best-selling author of *The Coming Plague: Newly Emerging Diseases in a World Out of Balance* (1994) and *Betrayal of Trust: The Collapse of Global Public Health* (2000).

EBEN KAPLAN is associate editor for CFR.org, where he writes primarily about terrorism and homeland security. Previously, he was a researcher at *Foreign Policy* magazine, and he has lived and worked in Mexico.

ANTHONY LAKE is distinguished professor in the practice of diplomacy in the Edmund A. Walsh School of Foreign Service, Georgetown University. Dr. Lake most recently served as assistant to the president for national security. He is the author of several books, including *Six Nightmares* (2001), *Somoza Falling* (1990), and *The "Tar Baby" Option: American Policy Toward Southern Rhodesia* (1976), and coauthor of *Our Own Worst Enemy: The Unmasking of American Foreign Policy* (1985).

PRINCETON N. LYMAN is the adjunct senior fellow for Africa policy studies at the Council on Foreign Relations and an adjunct professor at Georgetown University. Ambassador Lyman's career in government included assignments as deputy assistant secretary of state for Africa (1981–86), U.S. ambassador to Nigeria (1986–89), director of refugee programs (1989–92), ambassador to South Africa (1992–95), and assistant secretary of state for international organization affairs (1996–98). He is the author of *Partner to History: The U.S. Role in South Africa's Transition to Democracy* (2002).

TERRENCE LYONS is an associate professor of conflict resolution at the Institute for Conflict Analysis and Resolution and codirector of the Center for Global Studies at George Mason University. Lyons has participated in talks to resolve conflicts in Ethiopia and served as senior program adviser to the Carter Center's project on postconflict elections in Ethiopia (2005) and Liberia (1997). Professor Lyons's publications include *Demilitarizing Politics: Elections on the Uncertain Road to Peace* (2005) and *Voting for Peace: Postconflict Elections in Liberia* (1999).

Vincent A. Mai is chairman of AEA Investors LLC, a global private equity firm with offices in the United States, Europe, and Asia. Prior to joining AEA in 1989, he was a managing director of Lehman Brothers, where he was cohead of investment banking. He has served on the boards of several institutions, including the Council on Foreign Relations, Fannie Mae, and the Carnegie Corporation of New York. He is chairman of the board of Sesame Workshop and also serves on the boards of the Juilliard School and the International Center for Transitional Justice. Mr. Mai is the chairman of the Africa policy studies advisory board at the Council on Foreign Relations and chairman of the Africa advisory committee at Human Rights Watch.

J. Stephen Morrison is the executive director of the HIV/AIDS task force and director of the Africa program at the Center for Strategic and International Studies. He was executive secretary of the Africa Policy Advisory Panel, commissioned by the U.S. Congress and chaired by then Secretary of State Colin Powell. From 1996 through early 2000, Mr. Morrison served on the secretary of state's policy planning staff, where he was responsible for African affairs and global foreign assistance issues.

William L. Nash, a retired U.S. army major general, is the General John W. Vessey senior fellow for conflict prevention and director of the Center for Preventive Action at the Council on Foreign Relations.

John Prendergast is senior adviser to the International Crisis Group and one of the leaders of the ENOUGH Campaign. Previously he worked at the White House and State Department during the Clinton administration, where he was involved in a number of peace processes throughout Africa. He has authored eight books on Africa, the latest of which he coauthored with actor/activist Don Cheadle, entitled *Not on Our Watch* (2007).

ROBERT I. ROTBERG is the director of the program on intrastate conflict and conflict resolution at the Belfer Center for Science and International Affairs at the Kennedy School of Government, Harvard University. He is also the president of the World Peace Foundation. He was previously a professor of political science and history, Massachusetts Institute of Technology; academic vice president, Tufts University; and president, Lafayette College.

COLIN THOMAS-JENSEN is Africa advocacy and research manager at the International Crisis Group. Prior to joining Crisis Group, Colin was an information officer for the U.S. Agency for International Development's humanitarian response team for Darfur. Earlier, he served as a Peace Corps volunteer in Ethiopia and Mozambique. Mr. Thomas-Jensen has traveled extensively in East and southern Africa.

FRANK G. WISNER is vice chairman, external affairs at American International Group. A career diplomat with the personal rank of career ambassador, he previously served as ambassador to India (1994–97). Additionally, he was ambassador to Zambia (1979–82), Egypt (1986–91), and the Philippines (1991–92). Ambassador Wisner has served in a number of positions in the U.S. government, including undersecretary of defense for policy (1993–94), undersecretary of state for international security affairs (1992–93), senior deputy assistant secretary for African affairs (1982–86), and deputy executive secretary of the Department of State (1977). During the course of his career, Ambassador Wisner served in the Middle East and South and East Asia.

CHRISTINE TODD WHITMAN is the president of the Whitman Strategy Group, a management consulting/strategic planning partnership. She was administrator of the Environmental Protection Agency (2001–2003) and served as governor of New Jersey (1994–2001). Governor Whitman is the author of a book about the GOP called *It's My Party, Too* (2005), and is cochairman of both the National Smart Growth Council and the Republican Leadership Council.

Acknowledgments

This book is part of a new publishing venture known as the Caravan project. The goal of the project is to make books available to readers where, when, and how they want them. *Beyond Humanitarianism*, like all Caravan books, will be available in a traditional print edition along with eBook and audiobook versions, both available for download in their entirety and in chapters. The Council is excited to be part of this undertaking.

We thank Council President Richard N. Haass for his support of the Council's partnership with Caravan. Dr. Haass immediately saw the advantages of bringing together a wealth of Council content—drawing on CFR.org, *Foreign Affairs* magazine, and other Council publications. We are indebted to him for recognizing the growing importance of the African continent—a region that is becoming steadily more central to the United States and to the world in ways that transcend humanitarian interests—and for having the vision to explore new publishing avenues that will lead to greater public awareness about the issues confronting Africa today.

We also thank others at the Council who were instrumental in the development of this book. Senior Vice President and Publisher David Kellogg played a leading role in making this book a reality. He and Caravan's executive director, Peter Osnos, knew the Council had an abundance of good material that could be packaged in a creative way. They were the first to recognize that Caravan would be a useful vehicle to profile some of the Council's work. *Foreign Affairs* editor James F. Hoge Jr. and Vice President and Director of Studies Gary Samore do an excellent job of overseeing the Council's flagship magazine and think tank, respectively.

Former associate editor Molly Graham researched and brought together many of the articles and essays that appear in this volume. We owe her a tremendous debt. *Foreign Affairs* Managing Editor Gideon Rose and former vice president and director of studies James M. Lindsay were kind enough to spend time discussing how

Acknowledgments

best to organize and present the materials. CFR.org Executive Editor Michael Moran reviewed original Council Web content that might be relevant and interesting for the general reader. We thank him and his deputy editor, Robert McMahon. The Council's new associate editor, Lia Norton, was helpful with much-needed editing advice and production support. Research Associate Will Evans was supportive with research and logistics. Council Publications Interns Ernest Herrera and Patrick Roath were also terrific, combing through and checking every article and reference. Finally, we extend a special thanks to each author whose article appears in this book.

Princeton N. Lyman
Patricia Dorff

Index